THE
WARNER
BROTHERS

ALSO BY MICHAEL FREEDLAND

Al Jolson
Irving Berlin
James Cagney
Fred Astaire
Sophie
The story of Sophie Tucker
Jerome Kern
Errol Flynn
(In USA., The Two Lives of Errol Flynn)
Gregory Peck
Maurice Chevalier
Peter O'Toole

AND WITH MORECAMBE AND WISE
There's No Answer To That

THE WARNER BROTHERS

Michael Freedland

Harrap London

**For my parents
who mean so much**

Kol hakovod

First published in Great Britain 1983
by HARRAP LIMITED
19-23 Ludgate Hill, London EC4M 7PD

© *Michael Freedland* 1983

ISBN 0 245-53827-5

Designed by Michael R. Carter

Printed and bound in Great Britain
by Mackays of Chatham Ltd

CONTENTS

ILLUSTRATIONS

ACKNOWLEDGMENTS

This is a book I have wanted to write for years. The fact that I was able to do so was due entirely to the co-operation of a host of people who agreed to have their brains picked. Going along with that is reason enough to say thank you.

However, they did more than that. They provided insights into what I had always known would be a fascinating, fabulous world, but which I had only begun to guess at before meeting them.

So for their help, their knowledge and their agreement to meeting me over the lengthy time this book was in gestation, my warmest appreciation to:

Larry Adler; the late Joan Blondell; Hoyt Bowers; Max Burcutt; Sammy Cahn; George Chasin; Dane Clark; Bette Davis (in the course of an interview for *The Times*); Irene Dunne; Julius Epstein; Rudi Fehr; Bill Feldman; Abbi Greshler; Paul Henreid; the late George Jessel; Peter Knecht; Paul Kohner; Mervyn LeRoy; Joan Leslie; Bill Orr; Ida Lupino; Mrs Jean Negulesco; Gregory Peck; the late George Raft; Irving Rapper; Bill Schaefer; Melville Shavelson; Vincent Sherman; Sidney Skolsky; Milton Sperling; the late Morris Stoloff; Hal Wallis; the late Raoul Walsh; the late Harry Warren; Jack Warner, junior; Loretta Young.

I was given a great deal of assistance by the librarians of the Academy of Motion Picture Arts and Sciences, Los Angeles, and of the British Film Institute, London, while for researching the illustrations my gratitude is due to the National Film Archive Stills Library. Sincerest thanks too to that walking encyclopaedia of the cinema, Dennis Sykes, and to my son, Jonathan Freedland, who worked exceptionally hard helping to organize material, and compiled the Index; to my secretary Hilda Allberg; my friend and editor, Simon Dally, for extraordinary patience at what was a very difficult time for me; and lastly to my beloved wife, Sara, who has had to tolerate so much.

MICHAEL FREEDLAND
London 1983

vii

CHAPTER 1

IT ALL CAME TRUE

'Uneasy lies the head that wears the toilet seat.'

With that profound statement, majestic in its tone and sonorous in its phraseology, Jack L. Warner, the Last Tycoon in Hollywood, declared his philosophy.

Of course, no one knew what he meant—except that they had heard it a hundred times before. As he twisted his cigar the way George Burns and a score of lesser vaudevillians had done for years, it was a signal that he was still in total command. He knew what he meant, and you argued with him at your peril.

Ever since he had first shown that as far as he was concerned, he was *the* Warner Brother, people in the film city had regarded him as a frustrated comedian who nevertheless had an intuitive sense of what made successful movies. A clown with clout.

However, those who dismissed him as merely a clown were doing both him and themselves a disservice. On the surface, of course, it was easy enough to do. When a man invites Professor Albert Einstein for lunch and then declares, 'You know, I have a theory about relatives, too—don't hire 'em' how could you possibly take him seriously? Except that before you heard that remark you should have taken the trouble to understand that he had the power to make and break careers with one of those flicks of his Havana, and in producing some of the most exciting films ever made had created what was perhaps the most interesting major studio of them all.

Julius Epstein, one of those highly respected screen writers Warners had the good sense to employ, described Jack and the two brothers with whom he nominally shared power at the Burbank studios—Harry and Albert—as 'robber barons'. It's a good phrase, because it said a great deal about them.

Jack was the brother who made the headlines and whom the actors, directors and the other Hollywood personnel knew best.

Speak to the survivors of his era and you have the distinct impression that he was either a martinet or a pussy-cat. He was both. He was also Hollywood in its greatest era.

He was the mogul who typified the image which soon was to become the cliché: the belief that he had a divine right to have his own way. The intense work ethic which translated itself to a form of paternalism. The vulgarity which he and others explained away as showmanship. The desk at the end of an office so intimidating that an international star would quake in his custom-made shoes as he crossed the threshold, and walked a distance the trade would have described as a dolly shot away.

There were, of course, the girls—although no one suggested he used the casting couch for that purpose. He didn't have to. And there was that cigar. None of those things, however, made him a mogul or made either his fortune or those of his brothers—who, let it be said straight away, brought their own contributions both to the company and to the industry. What they had was the foresight to predict what cinemagoers in their country—to say nothing of the world outside—would want to see from their seats in a movie theatre.

It was Warners who brought sound to the cinema—and having done that, launched first the musical film and then the era of the gangster picture. Before anyone else thought about it they were warning the world of the menace of Nazism, and stirring a nation's conscience about the unspeakable conditions of men forced to work on one of those mobile Auschwitzes known as chain gangs.

'Combining good picture-making with good citizenship' was the studio's proud boast, and for as long as Hollywood held its unique position, it was never really to lose its hold on those words, even though the brothers Warner themselves made mistakes that would have crippled lesser and poorer people.

This is not yet another studio story. Certainly it is not another long critique of the films the Warners made. There have been too many of those. Instead it is a story of the brothers themselves, of the men who made the movies, and in so doing made themselves.

CHAPTER 2

DESPERATE JOURNEY

Working for Warner Bros was like making love to a
porcupine. A thousand pricks against one.

Melville Shavelson

The family Warner was like a million other Jewish people who were
embittered enough with life under the Tsars to want to get away
from their empire, and sufficiently strong and young to be able to do
something about making that wish a reality.

Ironically, in time four of the Warner sons would themselves be
dubbed Tsars, but it would be a good many years before Benjamin
Warner would appreciate the joke. What he assumed back in the
early 1890s was that his growing young family would work as hard
as both he and his pretty wife Pearl had always done in the Polish
village of Krasnashiltz.

None of the Warners had had any education to speak of, although
Benjamin had gone every day to the local Hebrew school, the
cheder, and now that his eldest son Hirsch was old enough to go too
it was taken for granted that he also should sample the benefits of
this spartan form of education.

No one knows how the Warners got their name. The original
family name—for it surely was not Warner—has been long forgotten, in much the same way as has their precise dates of birth. No one
bothered with such fripperies as birth certificates in Tsarist Russia.
Jack Warner junior was to inform me: 'I asked that question of my
grandmother several times and she couldn't tell me. But it was an
area of the Pale of Settlement [that part of the Russian Empire to
which the Jews were confined] where names beginning with "W"
were quite common.'

They were not a fanatically religious brood, but certain things
were taken for granted. The Jewish Sabbath had to be observed to
the point of never striking a match or even picking up a
kopek—about the only coin they ever saw—on a Saturday. And
there could certainly be no question about observing the dietary

laws which not only proscribed the eating of pork, but of any other meat which had not been ritually slaughtered.

In his autobiography. *My First Hundred Years in Hollywood,* Jack Warner said that his family were always surrounded by pigs as they walked the streets of Krasnashiltz. It seems unlikely. Their home was in the part of town known as the *shtetl,* where Jews lived in a world entirely cut off from the surrounding Gentile population. For them even to see a pig, let alone be surrounded by them, seems to be a breach not only of religious law, but of decency.

Jack Junior told me that the family were peasants. That too was unusual in Jewish life. More likely they scraped a living selling the gleanings of the soil around them. The milkman in *Fiddler on the Roof* was about as close to agriculture as Jews in that world of more than a century ago ever did get.

They found it desperately hard not merely to earn a living but to live at all. From one part of the Pale of Settlement to another, stories filtered through of Cossacks raping and pillaging as if taking part in a World Series of atrocity. There wasn't a *shtetl* in the land which, under the beneficent rule of Tsar Alexander, hadn't had its pogrom.

The effects of a pogrom were devastating, and not just for the people whose lives were directly involved—the ones who had lost beloved close relatives, whose shops had been sacked, who had themselves become maimed as a result of having their bodies clamped between cobble stones and horses' hooves. It all had a tremendous psychological impact on a population which never felt anything but totally vulnerable.

The Warners first thought of leaving Poland when their daughter Anna showed that she was developing into a sturdy child, and the realization that she too might before long become the victim of a Cossack rapist had become an obsession. They had already lost a baby girl, a victim of the plague of infant mortality which was taken so much for granted by all classes in the nineteenth century. There had been nothing they could do about that, but they could see no reason to expose their other children to unnecessary risk. Benjamin had made up his mind. He had to think of the future.

And that future was summed up with one word—children.

As Benjamin saw it, there was only one place to bring them up—America. But his first attempts to cross the Atlantic were stymied by the fact that it seemed as though he was faced always by another mouth to feed.

Their son Abe was born in 1884, two years after Hirsch. He was followed by Henry, Sam, Rose and Fannie—all of them in intervals of alternate summers. Henry and Fannie—their names indicate the certainty their parents had in the fact that they were all to be

4

Americans—did not survive beyond their fourth birthdays. But the others promised to grow healthily, and he knew he had to get them away. Since the Warners lived close to the German border this meant that it was a slightly easier decision for them than it was for those living in the Ukraine, or in even farther-flung areas of the Pale.

By the time he had made up his mind, Benjamin had changed his occupation. He had become a cobbler—perhaps he considered a new job the right sort of preparation for a new world.

What really persuaded him to make the trip in 1890 was a letter from Baltimore, a name which as far as the Warners were concerned could have been the capital of Paradise or of the second crater to the right on the face of the moon. It was where a man called Waleski—hitherto always regarded as the village idiot of Krasnashiltz—had settled, and now seemed the obvious destination for his own family.

Ben made the journey alone—almost a month it took—at first in cattle-cars not altogether dissimilar to the kind in which his children might have perished on the rails leading to Auschwitz had he decided not to go. He then graduated to the steerage section of a ship which should long before have lost its certificate of seaworthiness.

Waleski had written in that letter (in the ancient Hebrew script which European Jews had adapted to serve the requirements of Yiddish, the only language either of them knew) that America was perfect. And if he didn't actually add that the streets were paved with gold he seemed to imply it.

With that thought in mind the stench and the dampness and the sounds of vomiting from the mass dormitory below decks on the ship were difficulties Ben could tolerate. He wasn't the stereotyped image of the ghetto Jew: at twenty-six he was built like one of the oxen which were such familiar sights on the streets of Krasnashiltz, and he could cope with conditions that killed off lesser men.

There was little risk of his being left stranded at Ellis Island, the no-man's land on the Hudson where the fate of the immigrants was decided before ever they were allowed into New York. For thousands America ended before it began at that spot. A hint of TB, the suggestion of incurable eye disease, was enough to guarantee a grey-faced man or woman a voyage back to Eastern Europe.

Benjamin knew it was going to be so much better than Poland, a promised land which the Bible had overlooked.

It wasn't. He made his way to Baltimore, and found no gold. Instead there was dirt. The noise was intolerable. In comparison, the slums of the Maryland city made the hovels of Krasnashiltz seem like the bungalows of a country club—had he ever heard of such places.

5

Even so, he had a feeling things would get better. If it wasn't Baltimore the Beautiful, Ben was glad that he came. He could spy a purpose to life in the American city he had never experienced before.

Ten days after his arrival he finally found Waleski—a sheepish little man who had for months been waiting for the call of 'Luntzman' (countryman) to echo through the Baltimore slums, but who at the same time feared the retribution his deception would bring. He had so wanted the company of someone he knew that a small lie was worth the risk.

When the two men met they hugged—until Ben shouted in his ear: 'You lied. But I'm glad you did. If you told me it would be like this, I would never have come. But now I'm going to make a go of it.'

Becoming a cobbler was no bad move on Ben's part. He was in a trade which even in the poor section of town was badly needed. People who could never afford to buy more than one pair of shoes in a decade—if that—desperately needed to have the one pair they did own repaired.

Ben knew that. What told him so was the same kind of instinct which within a very few years would revolutionize the entertainment industry. He also knew that he wasn't the only shoe-repairer in town, so he had to provide something different.

What he offered was summed up in the sign 'Shoes Repaired While You Wait'. It had never been done before, and that little difference brought him in 3 dollars a day. Enough for him to send for Pearl and the children.

Business didn't exactly prosper. But with the arrival of his family he could begin to think of a future in America. Hirsch's name had already been Americanized into Harry, and soon after his arrival in the new country he was told he was old enough to go into the family business.

In *My First Hundred Years in Hollywood* Jack describes how Harry learnt the cobbler's trick envied by generations of small boys—throwing nails into his mouth, ready to be hammered into a leather sole or heel.

He learnt something else too—to search the floor for dropped nails for which he could find some good use. Once when he was President of Warner Bros film studios Ann Sheridan spotted Harry bending down as he walked through the lot, every now and again picking up nails which he then popped into his mouth. Such were the habits of childhood. Harry later designed a stick with a magnet on one end so that he could indulge his habit without making it seem quite so obvious.

Probably the most important of those Warner customs was simply the fact that the day was meant for working, and that you didn't waste God's given time doing anything else. From such ethics people wasted away—or created empires.

Ben had been pleased with the business he created, but he also knew its limitations. When he heard that a new railroad was being built in the area his mind turned to other things. He realized that there was probably going to be more money earned meeting the trackmen's daily needs than could ever be gained by hammering boots and shoes while his customers waited.

So Ben became a peddler. He took along Pearl's two brothers, Hyman and Barrel Eichelbaum, as partners to sew up the territory. Barrel soon vanished with a week's earnings, and convinced Ben about the wisdom of the policy of hiring relatives later articulated to Professor Einstein.

With Pearl and the children following on behind, Ben went on to Canada. In London, Ontario, in 1892 another son was born. He was named Jack—the middle initial 'L' came later because it seemed to add stature—he would say it stood for Leonard—and immediately became the apple of his mother's eye, and the object of his eldest brother's intense jealousy. Practically from that moment on, the emotion that was strongest between Harry and Jack was one of hatred.

Exactly when Jack's birth occurred no one now knows. He had no birth certificate either.

Like a lot of other people in similar situations—Al Jolson was one—Jack chose for himself a birthday in the summer: 4 August.

To Ben and Pearl, birthdays didn't matter very much. There was the family's living to earn, and Ben, the peasant-cum-cobbler-cum-peddler, was now convinced that there was no better way of making money than as a fur-dealer.

Ben's real forte was accepting other people's fantasies. A friend had convinced him that by taking his horse and cart to Montreal he could exchange his tin wares for fur pelts. He would open a store in the city and send back furs to the friend, who would translate skins into cash.

Needless to say, it didn't happen that way. His friend skipped off with the furs, leaving Ben with huge crates, not of the money he had been promised, but of shredded paper. After two years, and with another baby in the family—a boy called David—the Warners were totally and seemingly irrevocably broke.

They moved back to Baltimore. But Harry was already showing signs of the impatience which was to characterize the Warner outlook on life. Word had reached him that there was a Polish community in the Ohio city of Youngstown, who might be glad of his business acumen.

7

A fourteen-year-old boy like Harry didn't know what his father could have told him—that there was a great deal of difference between Poles and Polish Jews like himself. But it didn't matter. At Youngstown he found a tiny shop, sent to Baltimore for the shoe-making last and the other tools he used, and opened up for business.

In the belief that there was nothing like publicity to bring in the customers, Harry sat in front of a brightly polished window and began work. The result was precisely the one he had predicted. There were more people in Youngstown needing shoes mended than could be catered for by the existing cobblers, and before long the fourteen-year-old had sent for his father and brother Abe. Abe followed Harry's example, and had long decided there was no point in wasting any more time on going to school.

Business seemed to prosper, so Pearl brought the other children to Youngstown, and there they set up home. Ben was working with Harry in the shoe-repairing business, but as always he had other ideas for earning the family's keep. He decided to rent a bigger place of his own, and open up a new venture—a butcher's shop and grocery store.

For the first time in his life, Ben seemed to be settled, although he couldn't resist telling Pearl about the latest idea he had for making a fortune. She for her part nodded phlegmatically and got on with cooking the chicken soup, scrubbing the floors, mending the clothes—and giving birth to another daughter, who arrived in 1895, and was named Sadie. A year later their son Milton was born.

None of the children finished school. Abe called himself Albert, because he thought it sounded better to the local non-Jewish population. However, although he always used the name Albert in public, he remained Abe to those who knew him. He went to work in a steel-mill. It was on his first day there that he saw a man crushed to death by a huge ingot of the metal falling on his shoulder. The next day another man's leg was smashed.

He didn't go in the day after that.

'My mother told me to stay home,' he explained years later to *The New York Times*. 'She said, "Today may be your turn".'

Instead he found himself a job with a soap firm. It seemed to make a lot more sense.

Meanwhile Jack and Sam helped their father in the butcher's shop, cleaning up the various sections—one part of the store was reserved for the kosher food required by the comparatively few Jewish customers—and making deliveries.

Youngstown was a big Mafia centre at the time, and young Jack had to teach himself to keep one eye on the stock and the other on customers who might have a gun where their money belt was supposed to be.

When a youngster came in for an order and demanded a discount at the point of a stiletto Jack surreptitiously added the weight of his thumb to the meat on his scales. He was prepared for trouble. At the suggestion of a local policeman he bought a .32 Smith and Wesson revolver. And he almost used it. Once.

That was the night a man forced his way into the store and demanded the contents of the till, with his own gun pointing in Jack's direction. Had not two policemen arrived on the scene at just that moment Jack L. Warner might have been no more than an entry in the dust-covered files of the Youngstown morgue. The experience so frightened him that he decided that, even hidden, the gun attracted trouble. He vowed never to carry one again.

There was, however, something of the marksman in Abe's performance in the soap business. He was working for Swift and Company in Chicago, and finding business rather less than so-so. In fact his salesmanship was achieving nothing, either for himself or for his product.

As he told a reporter, 'At night, I would line up all the different kinds of soap I had to sell on the bureau in my hotel room and walk up and down in front of them, practising sales talks for the next day. I even carried a cake in my pocket, so that I could take it out and hold it in front of the storekeeper or the buyer the minute I got in the door, without waiting to open my suitcase. But still I couldn't get an order and was thrown out of some more places.'

It was in sheer desperation that he hit on a idea which he didn't have the guts to tell his bosses about. He upped the prices to his customers, but then threw in a free box of soap for every five that they ordered.

It was sheer psychology. The soap cost his customers exactly what they had been paying before—or rather what they had definitely not been paying before—and on the surface made no more for his company. But there was about it the philosophy of something for nothing, and the orders tumbled in.

Abe's idea soon became company policy. More than that, it revolutionized the sale of soap in America.

Years later he was travelling in the smoking car of a train and telling the story to a man who had said he was in the business himself. He told him that it was now the way every salesman went about his job. Moreover, it had become the established practice of not only that firm, but of the entire soap industry of America. Single-handedly and without realizing it, Abe had invented discount trading, variations of which would be introduced throughout America's commercial life. Still in his teens, he had established himself as an ace salesman, learning lessons he too would take far away from the world of soap.

9

Things were happening in the Warner family. Four of the brothers had quite separately had an experience which changed their lives. They had seen their first moving pictures.

Chapter 3

HOLD EVERYTHING

Why did a certain type of men do so well? They never went
to the USC School of Cinema. In aviation terms, they flew
by the seats of their pants.

Jack Warner junior

It may have been coincidence. It could have been heredity. While
other people saw shadows come to life on a blank wall and were
thrilled, Harry, Abe, Sam and Jack each came to a similar conclusion. They were not prepared just to sit and watch; they decided it
was a business they had to get into.

Abe saw his first movie in Pittsburgh, in a nickelodeon on
Pittsfield Street. He saw it once, and wanted to see it again. Every
Monday and Thursday the programme was changed, and every
Monday and Thursday Abe was the first to be waiting in line for the
show to begin.

'Then I began to figure out the attraction,' he wrote in 1929. 'If
these pictures have such an appeal for me that I never miss one, I
thought, then it must be a pretty good business to be in.'

He decided to give up the soap business and go back to Youngstown. Before he could say anything about his own idea, Sam got in
first: 'Abe, I've decided to go into the motion-picture business.
There's a guy who runs a nickelodeon here, and he's shown me how
to work the projector.'

Sam's idea of gratitude to the kind exhibitor was to go into
business as his competitor. But if there was one successful nickelodeon operator in Youngstown there was plainly room for another.

Sam had for years been known as the family showman. He was
the one who would sneak away to the circus or the local vaudeville
theatre and come back with stories of the magic offered by the
sawdust and the footlights. 'One day,' he told the family, 'one day,
I'm going to have a show of my own.'

Now the time had come. He was only eighteen, but that was old
enough to infect his father with whatever it was that had struck him.
Ben Warner agreed to pawn his watch so that Sam could buy a

projector. One came on the market quicker than he expected—the local nickelodeon operator had gone broke.

Instead of regarding that fact as a warning of the dire perils awaiting anyone venturing into the movie business, Sam persuaded the rest of the family that they could more likely benefit from the lack of competition.

Jack was hanging on his brother's coat-tails, counting the hours till the projector was theirs. He too had been to the local nickelodeon, and been fired by the same enthusiasm. It wasn't the prospects of financial reward that excited Sam and Jack so much, but it was precisely that which appealed to Harry and Abe. The two older brothers had seen dollar signs flashing between the frames of film projected in front of them, and that was why they backed Sam's initiative and his hunch so warmly. (In fact in later years Jack would say that it was Abe who first saw the business potential of flashing images on to a blank screen.)

The projector was theirs. So was a trunk full of tickets they would sell for their shows. And, oh yes, they also had a film to play to the people who would buy those tickets, a somewhat scratchy print of what had been the very first 'feature' film ever made, *The Great Train Robbery*. All over the country audiences had already screamed and ducked as the locomotive rushed towards them. In Youngstown that was a novelty still ready to be exploited.

The movie also had the same sort of hero who before very long would make a fortune for the brothers. A dog.

For the moment they had to concentrate on showing their film, which was easier said than done.

Having the film and the equipment on which to show it was one thing. Finding a place where they could do it was quite another.

Vaudeville theatres were not in the least interested in hastening their own demise by introducing this new branch of entertainment, although many of them disliked the idea for totally different reasons. They regarded it simply as a peepshow, and they wouldn't demean themselves by allowing it into their buildings. The few bright spots were the opera houses in the neighbouring town of Akron, where they were grudgingly allowed to fill in the gaps between the visiting show companies and the Shakespearean players who plied their trade from place to place like vaudevillians.

The brothers showed the film and a package of shorts interrupted by a vaudeville performance by a couple of newcomers to the business, Jack Warner and his sister Rose. Rose, now thirteen, played the piano while Jack led the audience in singing the ballads of the day, pointing to the lyrics on a screen behind him. Jack wasn't very good, but he would probably never be happier.

The same could be said about Sam, who was in his element manning the projector.

Abe sold the tickets, and did the business organization of the tour, while Harry stayed behind earning the more reliable kind of family income by mending shoes. He also offered the benefit of advice culled from his long and sound commercial background. He was, after all, twenty-three years old.

The big problem they faced was the one that came up all too frequently—when the film snapped. Jack always had to be ready with the sign that proclaimed 'Two Minutes Intermission', to say nothing of the pot of glue with which he would madly try to rectify the fault. Needless to say, it usually occurred during the most emotional moments of the film.

The pattern of the week never varied. On Saturday nights they counted up the week's takings and assessed their profits. More often than not, these amounted to no more than enough to buy each of the troupe a three-cent cup of coffee, and their streetcar fare home.

It was Harry's advice that something had to be done. They either had to get out of the business or find themselves a permanent theatre of their own. They had no doubt about the choice they would make. The difficulty was that local real-estate people weren't happy about having a peepshow in their midst—and for as long as they were called nickelodeons that was precisely what they were considered to be.

Finally they found a hall in a building in New Castle, Pennsylvania, and with money lent them by Harry took a lease there. The only trouble was that buying films cost between twenty and thirty dollars for each twelve-minute reel. In a permanent 'theatre' these had to be changed twice a week.

The brothers decided they could just about afford that. What they could not afford was to buy any chairs for their customers to sit on while watching their movies. It was Abe who had the solution: he went to a near-by funeral parlour and did a deal to rent the chairs while they were not being used for less secular purposes.

The trouble came when there was a hastily arranged funeral, and the undertaker had to reclaim his property in the midst of a chase across the prairie. The audience had to see the rest of the film standing up.

The customers were not the only ones who had to be satisfied by the performances at this first Warner theatre. There was also a little matter of not contravening the safety regulations imposed by the local council, who regularly sent inspectors along to make sure that both the projection equipment and the highly inflammable film stock were being used properly.

Film was an entirely new commodity—but the inspector was not.

13

He had no idea whatsoever what he was supposed to be looking for, and he was never seen in the Warners' projection booth, a room knee-deep in film (there was no take-up spool on the projectors in those days) without a cigar perched as precariously at the end of his mouth as Pearl White hanging from the edge of a cliff. Every time the white ash from it fell to the ground Sam would have to leave his projector to mop up the potential hazard. While he was doing this the film ground to a halt, because there was no one around to crank the handle.

Jack had by that time convinced himself, if not his brothers, that he was the potential star in the family and needed all the exposure he could get in front of the spotlight. After all, he had the benefit of a semi-captive audience. What he didn't have was a good name. It was an age when no self-respecting singer would dare to go on stage with a name that didn't have a distinctly Latin flavour about it. Jack Warner knew that—and decided to call himself Leon Zuardo. He thought it made him even more marvellous, although his audience couldn't really be sure.

He even branched out on the road by himself. In a blackface act with a local lad called Pike Richard, Leon Zuardo was in show business. He spent a season going the route from one tanktown to another—they were so called because they were the places where water was stored in sufficient quantities to cool steam engines passing through—before agreeing to heed Sam's advice to get back into the movie business and start exploiting other people's talents.

Sam was the brother whom Jack always called 'my favourite', but his advice was hard to accept. At fourteen, Jack had an urge to get up and be 'on'. He would never lose it. In later years he would complete the vaudeville image—with a little moustache modelled on that worn by an old comedian he admired.

All the brothers had, of course, tried even more other things before showing their movies. Harry, Jack and Abe had once sold bicycles, and Sam had predated the Las Vegas craze by having his own roulette wheel and other gambling machines (which needless to say never gave his suckers an even break!)

Their New Castle theatre was a different matter, however. They called it the Cascade, and on the box-office was now a sign that promised, in exchange for five cents admission, 'Refined Entertainment for Ladies, Gentlemen and Children'. It also still boasted a live performance by Jack and Rose. This was extraordinarily valuable in clearing the theatre between continuous performances.

The entrepreneurial spirit, however, didn't allow the Warners to stand still, and the brothers believed that there was more to the film business than simply showing movies to people sitting on undertakers' chairs. Again it was Abe who saw the financial possibilities of extending the brothers' activities, and this time he believed he could cash in on the money that exhibitors paid for the films they showed. If he could obtain enough cash to buy a great number of films, and then rent them to nickelodeons like the Cascade all over the area, he would not only have their cash, but the same films could earn money over and over again.

Abe took the idea further, and with the same type of salesmanship which he had used to get rid of those cakes of soap he persuaded a financier to part with 2,000 dollars. With the money in his wallet, he took the first train to New York, bought a stack of film, and the Warners' film exchange was in business.

They operated from Pittsburgh, and after overcoming the initial resistance of the theatre-owners—who took some time to realize they would be better off by renting twenty films for 100 dollars; ten weeks supply—they were soon making what appeared to be a fortune. Within ten weeks they had sewn up an area stretching as far west as Portland, Oregon.

Harry was the one who saw the excitement of those days bringing with it family responsibility.

'When we've made enough money we're going to retire Mama and Papa,' he said, and it wasn't an idle thought. It was an instruction to the other brothers that could not be disobeyed.

The first earned dollar was put away as though it were a token of the commitment they had made.

Jack found the whole thing invigorating, especially since it enabled him to use some of the double-dealing techniques of which he would later become the Hollywood master. In *My First Hundred Years in Hollywood* he describes how he would occasionally snip a few feet from the beginning of the films they rented. Conveniently, those feet also included the initial title frames. Thus if an exhibitor phoned to complain that he hadn't received, say, *My Old Kentucky Home,* Jack would conveniently have the title of that film to add to whatever he had available. It was a totally different picture, but no one ever appeared to be any the wiser.

It was Jack's ingenuity that also gave the cinema its first ever all-Black movie. At least, that is what he said it was. He didn't bother to tell the gentlemen who wanted to show films to Negro patrons that what he was getting was a pile of negatives that had been delivered to the exchange by mistake.

It was not a mistake Jack could afford to make when he moved to the South. He became Sam's assistant in the Norfolk, Virginia, branch, which they called the Duquesne Amusement Supply Company. Everything in the film garden seemed to be rosy. The brothers had a commodity they knew they could sell, and enough customers to be willing purchasers.

15

That was until Thomas Alva Edison entered the scene. The man who had always been regarded as one of the principal inventors of the cinema—there were others who equally frequently disputed that claim—had by now invented something else, a monopoly of film distribution rights. He and a group of other people who considered themselves to be the cream of the film-producing business set up the Picture Patents Company, which decreed that no firm could make or distribute films without a licence which they alone could award.

The result was that the Warner brothers were (for the moment, at least) broke. Sam had to sell the Buick car which he had just a few weeks before bought as a sign that they had 'arrived'.

Had he just been a businessman, Sam might have written it all off to experience and gone looking for new ways to recoup his losses, but he wasn't that kind of person. The smell of celluloid had gone from his nostrils into his bloodstream, and now his brain was filled with images that told him he had to get back into the game as soon as he could.

It was gaining the rights to a hand-tinted version of Dante's *Inferno* which brought Sam back into a projection booth. Because Edison's friends hadn't been able to go back in time to pick up any royalties from Dante, the film was theirs for the asking. All they had to do was find a theatre.

Sam found one in Hartford, Connecticut, but he did more than that. He also located an eccentric actor named Stephen Bush, and advertised in the local newspapers that 'Professor' Bush would read the masterly Dante lines to accompany the action at every performance.

There would also be sound effects—a home-made wind machine, operated by Jack.

The public saw the advertisement and came to see the movie. They were not disappointed. As far as many of them were concerned, this was a talking picture—in colour. The significance of that notion was not lost on Sam, but for the moment he was satisfied with the spectacle of the people trooping in to see his movie by the hundred.

The 'professor' was later fired for being drunk, but he took them on a tour of the country that seemed to get more successful with every stop they made.

It was in 1917 that the ill wind which had engulfed Europe in the First World War blew a great deal of good for the brothers. And once again it was Sam who set the wind in motion, and Harry this time who fanned the flames.

The Dante experience had convinced Sam that he ought to

16

extend his activities in the movie industry and Harry now who provided the means by which he could do it. A phone call from New York informed the other brothers they were now film-producers.

CHAPTER 4

THE MIDAS TOUCH

Harry was appalled by Jack's lack of loyalty to the
family. Jack, on the other hand, was fundamentally
self-centred. An endearing personality. Treacherous,
hedonistic and a tyrant.

Milton Sperling

Harry Warner had the same kind of gift with money that other
men have with women. He was not only attracted to wealth, money
seemed to seek him out and run after him. While the other brothers
had to nurse their wounds after the Edison débâcle, Harry was left
counting the cash he had saved from the venture, and which he had
now very comfortably invested.

However, as Harry Warner contented himself with seeing his
bank balance grow, he was not beyond a touch of envy for two of his
brothers at least, young men who seemed to be having a great deal
more fun than he was. The only way, he reasoned, in which he too
could enjoy a connection with motion pictures and still make money
was to produce his own movies. All he needed was a story.

He was convinced he had found one with *Passions Inherited,* a
tale with more sentiment in it than a soldier's letter to his
sweetheart. It was, Jack later wrote, a 'strictly clean hearts-and-
flowers plot, and not the kind of backroom sex formula that would
draw'. It was based on a poem written by Ella Wheeler Wilcox,
which Harry himself had read and had decided was beautiful—and
if he liked it, how could it fail to win the Great American Public?

The other brothers were brought in when Harry began to doubt
whether he had been right. He had already paid a certain Gilbert P.
Hamilton 15,000 dollars to direct the picture, and then added
another 5,000 when Hamilton said he couldn't finish the movie
without it.

The film was supposed to be made in Santa Paula in Southern
California, but none of the people Harry had sent out in search of
either Hamilton or his party (and, he might have added, his money)
had come up with any kind of success.

Finally he asked Sam to deal with it. Jack, on the other hand, who still laboured under a terrific inferiority complex where his eldest brother was concerned, believed it was something he could do equally well himself, and took up the chase.

He eventually found the long-haired moustacheoed Hamilton in bed with a couple of girls who should have been performing a different kind of action for his benefit. He had also provided himself with an expensive car on the proceeds of Harry's investment. Jack used some fairly choice language to persuade Hamilton to produce his film. Finally he did so, although he insisted he had a whole final sequence to make before he would let it out of his sight.

Jack also informed him that he would be doing no such thing. Instead young Warner himself found a nice clinch in the middle of the picture, duplicated it and tagged it on to the last frame Hamilton had shot. He wrote the titles himself—with his spelling and punctuation corrected by another member of the team—and before long he and Harry had a flop!

America had entered the War, and the only kind of hearts or flowers that the public wanted were the kind that went with khaki.

But the main thing was that the Warner Brothers were in business, making movies. Harry had the bug as much as Sam and Jack, and Abe indicated that he wanted to be part of the action too. One failure wasn't going to make them leave the industry before they had got into it.

First there was the War to contend with. Sam and Jack enlisted—only to be told that the best thing they could do was to make movies for the Army Signals Corps. They made one picture for the Army—about VD, with Jack himself playing a young soldier being taken for 10 dollars by an unprincipled doctor.

The brothers were so short of money that they haunted other New York studios, begging unexposed lengths of film ends on which they could shoot their picture, *Open Your Eyes*. One of Jack's 'co-stars' was a young actor named Ben Lyon. Shortly before his death, Ben told me, 'I once said to Jack, "I wish I had been as lousy an actor as you. I might have become head of a studio too." '

The film was eventually made, and the Army seemed satisfied. It was fine to show to the doughboys about to be shipped off to France. Jack later thought he could release it again for civilian audiences, but it would have been easier selling bathing costumes in Siberia.

Of course, it was all marvellous experience, and sufficiently impressive to convince Harry and Abe too about their knowledge of the movie industry. Harry was continuing his business career, making money where none had existed before with a series of deals. His younger brother, Abe, meanwhile was in the Army. He became a sergeant—although for ever after he would call himself the Major.

Jack Warner comments in his book that it wasn't a war that

exactly swept the country in patriotic fervour. What was more, it was difficult to persuade the people who were supposed to be involved in the propaganda industry that it was a war worth fighting. Even so, it began spawning a series of stories which caught the public imagination rather more than the conflict itself. And once more it was Sam who spotted the potential they offered.

Although he was something of a character in the family, a snappy dresser who was a great hit with the girls, an ideas man with a wild sense of humour, Sam was also the best-read of the clan. He devoured books which his brothers wouldn't even have known had been printed, and read parts of the papers that didn't contain dollar signs or words of less than three syllables. It was while reading the *Philadelphia Public Ledger* that Sam had an idea which changed everything for the family.

The paper carried the serialized memoirs of James W. Gerard, who had for four years been America's ambassador to the Court of Kaiser Wilhelm.

Sam read the episode it contained over and over to himself, and then waited impatiently for the next day's paper. When that arrived he devoured the current story too. For the rest of the week it was all he allowed himself to think about.

Finally he contacted Harry: 'This is our chance,' he said. 'If we make this into a film, we could have a fortune.'

He wasn't far wrong. Harry went to see the Ambassador and told him he could have a quarter of the profits that the film would make. They couldn't offer him any cash because they didn't have any.

Harry was persuasive, but so was the Ambassador. He said he had already been offered a great deal of money by another company, but there was something about the young Mr Warner that he liked. Before long they shook hands on a 50,000-dollar advance—which Harry raised by selling more shares in the picture to other people. It was a gamble, but at a time when one very rarely saw photographs, let alone movies, of real-life personalities one worth taking.

When *My Four Years in Germany* had its première Ambassador Gerard was in a box to acknowledge the applause of an audience which was at that moment giving him a standing ovation. It was a fair indication of what was to follow. The film made a million dollars' profit and the kids from Youngstown had become movie moguls—making just the kind of picture which would before long be their trademark.

The film's potential had been spotted right from that first night. The *Motion Picture World* declared it to be 'not a photoplay, but an historical document'. The brothers wouldn't have wanted to quarrel with any such judgment.

Business was bustling, and so it seemed were things at home. Jack was married to a pretty young girl named Irma Solomons, and they had a son, who contrary to Jewish tradition they named Jack Junior. But family life didn't interest him that much. How could it when there were films to be made and all the excitement they brought? Besides which, there were usually other young ladies who were always willing to take off their clothes and go to bed with him. Nevertheless he would usually avoid actresses, and made sure there were never promises of jobs in his pictures.

Harry and Abe were now both married too.

Harry also had a son, Lewis, whom he just knew would become the leader of the next generation of Warner Brothers.

As for Ben and Pearl, life was sweet. Customers at Ben's store heard daily reports of the success of 'My sons, the producers,' and indeed there was much to tell.

The brothers made a series called *Southern Classics of the Screen* which were pretty terrible, but brought in cash. It was the age of the serial, and no self-respecting motion-picture outfit could contemplate staying in business without one. The Warner contributions were two Helen Holmes vehicles, *The Lost City* and *The Tiger's Claw*.

They were by now operating from Los Angeles, which had already established itself as the centre of the film industry. Jesse L. Lasky, Cecil B. DeMille and Adolph Zukor knew what they were doing when they made *The Squaw Man* in a tiny, virtually uninhabited suburb called Hollywood. In the days when the only way to film anything was in the open air, the virtually perpetual strength of the Southern California sunshine had no competition.

Warners rented their studio space, first at Main and Eighteenth Streets and then in Culver City. Neither of these premises would have passed too close an inspection from the local sanitation department, but the Warners saw their business as producing completed films. No theatre patrons—the nickelodeons had by now gone the way of *The Great Train Robbery*—were going to ask questions about the place where their entertainment had been manufactured.

Neither at that stage were they too bothered about stars, although Helen Holmes was so curvy both fore and aft that she developed a following. Considering the quality of the pictures she made, that was fortunate.

If the villain's name in those pictures happened to be Jack L. Warner—as he remarked in his book, it wasn't easy getting actors on their budget—no one would mind very much. As for Jack himself, he was more than content to see his name on the front of all his pictures as 'Producer', a role he shared with Sam.

At one stage they thought they had signed a young lady who until a few months earlier had been called Gloria Swenson—she changed the 'e' in her name to an 'a' because she thought it sounded more American—at 2,000 dollars a week. But Gloria had gone off on honeymoon, and changed her mind. (As Jack wrote, it was a good job she did: they could never have raised the two thousand.)

Another find-who-never-was was Harold Lloyd. He actually had an unsigned contract with Warners when a bomb—which everyone had thought was a mere prop—exploded in his face at the beginning of a photographic session. By the time he was ready to go back to work—after having lost two fingers in the explosion, and wondering whether he would lose his sight—he signed a more lucrative deal for Pathé.

But there were other actors who did work for them. An Italian comedian called Mario Bianchi (or Monty Banks) was a great success in a movie called *His Night Out* written by a youngster called Ken Hawkes and his brother Howard. Jack always thought Banks a better comedian than Chaplin, but he didn't last, and is best remembered today (if at all) as the first husband of Gracie Fields.

The brothers were enjoying themselves. Abe now styled himself Treasurer, although Harry called all the financial tunes. For the time being, however, all four were involved whenever a decision had to be made.

When Harry complained that a customer owed the brothers 70,000 dollars for the rights to show films in his possession it was Jack who was sent to collect. He didn't get his money, so in lieu confiscated the films.

That was when Harry discovered there had been a mistake. Jack was sent round again, this time to apologize.

The customer, a dark, curly-haired man, complained vociferously to Harry, and the eldest Warner brother had a hunch that it might be in his best interests to try to make peace. There was just the possibility, he conceded, that the awkward exhibitor was about to become important enough to make life difficult for them all. He was proved right the following year, when a smiling Louis B. Mayer shook the Warners by the hand in Hollywood and said he couldn't remember a thing about the incident.

The brothers were happy to agree. After all, they had their cheque. It was a time when every cent counted—and producers were expected to take their cameras home with them at night, lest they fell into the hands of the local sheriff before filming could begin next day.

Perhaps the best contact the Warners could make at the time was a banker named Motley Flint. Whenever there was trouble raising money to pay for salaries or stock—and there frequently was—it was Flint who came to the rescue. He had an intuitive feeling about the business, and believed the Warners were men whom he could trust. In fact, he became one of the only true friends Jack Warner ever had.

In 1922 he lent them 25,000 dollars to buy a property at 5842 Sunset Boulevard. The place was torn apart, and almost a year later an elegant façade above the white colonnaded building proclaimed 'Warner Brothers West Coast Studios'.

The decision to open the studios cost them a small fortune they didn't have. But with Motley Flint prepared to accept their characters as collateral, a Hollywood studio building was investment enough to attract others, particularly actors. Stars didn't just mean fodder for the cameras; they also represented prestige in the highly competitive business in which the brothers were now active.

Actors approached by Jack and Sam—now the resident heads of the studio—were sufficiently convinced to sign contracts, supervised by Mr Flint and his lawyers. When one actor or actress accepted terms other performers were happy to follow their example. Jack and Sam were usually delighted to have them.

It was all a huge gamble, but the brothers would never be strangers to gambling.

Harry and Jack were still based in New York. Someone had to look after the business side of things, and the East Coast was the place to do it. They also appeared to be doing it very well.

Mere babes in the industry they may have been, but Sam and Jack were now turning out pictures that critics were beginning to notice. Movies like *The Beautiful And Damned* by a youngster named F. Scott Fitzgerald, and *Main Street* by Sinclair Lewis, two titles that ever so slightly were getting the brothers a reputation for social awareness.

The successful running of a Hollywood studio meant doing it your own way, by your own gut-reaction. That went for choosing your films, the people to act in them and, most important of all, the names of those people. When a Latin-looking type was taken under contract Jack thought he could be the Warners' answer to the ever-growing Valentino cult. Except that his name was Joseph Page.

'Let's give him a Spanish name,' Jack said to Sam and a group of cronies in the room at the time.

No one could think of one Jack liked.

'Well,' he said in desperation, 'what are the street-names around here?'

He was offered Pico, Santa Monica, Alvarado. . . .

Alvarado it was. Joseph Page became Don Alvarado. Ironically, Jack liked Page so much, and discovered he had so much in common with him, that in a few years he proved it by marrying his divorced wife, Ann.

But what really brought the studio riches beyond their collective previous imagination was the discovery of a performer whom Jack would say was the most reliable and most loyal of any employed in the history of the company.

His name was Rin Tin Tin, an Alsatian dog abandoned as a puppy in a First World War trench of the German Army. Lee Duncan, the American soldier who discovered the dog, thought he could be trained to perform in the movies. He brought the idea to Warner Brothers, who thought so too.

For years afterwards Jack would call the dog 'the mortgage lifter'. All he asked for in salary was a juicy bone, and his idea of a raise was a hamburger. He was a success from his very first film, *Where The North Begins,* based on a story by Duncan himself. In 1924 he made *Find Your Man,* and a year later, *Tracked In The Snow Country.* He became so important to the studio that there was a standing order among the state's pedigree-dog breeders for 'doubles' which could be trained to do the tricks that even 'Rinty' couldn't manage. Years later, when the original was too old to work, no one ever knew he had been replaced altogether. If only some of the human Warner actors were equally dispensable! It would have made the studio a lot more peaceful a place.

The rows between the brothers began in earnest about this time. Harry was demanding economies, while Jack and Sam were trying to get over the message that they could only afford to economize if they were making money. And the only way to make money was to produce the biggest pictures they could.

They dallied with the idea of epics, but *Noah's Ark* was the only one they ever made. It was a flop.

Jack, blessed with the kind of intuition that told him what was right for their own particular set-up—and which was to prove his greatest forte—was convinced that Warner Brothers, to make money, needed good stories. Reluctantly, he also accepted that they ought to look out for good actors.

He bought the screen rights to all the works produced on Broadway by David Belasco. At the same time, in what would before long seem a symptom of a peculiarly masochistic strain in his character, he secured the services of John Barrymore. Mr Barrymore would later provide Jack with the same kind of headaches offered by the bottleful by his protégé Errol Flynn.

Barrymore never saw the movies as much more than a means of subsidizing his only real love—excelling in unique Shakespearean performances on the Broadway stage. It wouldn't be long before he would insist on the strategic placement of cue cards at his feet before the cameras began turning. 'My mind is filled with the beauty of Shakespeare, Marlowe and Bacon,' he would explain. 'Do you expect me to crowd it with this shit?'

For the rest of his life Jack would regale friends with stories of how he personally had to yank Barrymore from bath-tubs filled with iced champagne. His early days at Warners were not invariably difficult, although he was more often drunk than sober. When he was not under the influence of alcohol he was cute enough to appreciate the value of his talent. Any suggestion by the Warners had to be countered by one of his own.

The brothers wanted him to make a new version of the *Don Juan* legend. He accepted—on condition that he first made a film based on the story of *Moby Dick*. The result was *The Sea Beast*. It was important for the studio to do his bidding. Barrymore represented class, and they thought that was worth paying for—to the tune of 76,000 dollars a picture.

There were other newcomers to the Warner lot, including an actor named Mervyn LeRoy who really wanted to be a director. He and Jack got on like a studio on fire. They had first met years before when Mervyn was selling newspapers in San Francisco. More important, both fancied themselves as vaudevillians at heart.

Another acquisition was Darryl Francis Zanuck, who arrived as a writer and was before long to be the studio's senior producer. Jack spotted his potential immediately—except that he looked as if he hadn't yet graduated from high school. Jack told him he had a future. 'But even if you don't need glasses, find yourselves some window-panes to make you look older.' He also told him to grow a moustache.

Least noticed of all at the time was a youngster employed in the publicity department by the name of Hal B. Wallis.

What the brothers looked for above all else in their employees was a sharing of their own zest for life.

The film business itself was still in its infancy, and Sam in particular thought it had a long way to go. It was not a view shared by others in the industry. New techniques had already been introduced—the close-up, the use of Panchromatic film—and to the opposition it looked as if it had surely gone as far as it possibly could.

But there was a rival medium jumping on the bandwagon—radio. The studios took fright and tried to do everything they could to discourage the listening habit. A massive publicity campaign got under way to remind audiences of the excitement that was theirs only in a theatre.

Again, that was not the way the Warners saw it. Sam believed that any opposition had to be joined, if not beaten. That was why he established his own radio station, KWBC—the last three initials stood for 'Warner Brothers Classics'—in a disused building adjoining the studio lot. Their competitors scoffed, but even Harry thought it was a good idea, and made a speech telling them how wrong they were.

'My attention has been drawn,' he said in April 1925, 'to a general tendency within the amusement field to fight radio. The identical arguments of only a few years ago in an effort to minimize the popularity of motion pictures are being dragged out and pointed at an entertainment which now has millions of supporters.

'The cry of "the pictures will ruin the theatre" is within easy memory. They didn't, although there is no doubt that pictures inflicted considerable damage to the cheaper theatrical attractions. To this is now added a new alarm: the radio will ruin the theatre and the pictures. It will not if it is used intelligently.'

Whether Harry had his brother Jack in mind when he said that we can never be sure, but what is true is that while Harry was making his speeches, and watching the balance-sheets in his New York office, Jack was having himself a huge ball.

Not only was he watching films being made that he had personally bought but he surveyed their progress in the rushes, and much of the time did his own editing. He was also keeping more than a watching brief on station KWBC.

Every night, he would march in with a posse of minions, an emperor surveying his newest field of conquest. Nor did he just watch: every night he would take over the microphone from the resident announcer and introduce the acts.

Most evenings his favourite guest was that well-known artiste, Mr Leon Zuardo, now reincarnated to the very considerable delight of Jack L. Warner if of no one else.

Like many of his generation, Jack's idol was Al Jolson, a man from a similar Jewish immigrant background to his own who had nevertheless made a huge success at the one thing at which he himself had failed—singing and joking on stage. Now it was his chance to be like Jolson. For the benefit of his radio audience Leon Zuardo affected a deep, mock-Southern voice similar to Jolson's—and worked so hard on it off the air too that it became his own natural tone.

For his apparently grateful audience—no one ever told him what he really thought—Jack would generally manage to feature a medley of Jolson songs. His favourite was 'When The Red Red Robin Comes A Bob-Bob-Bobbin' Along'.

Hal Wallis was one of those who were expected to enjoy these supposedly impromptu but well-planned performances. As he told me, 'Jack used to think he was marvellous. In fact, he was awful—and nobody said anything good about him. But the audience

26

would cheer him and he took it as a signal to go on and on. I suppose it had a lot to do with the fact that radio was such a novelty.'

There could also have been another reason: the audience was made up chiefly of Warner Brothers employees.

Radio was not, however, the big money-maker that the brothers had anticipated. And they needed one badly. In 1924 the company was said to be worth 220,000 dollars. The following year, published figures showed its value had decreased by half. By February 1926 the brothers were forced to report a net loss of 333,413 dollars for the previous six months. In June came a statement that the last half-year had seen the deficit grow to 1,337,826. All dealings in the company's shares came to a halt.

This decline was partly explainable by another example of Warners' profound belief that if they didn't expand they would go under. Patently, they didn't realize that they stood to go under all the sooner if they did expand. They bought the Vitagraph company, and a pack of further financial problems, but Vitagraph had a vast nation-wide distribution set-up which they were convinced could only benefit them considerably.

The people who were not impressed were the men of Wall Street. The stock exchange thought the Warners had taken leave of their senses. Even Motley Flint couldn't help stem the flow of the tide. It was now Harry who went cap-in-hand to the finance houses of New York.

That was a lot less simple than it may seem. The American financial empire (for all the allegations of Jewish domination already being circulated by right-wing extremists) was notoriously antisemitic, and it was plainly delighted to see the troubles of a Jewish-owned organization. Eventually, at what seemed punitive interest rates, Harry managed a deal to bail out the family firm.

He also developed a method of postponing the excursions into the red. All payments to people in Los Angeles—which meant all the actors, actresses and studio staff—were made on cheques drawn on New York banks. Since the return journey from coast to coast was at least eight days, there could always be a minimum of those eight days before the cheques were paid.

There were times when they would conveniently forget to sign them, too.

For the firm's New York employees, the entire operation was put in reverse. Meanwhile, in an effort to show just how industrious and sincere Warner Brothers were, a member of one Wall Street firm—albeit one of the few Jewish companies—Goldman, Sachs and Co, was appointed to the board.

At the same time, almost as a gesture of defiance, Warners entered the radio field on the East Coast too. They took over the

Newark, New Jersey, station of WAAM, using the call letters WBPI. They also bought the Piccadilly Theatre on Broadway. The financial district thought they were even more crazy, but it confirmed the Warners' belief that standing still meant going backwards. The arch-apostle of that belief was now, as ever, Sam, who for the moment was not popular with his two elder brothers, to say nothing of his parents.

Sam had married Lina Basquette, *première danseuse* in the current edition of the Ziegfeld Follies. Although the marriage had been solemnized at the home of Dr Nathan Krass, the rabbi of the Reform Temple Emanu-El in New York, the first wedding of a Warner brother outside the Jewish faith brought a great sense of shock, if not outrage.

He was not only a member of the family, but also of the company, so they were not about to make him an outcast. But it was only Jack, who had always idolized him, who treated him with anything other than coolness.

It was not a situation that could last. For one thing, Lina had given birth to a daughter, Leta, and the Warner grandparents didn't want her brought up outside the family. For another, Lina was sickly, and would die while her child was still an infant.

There was another reason. Sam had been working on an idea which almost everyone else thought was further proof of his madness. *He* thought it could make the whole industry change overnight—pictures that talked.

CHAPTER 5

THE MIRACLE-WORKER

It was a factory. They were turning out a product.

Joan Leslie

There was something missing. In fact, there had been ever since, quite independently of each other, Thomas Alva Edison and William Friese-Greene devised methods of showing that images could be made to move when they were projected on to a screen.

It was one thing to be mown down by an approaching express locomotive, but quite another for it all to happen in complete silence. The cinema industry's answer to that, of course, was simple—music: an out-of-tune piano played by a maiden-lady schoolteacher in the neighbourhood Bijou, or a symphony orchestra in its full glory in a Broadway or London West End picture palace.

It should be said, too, that the public were happy enough to accept things as they were. Those who made a weekly trip to their local cinema hardly conceived of things ever changing. They never considered that movies had to talk, any more than any of them gave a moment's thought to the notion that the pictures in their daily papers should suddenly get up and dance around, or that those in the family snapshot album would suddenly find a voice.

The people who weren't so sure were the movie-makers themselves. 'I always knew that the absence of sound meant that an essential element in the making of pictures was missing,' Sir Michael Balcon, the eminent British producer, once told me.

Knowing that there was an absent dimension and doing something about it were inevitably two completely different things. At the turn of the century Edison himself had been toying with ways of giving voice to his own invention, the Kinetoscope, and by 1913 had declared that 'All the problems have been cured.' They hadn't.

It was virtually impossible precisely to synchronize sound with movement, and when it was in time people couldn't hear it. No one had yet found a way of amplifying a gramophone record—for that was how he thought the sound should be transmitted.

The invention of the valve, or vacuum tube, by Dr Lee De Forest changed everything. It meant electrical recording was now a reality. In the 1920s De Forest himself developed his own system of sound-on-celluloid. He called it Phonofilm, and opened a laboratory with an impressive fascia for all to see. It was the 'Home of Talking Pictures'—the first time that phrase had been used.

Nevertheless, the industry itself was not sufficiently impressed with the invention to risk sinking into it either its money or its library of film projects. What it had seen it didn't particularly like—a man talking to a duck; a girl saying she was the Queen of the Fairies—all good stuff for the fairground, but the cinema had grown up. It wasn't remotely interested in what would today be called gimmicks. The industry had become an art-form, and it didn't want to demean itself. De Forest thought it was wrong.

What no one knew was just how revolutionary it all could be. Except perhaps Sam Warner.

He had met a certain Major Nathan Levinson, a genius with the electrical equipment used by the American forces in the War, and now anxious to see his experience put to civil use. Levinson was helping Warners with their radio station when the subject turned to sound films.

Levinson had seen some experiments his company were doing in their New York office, and knew they offered a completely different perspective to the whole business of film-making. Moreover, he knew something about the Warner brothers, particularly about Sam. The talk in the trade was that the company had invested in radio because they were in financial trouble. Levinson knew the brothers paid their bills—and also that they were still desperately searching for ways of being sure that they could continue to pay them.

Most of all, he appreciated the fact that 37-year-old Sam would greet a new technical development like a spring lamb seeing a wide-open field. He invited him to New York, and, just as he predicted, Sam ran to accept.

It was, Sam later told his brothers, the most exciting day of his life. There he was, invited into a viewing theatre no bigger than a large office, and pictured on a screen in the darkened room, a man sat down at a piano, removed his gloves, looked towards the camera, smiled and began to play. Soon he was joined by other musicians, who also began to play. But that wasn't the significant part. Sam also heard them.

And what he heard was not only well amplified but sounded the way a band should sound.

'How's it done?' Sam wanted to know. The answer was that the soundtrack was on a 33·3 revolutions-per-minute disc played from the centre outwards—the opposite direction from that used by conventional gramophone records. A series of gears had connected it with the camera when it was made, and the same process was now in use with the projector.

All Sam could say was, 'I've got to tell the others about this.' Major Levinson knew he had made the most important sale of his life.

Sam realized this was the one moment Jack would regret being based in California, but it was not a time for sentiment. Harry was the one who controlled the company purse-strings—such as they were—and Abe was the Treasurer. When he phoned Harry to say, 'This is the opportunity we've all been waiting for', the only answer he wanted was, 'When can we see it?'

A second showing was arranged for later that week, and Harry and Abe were invited along to relive Sam's experience, if not perhaps his thrills.

He did not tell them that they were going to see a sound film.

'If they had said talking picture, I never would have gone,' Harry wrote years afterwards, 'because talking pictures had been made up to that time several times, and each was a failure. I am positive if they had said talking picture, I would not have gone.'

But go he did, and leave he did, if not quite as enthusiastic as his younger brother, then at least convinced it was something at which the family business ought to have a try.

As canny as ever, Harry first wanted the advice of Waddill Catchings, investment banker for the Wall Street firm which was now represented on the Warner board. Catchings seemed rather more enthusiastic than Harry. And that was all the eldest member of the outfit needed to know.

When Harry saw a jazz band performing on the screen he knew exactly where he had to go from there. For once not leaving the production ideas entirely to Sam and Jack, he phoned Catchings the next day and told him, 'I've decided what we must do. No wonder this hasn't taken hold. It needs to be sold with showmanship.' And then he added, 'If people can be made to play instruments on the screen, they can be made to sing too.' Prophetic words.

But it was a move that had to be made quickly. Quite suddenly they were not alone. The Fox studios had been toying with a new sound-on-film process, developed by Theodore Case. Unless Warners acted at once, they would lose the race before it had begun.

Warners made the corporate decision to enter and win.

Harry's idea was simply to put into production more of what he had seen at the surprise demonstration; to take top acts from all over America and turn the local cinema into part of the biggest vaudeville circuit in the country.

31

A deal was struck with Western Electric, the manufacturing arm of the telephone firm, and a new company was formed between them. They called it Vitaphone, a convenient development of Warners' own Vitagraph organization.

The old studios in Brooklyn which the brothers had first used in the War were brought back into business, and a series of short subjects was filmed there. Some featured poor vaudevillians who had never been able to make any real impact or money in their lives. Others starred people who very definitely had made both. Caruso sang 'Vesti la Giubba' from *Pagliacci*. Eddie Cantor rolled his banjo eyes. George Jessel spoke on the telephone to his mother—and, most promising of all, as it turned out, Al Jolson came through the door of a log cabin and sang 'April Showers'.

The shorts, it was decided, would be sandwiched between other Warner Brothers features. Within weeks they became a staple part of the Warner diet. Producers were told by Harry (in one of his few recorded demonstrations of wit), 'We don't want 'em good, we want 'em Tuesday.' Sam, who regarded each as an art-form, was furious.

Art or novelty, the shorts didn't make any great impact.

Cinema audiences had been used to having live vaudevillian acts featured between their movies. Some theatres already had electric organs. In the plushest cinemas there were the great symphony orchestras. To the people who were used to these things, the Vitaphone shorts were little more than an interesting diversion.

The brothers were not in the business to make diversions. If the cinema had escaped from the peepshow once, it was not going back there now. Sam decided they had no choice but to go full pelt to make Vitaphone a success. For if it failed, they would sink with it.

He persuaded the other brothers to make their next big movie with a Vitaphone sound-track. The film they chose was *Don Juan,* with John Barrymore in the title role and the beautiful Mary Astor as his co-star. There would be no dialogue, but every action on screen would be synchronized with musical accompaniment, and there would be sound-effects—every time Don Juan fenced, the audience heard his blade tangle with that of his opponent.

The New York Philharmonic were retained, and Sam took charge of the production. The score was written by Edward Bowes, soon to be known all over the United States as 'Major Bowes' of the radio show *Amateur Hour.*

Sam wouldn't allow anything 'amateur' to encroach on this, the most expensive film Warners had produced to date. When the noise of passing traffic got unmanageable he moved the orchestra from the studio to the Metropolitan Opera House. When even the opera house wasn't sufficiently soundproof—the noise at times was so violent it jogged the recording stylus—he insisted that all the recording be done at night.

It was a sensible move. Only afterwards did he realize the cause of the noise. An extension to the New York subway system was in the course of construction.

The people working on the film knew how important it all was. Even Barrymore himself was well behaved—which, as Jack Warner was to remark in his memoirs, was quite remarkable, considering the quality of Prohibition gin—and only crashed through one glass window.

Finally, at the Warners Theatre in New York on 6 August 1926, the film had its world première. However, the audience, who were used to hearing the greatness of a full symphony orchestra in Broadway theatres, reserved judgment. No matter how brilliant the recording, the discs could still not compete with the sound of a live performance.

The evening as a whole, however, was something else. The very same audience that was too blasé to appreciate the musical accompaniment to the main feature was enchanted by the shorts that made up the programme. These were people who had never been exposed to the 'peepshows' of the past few months, and the sense of being present at something totally new grew as one 'act' followed another.

The New York Philharmonic had a film to themselves—on screen this time—playing *Tannhäuser,* and opera singers Marion Talley and Anna Case performed. So did a certain Roy Smeck, who played the banjo. Efrem Zimbalist and Mischa Elman played their violins, and Harold Bauer was at the piano. Martinelli from the Metropolitan Opera sang 'Vesti la Giubba' (now accepted as *the* cinema aria).

They all made up one of the most fascinating evenings in theatrical history. Perhaps the most interesting part of the whole programme was a speech on film—a message from Mr Will Hays, who had recently moved from Washington, where he was Postmaster-General, to become Hollywood's 'voluntary censor', the President of the Motion Picture Producers and Distributors of America.

The Warners audience roared their approval as the head of what was already known as the Hays Office declared, 'To the Warner Brothers to whom is due credit for this, the beginning of a new era in music and motion pictures, I offer my felicitations and my sincerest appreciation.'

It was Mr Hays's perfectly synchronized enunciation that made Sam that night think of what was in store for the company. . . .

'If Hays can talk, so can our actors,' he said excitedly to Harry, who replied, 'Rubbish' or words to that effect. 'This is for music, not words.'

In the coming months Harry was to be proved wrong, but he wouldn't budge. For the moment, however, he had to admit it was an important night.

Variety proclaimed loudly that it approved. 'Vitaphone will get 'em—men, women and children. It's the unprecedented success of filmville. The Warners have an achievement.'

Jack Warner meanwhile had to be content with making his assessments second-hand. He was the only member of the partnership not at the Warners Theatre that night. Someone had to stay behind in Hollywood to mind the store—and to assess immediately the reactions of the opposition as he planned the film's West Coast première.

Two people who enjoyed every moment of it, however, were the senior Warners, Pearl and Benjamin. They had been brought to New York from Youngstown by their sons, and treated by them as the distinguished guests of honour.

In his book Jack Warner recalls a letter they wrote him after that evening:

Dear Jack,

We never dreamed that we would live to see such a performance, and above all that we would be the parents of such wonderful boys. It is our fondest hope that we will live to a ripe old age so we can see you boys grow on and on. When four marvellous boys like you stick together through thick and thin, there is no question but that you will attain all the success you hope for. And, Jack dear, we want to tell you that the only thing that marred our happiness on opening night was that you weren't there.

Lovingly,
Mum and Dad.

If no one could yet be sure that Vitaphone represented the only way the cinema could go from now on, there was no doubt that it caused a stir. And while people were still talking, Fox had also made its plunge into the sound market—with special editions of their Movietone newsreels.

People could hear as well as see Benito Mussolini greeting the American public and, most sensational of all, the return of Colonel Lindbergh to the United States after the first solo air crossing of the Atlantic Ocean.

They marvelled not only at the welcome from President Calvin S. Coolidge, but most of all at the sound of Lindbergh's plane, *The Spirit of St Louis,* touching down.

That event would continue to haunt the Warner Brothers and be responsible a generation later for one of the most spectacular losses the company incurred, but for the moment it served as a spur.

It wasn't easy to keep a secret in Hollywood, and the word was very definitely that while Fox were encouraged by their Movietone success, they had no intention for the moment of using the system to make sound feature films. Indeed, there was an unwritten agreement between the studios that none would do so for a year—if one of them succeeded to the extent that audiences demanded movies nobody could deliver, they would all be left panting in the ring, simultaneously knocking each other out.

Sam Warner, however, was not to be swayed from his conviction that Vitaphone offered the company the only way out from being totally swamped by the much larger and richer competition.

'It's still a fight', he told Harry, 'and we either win it now or lose it tomorrow.'

It wasn't easy to resist that sort of persuasion. The brothers agreed to search for a story on which they could build the achievements of *Don Juan*. However, Sam wasn't going to be satisfied with a mere background musical score. This time there would have to be musical numbers integrated into the plot, similar to the ones that had proved so successful in the shorts at the *Don Juan* première.

'What about dialogue?' asked Sam. 'Nonsense,' said Harry. 'OK, no dialogue,' said Jack. Abe, who was beginning to worry about the whole idea of making films for theatres with no equipment to show them, shook his head.

They looked through the library of properties they had bought but not yet made, and agreed they had a title which might lend itself for what they had in mind.

CHAPTER 6

THE JAZZ SINGER

I always thought Jack was a little paranoid. But he
could predict what people would do.

Bill Orr

The Jazz Singer was the rage of Broadway, but no one expected it to
be much else. It was a New York story that was unlikely to transfer
to the sticks. When Warners bought the screen rights to Samson
Raphaelson's drama it caused no more than a few nods in the
Hollywood community. A paragraph in *Variety* duly recorded the
purchase, and that was that—a silent film called *The Jazz Singer* had
definite limitations.

It was one thing, perhaps, to expect audiences to relate to mute
mouths reciting lines later shown in sub-titles; quite another to
expect them to be entertained by a man supposedly singing songs
they couldn't hear.

In live theatre terms, however, it had been a different story.

George Jessel, still in his twenties, had a personal triumph in the
musical show which the advertisements in all the New York papers
said would run and run. Certainly it looked set to do just that.
Takings never dropped below what the show-business set would
have described as 'socko', and when the screen rights were bought it
was tacitly understood that the man who had been such a hit on
Broadway would, in the fullness of time decreed by the box-office,
repeat his success on the screen.

There were good reasons for Jessel himself to think so. Firstly,
Jack Warner had told him so. Secondly, he had done rather well for
the studio in the couple of years preceding his Broadway opening.
Private Izzy Murphy and *Sailor Izzy Murphy* were a couple of
nonsense pieces about a Jewish boy falling in love with a Catholic
girl. However, they made money and represented, it might have
been thought, a fairly good apprenticeship for *The Jazz Singer,* the
story of a cantor's son who chooses the stage instead of the
synagogue, and at the same time falls in love with a Gentile.

As far as the studio was concerned, too, it seemed an open-and-shut case. They were in no great hurry to make the movie because they knew it would be little more than a filler, a product to satisfy the exhibitors but nothing exceptional.

And there was that business about the title. The studio could possibly have reverted to the original name of *Day of Atonement*, and then made the cantor's son an actor instead of a singer. Short of that, it wasn't going to be easy to get over the message that the young man wanted to sing for a living.

Such were the problems of silent pictures.

Now, quite suddenly, the title *The Jazz Singer* stood out in capital letters. Alan Crosland, who had directed *Don Juan*, was brought in to take charge of it. As the father he cast the perhaps significantly named Warner Oland, who would go on to play a whole pagoda-load of Charlie Chan roles (he had played Cesare Borgia in *Don Juan*). Eugenie Besserer was lined up as the jazz singer's mother, and May McAvoy would play the love interest.

The star of the piece? George Jessel, of course. Jack Warner took a train to New York, entertained Jessel to a superb dinner at Delmonico's, and casually dropped the news of his star's acquisition to the waiting Pressmen.

That was when the situation changed. Jessel, who was greatly enjoying all the trappings of sudden stardom—to say nothing of what was about to become international attention for the first time in his life—decided he was not going to be rushed into anything.

'After all,' he told a somewhat incredulous Jack Warner, 'if I'm going to risk my career on some new-fangled invention, I think I ought to be appropriately compensated.'

Jessel believed he had got all his shots into court. What he did not appreciate was that Warner was himself a fairly good tennis-player. He cried 'Fault!' and, without telling Jessel, started looking elsewhere.

In his book Jack recalled that he had first agreed to pay Jessel 30,000 dollars and then shook hands on 10,000 more. The star, however, wanted it in writing before he would agree to take the train West. Warner thought his word should have been enough, and called the whole deal off.

That is not the way Jessel himself saw it, although there was broad agreement that money was the stumbling-block, and that other artists were then approached. One of them was Eddie Cantor, who turned it down because he didn't want to upset an old vaudeville partner—George Jessel.

Jessel and Warner agreed too on the fact that the next to be approached was Al Jolson, but this is where their stories part company. Warner said that he got his New York representative to 'talk turkey' and find out how much Jolson wanted for the role. He said 75,000 dollars, and it was agreed there and then—while Jessel licked his wounds, fully aware of what was happening.

The story Jessel told me is rather more colourful. Both he and Al had spent the night with a couple of show-girls at New York's Biltmore Hotel. The following day was a Sunday and they had arranged to use the morning playing golf. However, Jolson knocked on Jessel's door and said, 'Georgie, I'm not that keen on playing golf today. I know you're tired, too. Why don't you go back to sleep? I'm going out for a walk.'

Jessel turned over and went back to sleep. 'The next day, I woke up to read in the papers that Jolson had signed with Warner Brothers to make *The Jazz Singer*. Is there any wonder I felt bitter? I felt sick. It was my part and partly my story. Jolson got the role because he put money into it.'

This is totally contrary to what Warner had written in his autobiography, but since Jack was not a man to allow the truth to interfere with a good story, there is reason to treat his view of the past with a certain reserve. Warner also denies that Jolson was paid in shares for his agreeing to sign for the role—which virtually every Hollywood historian from Darryl Zanuck downwards, to say nothing of Jolson himself, had always claimed. It was widely reported at the time, and ties in with Jessel's claim that his rival 'put money into it'.

What is not subject to doubt is the fact that Al Jolson not only revolutionized motion pictures on Warners' behalf by starring in *The Jazz Singer,* but that he also did it uniquely. Even Jessel admitted to me, 'He was better at it than I would have been.'

The Jazz Singer began life as a magazine story written by Raphaelson while he was still a student at Champagne, Illinois. It was Jessel himself who read the piece and suggested that his 'Day of Atonement' would make a marvellous Broadway play. It had the germ about it of the old traditional Jewish story of the cantor who dreams about singing in one of the grand opera houses of Europe.

Ironically, Raphaelson told me, he had Al Jolson in mind when he first wrote his piece. More ironically still, it was very much Jolson's own story. He too had been a cantor's son who ran away from home to sing in front of an audience in a theatre, rather than before the Ark of the Law in a synagogue. It was therefore a story into which Jolson could put his heart, to say nothing of his own very different approach to show business. He was not an actor.

He was the kind of entertainer who needed to make love to an audience. It wasn't easy to do that to a camera.

However, it wasn't Jolson's acting that made *The Jazz Singer* such an important part of cinema history. It was, after all, intended as a

38

silent film with musical extracts. That was the plan Harry and Abe had agreed to. That was the plan to which Sam and Jack were working at the Sunset Boulevard studios. What none of them had reckoned with was that very individual Jolson style which had, at the age of forty, already earned him the title 'The World's Greatest Entertainer'.

When the script said that Jolson should sing that was precisely what everyone expected would happen. Al has to respond to the cheers and calls from a night-club crowd and then go into his first big number in the picture, 'Toot Toot Tootsie, Goo'Bye'.

Alan Crosland had never worked with Jolson before, and didn't know quite how to react to what happened next. He had given the signal for sound recording to begin. The cameras were turning, and the musicians were poised for the conductor Lou Silvers to raise his baton. He did—and that was when Jolson did precisely what he had done on the stage of New York's Winter Garden theatre a thousand times before.

'Wait a minute,' he cried. 'Wait a minute. You ain't heard nothin' yet. Wait a minute, I tell yer. You wanna hear "Toot Toot Tootsie"? All right, hold on. . . . Lou, listen. You play "Toot Toot Tootsie". Three choruses, you understand, and in the third chorus I whistle. Now give it to 'em hard and heavy. Go right ahead. . . .'

And then he did what he was supposed to have done at the beginning. He sang 'Toot Toot Tootsie'.

Now, nobody could have written those opening words for him. They would never have passed the careful eye of a script editor. But they were very much Jolson. They symbolized the way he performed. They meant that the other people on the studio sound-stage were real, and it was to them, not a whirring camera, that he was singing. More important, they meant that the silent film was about to be consigned to the scrap-heap.

But there was the question of Harry and the other people who thought they had to do his bidding. Wasn't it defeating the whole purpose of Vitaphone? That was the point at which Sam took charge. The lines, he said, should stay. He was well aware of the effect of that decision.

It meant that the talkies had arrived.

Sam saw the potential of it all the moment he made the decision not to ask Jolson to re-record 'Toot Toot Tootsie' (of course, getting him to do so would have been another matter entirely).

He immediately suggested that Al record a new all-sound sequence for the movie. Between them they chose the scene where the putative Broadway star Jack Robin comes home on the eve of the birthday of his father, Cantor Rabinowitz. The cantor is out, but his mother welcomes the return of the prodigal son with love, warmth and (we can assume) chicken soup. The schmaltz came from Jack —who sits down at the piano and begins to warble Irving Berlin's new hit 'Blue Skies'.

Sam and Jolson spoke about a verbal bridge between the two choruses of the song. 'I'll get a few lines written,' he said. 'No, don't bother,' said Al. 'You know I always make things up as I go along.'

Sam knew all right, and agreed. What came out between those choruses was pure Jolson. Most film history books have recorded that Al just said, 'Come on, Ma, listen to this.' In fact, his lines were much longer:

'You like that, Mama? Well, I'm glad of it. You know I'd rather please you than anybody I know of. Darling, will you give me something? Shut your eyes, Mama. . . .'

It's a lovely moment, even ignoring the impact it must have had on audiences hearing those words for the first time. Jolson tells his mother he's going to steal a kiss, just as he will when he takes her into the 'Dark Mill' on Coney Island. He's going to buy her a new pink dress and then they'll all move to the Bronx, so that 'Mrs Friedman, the butcher's wife, . . . she'll be jealous of you'.

It all comes to an abrupt end while Jolson sings the song 'jazzy, like I will on the stage'. His father walks in, shouts 'Stop'—and the picture goes silent again, apart from the ubiquitous musical accompaniment.

Naturally enough, it wasn't an easy picture to shoot. Much has been written about the hiding of microphones in flower vases, telephones, in women's dresses. It all happened, and more.

Huge carpets were hung on the walls of what had now become sound-stages, to try to keep out the noise of passing traffic.

The constantly whirring cameras had to be concealed in sound-proof booths so hot that the operators either fainted or fell out of the enclosures at the end of a take, writhing in sweat and agony.

Above all, there was the simple problem of fitting in sound to match the pictures, a difficulty heightened by the Vitaphone process. Every reel of film had to be matched by a corresponding disc, and while it was easy enough to cut and edit a strip of film, you couldn't do anything of the kind with a disc.

Consequently, once the film had been shot and the musical accompaniment added, that was the way it had to remain. It was also one of the reasons why Warners were so unwilling to produce a 100 per cent talking picture. If they had done so it would have had to have been shot at the rate of 1,000 feet a time, with no scope for retakes whatever.

As things were, Alan Crosland had first to shoot the non-singing scenes, edit and assemble them, and then add the sound segments. Because these had to fit precisely into the thousand feet and then on

40

to the wax record, they had to be perfectly timed. Had there been computers in 1927, this wouldn't have provided any problems at all. As it was, the methods the studio had to employ would have done credit to Henry Ford's Detroit production line.

Blank film was first inserted where the musical scenes would go. It was in this space that the precisely timed sound sequences had to be placed. They were shot on adjoining stages.

If in the first reel, for instance, there were three songs, three stages had to be ready side by side with three camera teams, each ready to take over immediately from the one before.

The silent scenes were projected on to a screen overhead, and when it was time for a song, or the piece of dialogue, work had to begin the very moment the blank piece of film came up on the screen.

There was an adjoining set for the orchestra—complete with its own sound circuit. Each of the sound stages had its own circuit, also. This gives some idea why singing 'Toot Toot Tootsie' provided so many technical headaches.

Of course, every stage of this new 'Vitaphoning' process was being carefully leaked to the Press by Warner's new publicity executive Hal Wallis. Jolson was to prove the most receptive subject with whom he had so far had to deal. There were none of the drunken histrionics of Barrymore or the prima donna activities of a host of leading ladies.

For his part, Jolson (who liked to consider himself the King of Broadway) loved being fêted as the new Emperor of Hollywood, and Jack Warner was more than willing to co-operate. He arranged for Douglas Fairbanks and Charlie Chaplin to be photographed with Jolson, to all appearances paying him homage. Together they went to the nightspots, and to the most fashionable tourist haunts.

But most significant of all, Jack showed him a deference he gave to no one else. If Al Jolson approached Jack's office and asked, 'Is the great man in?' (the terminology radiating into the Warner room was guaranteed to put him in a wonderful mood) he was certain to be shown immediately into the sanctum.

For hours after his departure Jack would regale anyone who would listen—and if you valued your job at Warners you listened and laughed at the appropriate moments—with what 'Jolie' had said.

There were other sides to the publicity surrounding the making of the film. It wasn't universally seen as the rock on which Warner Brothers' future fortune would be built. For everyone who decided that the studio was creating a huge money-spinner there were others who were convinced that it was merely helping itself along an ever more ruinous course.

The result was that people who might have been content to wait for bills to be paid now sent process-servers to Sunset Boulevard demanding immediate payment. Evading these people became a full-time exercise for the brothers and their executives. Day after day they used new entrances to the building, going through doors they previously hadn't even known existed.

Nobody outside of the Warner empire really had any idea how *The Jazz Singer* would turn out. Harry and Abe were increasingly sceptical, especially since the costs of production seemed to escalate with every new development. But to Sam and Jack it was not just the most marvellous thing that had happened to them, it was the crock of gold at the end of the rainbow, the one factor that would alter the course of film history—and it was all due to them.

Arrangements were all set for the world première at the same Warners' theatre where *Don Juan* and the accompanying programme had heralded it all. It was going to be the biggest evening in movie history. Sam was convinced of that, and Jack was carried away by his enthusiasm.

It was in the midst of this frenzied enthusiasm that one problem—to which no one had even given a moment's thought—changed everything. Sam was struck down by a mysterious illness. Jack recalled that his brother became 'weak and listless' with black rings under his eyes, but insisted that the younger brother still go off to New York to complete arrangements for the 6 October première.

Jack went alone, not realizing that Sam would almost immediately be taken to the California Lutheran Hospital.

Harry and Abe, with two New York specialists accompanying them, took the first train they could across country. A few hundred miles out of Manhattan, they received a telegram saying that Sam had had a severe stroke and was not likely to survive.

Jack followed his brothers almost immediately afterwards.

The doctors tried to charter an aeroplane—a pretty rare and not hazard-free move in 1927—but the only one they could find was laid up for repairs.

The torment of the slow 2,500-mile train journey was almost more than Harry and Abe could bear. Less than halfway across the country, they chartered a train of their own. But it wasn't quick enough. Sam had to have two emergency operations. By the time the brothers reached his bedside he was dead.

Twenty-four hours later *The Jazz Singer* opened at Warners' Theatre. None of the brothers was present to see Sam's faith vindicated.

Appropriately, the première was held just a couple of hours after the end of Yom Kippur, the Day of Atonement which played such a big part in the film's story. It was a strange occasion. That very day, the New York papers had given considerable prominence to Sam's obituary and his death was in the minds of a number of people, but at the theatre no one mentioned it. The message seemingly was that the show must go on, and go on it did—to rapturous applause. The cheers that greeted the shorts at the *Don Juan* première the previous year were the pitter-patter of a shower compared with the storm of that night.

Most people hadn't known what to expect, and those who thought they had were overwhelmed by seeing and hearing Al Jolson in this somewhat maudlin monochrome film.

Jolson went on stage to say how moved he was by the audience's reaction. 'Folks,' he said, 'I was so happy that I couldn't stop the tears.'

The critics were as affected as anyone else. The next day Mordaunt Hall wrote in *The New York Times*, 'The success of this production is due to a large degree to Mr Jolson's Vitaphoned renditions' and 'The Vitaphoned songs and some dialogue have been introduced most adroitly. This in itself is an ambitious move, for in the expression of song the Vitaphone vitalises the production enormously.'

He added:

The Warner Brothers astutely realised that a film conception of *The Jazz Singer* was one of the few subjects that would lend itself to the uses of the Vitaphone. It was also a happy idea to persuade Mr Jolson to play the leading role, for few men could have approached the task of singing and acting so well as he does in this photoplay. His 'voice with a tear' compelled silence and possibly all that disappointed the people in the packed theatre was the fact that they could not call upon him or his image at least for an encore.

They had to content themselves with clapping and whistling after Mr. Jolson's shadow finished a realistic song.

All that was not to say there were not a few reservations on the critic's part.

There are quite a few moments when the picture drags, because Alan Crosland, the director, has given too much footage to discussion and to the attempts of the theatrical manager to prevail upon Jack Robin not to permit sentiment to sway him when his great opportunity is at hand.

There are also times when one would expect the Vitaphoned portion to be either more subdued or stopped as the camera swings to other scenes.

43

The following Sunday, Mr Hall had forgotten most of those criticisms.

On the opening night [he wrote] one almost forgot that the real Jolson was sitting in a box listening to his own songs, for it seemed as though in the darkness Mr Jolson had crept behind the screen and was rendering the songs for his black and white image.

That, of course, was precisely what the less sophisticated movie audiences were thinking. In the whole of the United States, only seventy-five theatres were wired for sound. But things didn't stay that way.

Variety wrote of a 'Talking Picture Sensation', and suddenly the rest of Hollywood shuddered.

Warners themselves switched a batch of also-ran films to be 'Vitaphoned', while their competitors were not sure what had hit them. Contrary to the popular image of what happened, the moguls didn't immediately pick up their white telephones and bellow, 'Bring in the engineers! All our pictures are now going to be talkies!' They were stunned.

A few still believed that *The Jazz Singer* and all that it had spawned were passing fancies, fairground stuff that once the novelty had worn off would be exposed for the vulgar gimmicks that they were, but when the takings at the Warners' Theatre box office were added up—the film would run uninterrupted for thirty-five weeks at the New York playhouse, and longer still in the Los Angeles theatre of the same name—incredulity had changed to panic.

More and more theatres were being converted by Western Electric engineers, and operating the new equipment. As each one played their print of *The Jazz Singer,* so it reported record ticket sales.

The result was predictable. The other studios did start following suit. Films that were virtually complete were converted to sound. The producers and stars who held out—Chaplin was the supreme example—were made to look old-fashioned and somewhat foolish.

What Sam Warner had probably not foreseen was the effect his faith in the new medium would have on the careers of a hundred or more top actors. Stars whose bodies were the personification of vibrant manhood or sensuous femininity were suddenly found to have voices that were more suited for a dressmakers' tea-party or the neighbourhood fish-market.

The moguls were cruel, too. The classic case was that of John Gilbert, whose voice was recorded at the wrong speed by MGM engineers, and so was immediately dismissed by Louis B. Mayer for being effeminate. He never recovered.

There was still another result. The silent film which had for years been considered an international medium—only the titles had to be changed to suit the language of the country in which a movie was being shown—was now being replaced by pictures that could only be enjoyed by people who understood the spoken word.

For the time being, that at least didn't matter. *The Jazz Singer* had more than enough silent footage for it to be shown in practically every country that had movie theatres. You didn't have to know the language to be moved to jumping up in your seat when suddenly you heard a voice on the screen start singing.

Simultaneously, theatres from New York to Nanking were being fitted up with sound equipment, and those that didn't yet have it were showing *The Jazz Singer* as a silent picture. Strangely, it didn't seem to be important. As if carried away by the momentum of all they had read, audiences everywhere clapped the film just the same.

Some people tried to explain it as being all part of Al Jolson's magnetism, although without his voice his ciné image was literally just a shadow of his stage self. However, there was an attraction to people in seeing an historic film, even though the reason for its importance was lost on them.

As far as Warners were concerned, Al Jolson was the hottest property around, and they continued to treat him that way. His second film for the studio was *The Singing Fool.* It contained a few more lines of dialogue but was also mostly silent with the same sort of musical accompaniment. The story was even more sentimental than that of *The Jazz Singer,* and Jolson would have had to have granted that his acting was far worse. But the film contained a song called 'Sonny Boy' which gave him what was perhaps the biggest hit of his career, a sentimental piece of nonsense written by De Sylva, Brown and Henderson as a joke. They were so ashamed of the song that they couldn't even bring themselves to mail it, and got the hotel bellboy to do it for them. However, 'Sonny Boy' helped *The Singing Fool* become the biggest box-office money-spinner there had been to date—a position it would hold for ten years, right until the showing of *Gone With The Wind.*

Warners, with the flair for publicity that Hal Wallis had brought to the studio, decided to stage the opening of *The Singing Fool* on Jolson's own plot of Broadway soil, the Winter Garden.

The picture made five and a half million dollars. Warner Brothers no longer had to send out their cheques drawn on banks 2,500 miles away, and by the end of 1929 chalked up a net profit of 7,271,805 dollars—compared with a loss of 98,972 dollars in the year of *The Jazz Singer.*

They were no longer an also-ran among the Hollywood producers. *The Jazz Singer* had made them a major studio. To go with his new station in life, Jack Warner—now virtually in sole control in Hollywood—was acting the part to perfection. He was talking big and acting bigger. His cigars grew longer, his expressions more extravagant. And his ideas and aspirations multiplied along with the figures on the company's books—much, of course, to the temporary delight of Harry, who usually found it very difficult to be happy about anything to do with his younger brother. Abe, on the other hand, seemed more than content.

If the brothers were afraid of being branded too far-seeing by half, Harry managed to put things to rights. In May 1929, as the talkies were becoming firmly established, he declared that people would never accept films in colour. 'It would be too taxing on the eyes,' he declared.

But people listened to him. The Warners seemed to know what they were talking about.

It was due to the man who had been in charge of the Vitaphone 'shorts' programme that sound moved the next step forward.

Bryan Foy, one of the Seven Little Foys of vaudeville fame (their father was the famous Eddie Foy senior), had the knack of spotting a feature-film idea in a story in a newspaper.

One of these ideas became *The Lights Of New York,* intended as a two-reel film about gangsters in the then contemporary world of Prohibition. Without telling anyone, Foy (everyone called him Brynie, and that was how he was known for his next thirty-six years at Warners) decided to master the problems of Vitaphone and make it an all-talking picture.

Jack Warner was conveniently out of the country at the time. He and Harry had decided to try to mend their fences. With Sam gone, Harry's sense of family unity had persuaded him to try to curb his hatred for Jack, whom he had to admit had done his bit to put the family firm back into the black. His younger brother was sufficiently subdued to accept the offer at face value, and the pair went to London, Paris and Berlin, officially to supervise the premières in those cities of *The Jazz Singer.*

It would be about the only time that Jack was not able to take charge directly of the Hollywood output. Brynie decided it was a case of the mouse playing in the cat's absence, and took a gamble he knew perfectly well Jack was not ready to take himself. He also knew that Abe, constantly frustrated at seeing his brothers having all the fun, would be only too glad to exert a modicum of authority.

In his book Jack was to say that he approved of the project from the start, and was so full of money at the time that he benignly handed over the cash on request. It wasn't quite that way. Before he heard details of the financial take, Jack was furious—which was understandable, since he had Harry breathing down his neck at the time.

When the second all-talking Warners film—none of the other studios had yet come up with one—*The Terror* was shown in August 1928 *The New York Times* called it 'A Titleless Talking Film'—in other words, there were no titles between scenes; all the dialogue could actually be heard.

Once more, every conceivable sound effect was over-used. There weren't even any visual credits at the start. Instead, as Mordaunt Hall noted, 'Even the main title, the cast of players and the names of those who have contributed to the making of this audible film [*New York Times* language for "the talkies"] are announced from the screen by the shadow of a masked man.'

That sort of thing didn't last long; a fate not a few people hoped would be in store for the talkies themselves. Mr Joseph N. Weber, President of the Federation of Musicians, said that his eight hundred local branches were all convinced that talkies would not last. It was wishful thinking, but when he conducted his own poll, 'three-fifths of the audiences have expressed their preference for personal appearance of musicians to mechanical music'.

It was no compensation to suggest that the loss of work for cinema musicians would be made up by all the employment now to be offered by the studios. Hollywood was fussy about the quality of the men it employed, and the only ones who stood any chance of getting work either lived in California or were prepared to go there. A piano-player in Duluth, Minnesota—to say nothing of those in Britain or virtually any other country in the world—who had been working in a cinema every night of his life was almost certainly going to be unemployed, and that applied to the musicians in the big theatre orchestras, too.

The last people to worry about that, frankly, were the Brothers Warner, who saw every development of the sound-film as a further enrichment to their status. In September 1928 they took over a two-thirds interest—William Fox held the other third—in First National Pictures, which had been one of the Big Four (the others were Metro, Essenay and Lasky Famous Players) in the days when Warners were forgetting to sign their cheques, and which was described at the time as the 'largest in the American amusement industry'.

This move was important to Warners for two reasons. Firstly, it gave them access to the still considerable First National reputation and their muster of stars and technicians, to say nothing of the superb studios they ran at Burbank, several miles away. But perhaps even more important, the deal also gave them more than four thousand theatres all over the country, which they immediately saw as a marvellous potential outlet for the Warner Brothers product, without any competition, arguments or bribery of film-exhibitors.

The figure quoted for the deal—a mere 250 million dollars—was happily financed for the company by Wall Street, which was now bending over backwards to show how marvellously unprejudiced it was in making money from people like the Warners.

'Albert Warner', it was announced, was to become head of the company's theatre division, which he ran as though each unit was his own little business. It was a good recipe for success.

Harry stayed in New York to look after the ever-bulging company purse, while Jack occupied himself more and more with running the studio—or studios, for he decided First National would continue to run as a separate entity. But it would be a Warner entity, with Warner men taking over the seats of power.

As Head of Production at First National he placed Darryl Zanuck, who continued to amaze everyone around by being the fastest writer in Hollywood. Given an idea for a film on a Friday, he would have a complete shooting script the following Monday.

Zanuck used to say that his early success was based on the premise that he was going to be a no-man instead of a yes-man. Jack asked him—as he did all his writers and producers—what he thought of films, and he would tell him he thought they stank.

The only difficulty in running the two studios was that Burbank was not equipped for sound, and Warners were the last people even to think about making silent pictures in 1928. Western Electric were consulted, and once more came up with a solution. They installed microphones at First National, but linked them by telephone line with the rest of the equipment at Sunset Boulevard. The results were no different from those achieved at the Warner studios.

Weary River, Naughty Baby and *Synthetic Sin* were among the first of these.

As Jack Warner wrote, the company was knee-deep in money, and every new development just served to increase its wealth. And to keep Jack busy and away from home. His wife Irma and their son, Jack Junior, hardly saw him now. Business was a good excuse for his absences, but there were usually other women at the root of his seeming lack of concern for his family.

Still, he kept both Irma and Jack well fed and well clothed, and when he said that he was engaged on business the results of that business were obvious for all to see. But then everyone seemed to be doing well in America.

Then in September 1928 the first inkling could be seen of things changing, if only slightly. A violent turn-over in the market hit what the financial papers still persisted in calling 'the amusement market'. The biggest to be hit were Warner Bros (the company was now using the abbreviated form for all its official dealings). In one day

Warner shares, which had been the most bullish on Wall Street, dived nineteen points.

They recovered before too long, but Harry thought he could read some writing on a distant wall. Shrewdly, he started investing company money in a whole range of industries he could see were doing well. When he thought he had gone as high as he could he pulled out. It was an experience that was to bode well for him.

He also decided to give a great deal to charity—an example avidly followed by Abe, who, believing that the best charity began at home, gave his father Benjamin an interest in one of his theatres. The old man was so thrilled that he walked around with a shirt bearing the name of the theatre at Niles, Ohio—a move that seemed to foreshadow the T-shirt and sweatshirt craze that would come fifty years later.

Abe in particular was enjoying the prosperity and high standing in which the brothers were now held. The US Signals Corps, sensing a certain wisdom in backing a winner, awarded him a commission in the Reserves. From then on the former sergeant could claim his self-awarded title of 'the Major' had been legitimized. In the studios and the whole film business thereafter, that was how he was known.

But he sometimes worried about his brothers. He liked to show that he knew as much about picture-making as any other Hollywood mogul, which wasn't quite true.

In an article in *The New York Times* early in 1929 he declared forcibly:

As rapidly as theatres throughout the country are being fitted for the audible films, it is preposterous to suppose that the time will ever come when all houses, the length and breadth of the United States will be so equipped. The sweep of the talking picture does not necessarily mean that all film goers will want nothing else. An occasional audible picture will suffice for some audiences whose steady and uninterrupted patronage will continue to be accorded to the silent picture. Neither field conflicts with the other.

The whole philosophy of Warner Bros at the time was to prove that the silent film was dead, that theatres had to wire for sound and that their cinemas would be in the forefront of doing just that. There were tough words in the family for Major Warner after that.

People in the Warner employ were not exempt from mistakes either. When they were found out—as they usually were, by a team of private investigators hired as doormen, carpenters or other workers—most feared for their lives. Jack was in charge, and he already had the reputation of being a young man anxious to show that his age was going to be no bar in making him too tough to tangle

49

with. Irma and Jack Junior had reason to know this to their cost.

At the studio—which was much more home to him than his now palatial house ever could be—his toughness seemed to know no bounds. There was one way of doing things—Jack's way. But there was a heart beneath the celluloid.

A veteran cameraman was assigned to work on a baseball picture. There were some marvellous shots out in the field, with the sort of action to send sports writers into raptures. The old man was as excited as everyone else, till it came to developing the film. That was when he realized that the lens cap had been on throughout the whole day.

Jack had to know. After all, he saw the rushes every day, and on this occasion there was nothing to see. The man quaked. Some younger executives were getting ready to enjoy the ensuing sport but there wasn't any. There wasn't even a Jack Warner joke —although he'd laugh about it often enough in the future.

He heard the story, smiled, twisted his cigar and said:

'I guess that's what they call human error.'

The unions were not always so sure about the human factor operating at Warner Bros. In fact, so many suggestions were made about Jack's parentage that it was frequently taken to be totally irrelevant. The big rows were still to come, but even in 1929 Actors Equity Association was suing Warners for making contracts with non-union members.

The main point at issue was that the union alleged Warners were not paying enough to small-time actors who were now expected to speak as well as emote in the 'Talkies'. Equity sued for a million dollars, but the issue was settled out of court.

Everyone was now talking big money. They also talked about more mergers—between Warners and Fox (who had sold their interest in First National to Jack and his brothers), Warners and Paramount, and Warners and MGM. The stories were denied so often that commentators believed they were true, and astronomical figures were quoted. But these too died down.

The studio was, however, still very much on the rise. It took over Brunswick records for 10 million dollars, and spent a similar amount on buying studios in Germany.

All over the United States new theatres were being built, and not so new ones were coming on the market. Whenever they could Warner Bros bought them. But there was one for which they had more affection than all the others put together.

It was a 3,000-seater in their home town of Youngstown which they were building for a million dollars. The project was intended, the brothers said, as a memorial to the man who had really been responsible for starting it all—Sam. After all, if he hadn't persuaded

50

Harry, much against his will, to go into a darkened room and see a man take off a pair of gloves, Warner Bros might now have been broke. Most other people were. For, as *Variety* had put it so succinctly, it was the time when Wall Street laid its egg.

CHAPTER 7

TOO MUCH, TOO SOON

He was a great showman—and always made me laugh.

Mervyn LeRoy

The Wall Street disasters had a strange effect on the motion-picture business. While everyone else was going broke, the studios were busier than they had been for years. Millionaires from other industries were throwing themselves out of skyscraper windows, but the film moguls were reaping the benefits of an investment which even they had never really appreciated.

Ordinary decent middle-class people might now be lining up at the soup kitchens, but they were also doing something else—going to the movies. Men unable to break the habit of a lifetime would leave home in the morning to go to a job that no longer existed, and which they hadn't the courage to tell their wives they had lost. They would sit in the parks, and then when the theatres opened, stay in the comforting dark of the cinemas until it was time to go home. Whole families would sacrifice a few cents from their relief money for two or three hours of escapism, and then crawl back to what served as home in a shanty town.

This could mean only one thing to the studios: a demand for more films which just had to be met. Paradoxically, it had an additional effect on film-makers like Warners, who also had their own theatre chains.

Theatres in some towns were filled to capacity for the first three or four days of the week, and then empty the rest—because the hungry demand had already been satiated.

This meant that it was wise to change programmes halfway through the week. So still more films had to be made, which would then also be leased to the independent exhibitors. Naturally, the demand for more films meant more work for the studios.

That, of course, wasn't the whole story. Like most other people, the studio bosses had invested money in institutions which had gone

Jack L. Warner in the '20s, when it was all happening

Albert ('Abe') Warner

Sam Warner – the Brother with the ideas, but who never saw the triumphs

Harry Warner, who saw himself as head of the family and protector of its good name

The Warner Brothers – and parents and sisters – soon after their arrival in America

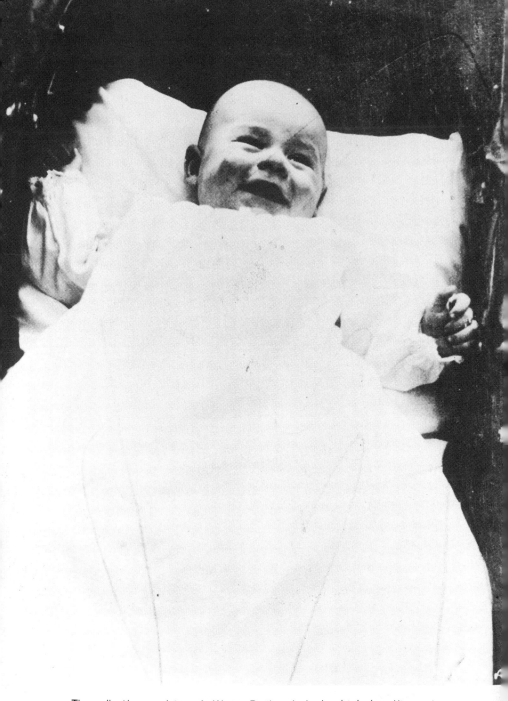

The earliest known picture of a Warner Brother. Jack, showing he loved it even then

A scene from the first Warner success, *My Four Years in Germany*. President Woodrow Wilson would later complain that the German atrocities in the movie were exaggerated

The Brothers 'in office'. Left to right, Sam, Harry, Jack and Abe

The dog that saved the studio – Rin Tin Tin

broke overnight. People sold studio shares with everything else, and there weren't always enough men around with the money to buy them at a decent price.

Some studios did have to file for bankruptcy. Warner Bros didn't. Harry said, 'I don't want our widows to suffer.' Even if for a time the trains rattling between the West and East Coasts did once more carry bundles of cheques that wouldn't be honoured for more than a week.

But the studio was working at such full pelt now that although there might be temporary cash-flow problems, the promise of riches to follow still seemed real.

Motley Flint knew that, and told the brothers not to worry about being able to pay their bills. He trusted them. Besides which, he had a kind of insurance policy in the shape of a masseur known as Abdul the Turk. An illiterate former boxer, Abdul Maljan had come to Hollywood to work as Mack Sennett's bodyguard cum masseur, and had later graduated to Douglas Fairbanks senior, and a number of other top stars.

It was Motley Flint who suggested that Jack might do worse than add a steam-room to the studio lot when he moved with the other executives from Sunset Boulevard to Burbank. And while he was about it, why not give Abdul a try?

Abdul came—and stayed for twenty-three years. The steam-room was built next to Jack's own private dining-room, close to the personal barber shop which he and a very select band of friends used every day.

Abdul was more than a masseur. He was one of those confidants that big, powerful men like to have around them in much the way that wealthy dowagers used to take companions. Jack could tell him things that he would never dream of telling Irma or even her brother, 'Doc' Solomons, now one of his closest friends. Certainly Abdul knew a great deal about the way the studio was run to which neither Harry nor the Major was ever privy.

Lying on his slab, Jack felt as relieved of his burdens as a devout Catholic in the confessional.

He was also doing himself and the studio a great big favour. Abdul was the soul of discretion, but he also knew when it was sensible to have his say. What he told Motley Flint about the way Jack ran Warner Bros and First National convinced the banker—if he had ever had any doubts in the first place—that the studios were very much a going concern.

There were rumours of mergers that never amounted to anything. But the company continued to expand in other directions—buying up more theatres, more radio stations, music publishers.

The financial scurrying from company to company was Harry's

concern. The theatres were Abe's. Burbank, sweltering in the San Fernando Valley summers, was Jack's personal fiefdom.

It was a situation he cherished. Being with the stars, planning the deals, doing somersaults with the contracts and discovering meanings hidden within the small print that even the lawyers didn't know were there were his idea of excitement.

What he also had was the tremendous instinct for what made good movies. He wasn't always right. In 1930 he was stating loudly and clearly that he was sure that the close-up, the first cinematic effect that took the cinema away from the peepshow and established it as an independent art-form, was dead. 'It's going to be replaced by three-dimensional films,' he declared.

It was a faith he would keep stored up within himself for the next quarter-century.

More often than not, however, he was right.

Over the years Jack would claim for himself the prescience for deciding to risk small fortunes on the kind of films that would later be regarded as Warner Bros specialities.

Others would do the same—a band of men who while still aged under thirty were performing miracles for the film industry.

Jack Warner always said it was his idea to turn into a movie a huge best-seller by W. R. Burnett called *Little Caesar*. The man who put the notion forward had inside him the force that set into gear the whole genre of the gangster film.

Was it Jack Warner? 'I got the idea first,' said Mervyn LeRoy when I put the question to the man who directed the picture—'a great director with a small "g"', as Jack described him.

'No, it was my idea,' said Hal Wallis when he recalled what became the first big picture he ever produced.

Such are the tricks played by time and by the pride of men who know a milestone in film history when they see one.

In a way, the entry of these two men into Warner Bros was just as significant. Mervyn LeRoy first arrived on the Warner scene as an actor, had a row with Jack, was fired, moved over to First National as a director, had a row with that studio and was fired again—only to bump into Jack Warner on his way out. Jack was making his first tour of his new studio, and ordered that LeRoy be reinstated. They became close friends for life, and Mervyn LeRoy directed and produced some of his finest movies.

Nothing at Warner Bros could be divorced from the problem of personalities.

There were no hotter rows than those constantly in operation between Harry and Jack. One of the biggest was over Hal Wallis. Jack decided that Hal was worth more than he could afford, so he gave him the additional opportunity to work as a publicity adviser to

54

other people. When Harry heard that he was not devoting all his time to Warner Bros he sacked him. Jack was furious, and as much to annoy Harry as because he needed Wallis, he ordered him back. Before long he appointed him head of production at Burbank.

Wallis had wanted to go on to production for years, but he had been doing so well running the Warners' publicity operation that Jack said he couldn't be spared. Until, that is, the company took over First National. Now he wanted his own man at the studio.

Wallis got his wish and became a producer.

Only days later, Jack had a violent row with the then studio head, Al Rockett, over the kind of films First National were making. Rockett was fired, and Wallis was installed in his place.

From then on the two studios, which were prevented by law from totally merging for two years, were in competition with each other. The competition did them both good, but it was First National that made people think, and *Little Caesar* made them think more than did any other film.

It was really the first gangster picture to see hoodlums as humans. There were few who didn't have distinctly mixed feelings as Edward G. Robinson, dying in a rain-swept gutter, called on a superior power to save him. 'Mother of Mercy,' he whimpered. 'Is this the end of Rico?'

It will be a question remembered for as long as there are pictures. If the Hays Office hadn't been so sensitive he would have said, 'Mother of God . . .' but Mother of Mercy was enough.

'I've always been grateful for *Little Caesar*', Robinson once told me, 'because it proved that with looks like mine, there was hope for anyone who wanted to become a movie-star.'

That was, of course, understating things and under-selling himself. Jack Warner, who according to Wallis told him to go ahead and make the film without reading a word of the book, wanted to sign Robinson to the usual Warner contract that made the star rich, but gave the studio rights not totally dissimilar from those of a Southern plantation-owner.

Robinson, who nourished ambitions to return to the Broadway stage, wasn't having any, and finally did a deal on the basis of a fee for every picture he made rather than taking a weekly salary.

He was to write in his autobiography, *All My Yesterdays*, 'I became a businessman. I looked at the small print. I demanded—and finally got—four months off each year to do a play. That I never used it was not Jack Warner's fault, it was my own. But I realised that I was in a web just short of being corrupt in which it was vital to protect yourself . . .'

Robinson didn't entirely enjoy being a gangster. For one thing, he hated the sound of gunfire. And that meant a few problems for

Mervyn LeRoy. 'Every time he squeezed the trigger,' Mervyn told me, 'he would screw up his eyes. Take after take, he would do the same thing. In the end, we had to tape up his eyelids to make sure it wouldn't show.'

Robinson had been brought in by Hal Wallis for the much smaller role of Otero. However, from the beginning he was determined to play Rico, and it was his Rico that established the archetypal Warner gangster—which was much the same as saying he was the archetypal Hollywood hoodlum. With *Little Caesar* Warner Bros became known as the Gangster Studio, an appellation that when used by some of its actors was not always entirely complimentary.

Jack Warner, however, saw it all as a distinct triumph—mainly for himself, for having the foresight to say yes (and, as the years went on, for spotting the book in the first place).

Of course, he didn't remember some of his mistakes.

LeRoy wanted for the subsidiary role of Masaro a young actor whom he thought was manly, exciting, and sexy enough to have all the women in theatre audiences eating out of his hand.

'Nonsense,' said Warner—at least that is the word Mervyn LeRoy remembered him using. 'He has ears like an elephant.'

Later he called him a 'big ape' and chastised LeRoy for wasting 500 dollars on the test.

As a result, Douglas Fairbanks played Masaro and Clark Gable was lost to MGM.

Little Caesar's creator, Mr Burnett, didn't like the way that Fairbanks and Robinson worked together at all. He was sure they acted like a pair of homosexuals—a conclusion not reached by anyone else involved in the picture.

Not only did the film establish a new image for the cinema, but as much as any other Hollywood production, it confirmed that the 'talkies' were here to stay. The silent film was assassinated, and not just non-talking pictures. *Variety* recorded: 'Vaudeville in 1930 stood motionless as a treadmill that moves backwards.'

From *Little Caesar* on, it was success and stars all the way. What the Rico story had done for Edward G. Robinson *Public Enemy* did for James Cagney, who as a result of pushing half a grapefruit in the face of Mae Clarke embarked on a career both of stardom and of rows with Jack Warner.

Public Enemy, based on a story called *Beer And Blood*—again the Hays Office intervened and wouldn't allow the word 'blood' to appear in a title—said so much about Prohibition that audiences could practically smell the bootleg hooch when it poured from the bar taps on screen. For years afterwards small boys—including one Francis Albert Sinatra— would scare their mothers out of their lives by falling head-first through their front doors just as the bandaged corpse of Tom Powers (Cagney) did in *Public Enemy*.

Jack Warner was delighted that they did. It was wonderful publicity for the film.

Every now and again, Harry Warner would get jealous of his younger brother's role in all this and exert his authority as President of the company. Sometimes he was right.

When he saw a German film called *Moon of Israel* he took a boat to Germany and hired the director, a young Hungarian called Michael Curtiz. What he was also hiring was a Warner Bros institution. Curtiz has gone down in history as the man who when he wanted riderless steeds for a scene in *Charge of the Light Brigade* ordered, 'Bring on the empty horses.'

He also referred to everyone—including his actresses—as 'that sohnofabeetch' and mangled more English words than Sam Goldwyn. Also like Goldwyn, he knew how to make brilliant pictures.

Curtiz arrived with Harry in New York to the accompaniment of bands playing and flags flying.

'All for me?' he asked innocently. Harry didn't have the courage to tell his new friend that it was the Fourth of July.

For Jack it seemed like the Fourth of July every day of the year. Everything was going well for him—at the studio, of course, and also in his private life. Irma and Jack Junior didn't see much of him, but then they knew they always came second to his work. And yet he was obviously having a good time even when he wasn't at the studio.

There were always women in his life, although Irma rarely knew who they were. Only Abdul could give an up-to-date account of the hairdressers, secretaries and artist's models with whom he was sleeping.

The only women excluded from his bed were his own employees. That was a rule he never broke, and he tried to insist that his executives followed his example. Sometimes they did. Others said it was more difficult.

On one celebrated occasion a famous Warner director found suppressing his natural urges in the face of a ravishing young starlet just too much. She had worked her charms on him so effectively that he couldn't get her to the nearest available sound-stage quickly enough. Once there he locked the door firmly and switched on the red light to ensure that no one would try to get in.

Inside, he removed the girl's clothing. When they began to make love a huge cheer went up from an assembled gathering of propmen, electricians and carpenters. What he had not remembered was that the set was open at the top, and every available crewman on the lot had climbed to the flies to enjoy the show. But the director was not without ingenuity—he wouldn't have lasted at Warners had he been so. 'My God,' he shouted at the girl. 'What in heaven's name do you think you're doing? Go Away! AWAY!'

There were other girls who were rescued from studio offices by secretaries saving their bosses from themselves. It was a familiar story that young ladies in a state of undress would be interrupted in their operations by the announcement, 'Washington on the line.'

Jack would tell the tales to his guests for the rest of his life, spicing them a bit more every time. Even those who didn't like him would admit that he was good fun to be with.

Darryl Zanuck once wrote, 'What a boring guy Harry was! Jack was unreliable, but never boring.'

Zanuck was able to prove it with the altercations they had week after week—usually over money. 'I think,' he once said, 'the studio motto should be, "When not in use, turn off the juice".'

If it was, then it was partly thanks to Motley Flint, who continued to keep a friendly eye on the company. He stayed close to them until 1930, the year when he was murdered.

His company, the Security First National Bank, were being sued by the young David O. Selznick in the California Supreme Court. He was demanding 250,000 dollars which he claimed the bank owed him.

At one stage Flint bent down to talk to Selznick's mother. As he did so a shot was fired and he collapsed in a pool of blood. He died instantly. Later Frank D. Keaton was indicted for murder. He said he was a victim of the crash of the JULIAN Petroleum Company, for which he held Flint responsible.

It was a shock that all three brothers took very hard. Flint had been a friend when they needed one most.

Had they had the benefit of his advice, Zanuck might have stayed on the payroll.

The big row between the brothers and the studio head came during one of the frequent economy drives instituted by Harry during the early 1930s.

The company President decreed there had to be an agreement by which everyone in the studio took a salary cut. Despite union opposition, most of the employees agreed to do so. Zanuck was not among them.

His intransigence angered Harry, who didn't like him much anyway. As much as anything, he was embarrassed by him. Zanuck was so talented there was a time he appeared to be writing almost every film script the studio produced. Harry had ordered him to use pen names. But there had never been any bigger rows than the one now over money.

In the middle of the dispute Harry and Zanuck were dining at the Hollywood Brown Derby—not together; the eldest of the Warner Bros did not like eating out with the hired help.

But Harry spotted him sitting at another table and gestured that they should go outside together.

Zanuck returned a few minutes later, visibly shaken, his face alternately scarlet and purple. The next day he was out of Warner Bros and ready to begin a brilliant career with Twentieth Century—soon to become Twentieth Century-Fox—Pictures.

Warner had simply told him he wasn't running things properly, that the studio was a family concern and that if he wasn't grateful for all Harry and his brothers had done for him he ought to be ashamed of himself.

The studio then issued a statement that said baldly:

> Due to a disagreement of policy in company management, Darryl F. Zanuck handed his resignation to Warner Bros Picture Corporation, which the company accepted. The resignation is effective April 15. The business policy of the company will in future be handled by Jack L. Warner.

Zanuck's place was now taken by Hal Wallis, who was given control of the output of both the Warner and First National studios. It was the first sign that the two organizations were in fact one.

The only intimation Wallis had of any change in his authority was when he arrived at the office to see his name taken off the door by a carpenter. When he complained at what he assumed was summary dismissal he was given the good news.

Jack was sitting in his office, a broad smile enveloping his face. Harry was standing behind him.

All Jack said was, 'Now you're it.'

He was—and Warner Bros were never the same again.

For all that, it is Zanuck to whom Wallis gives credit for his own success—and not simply for providing shoes into which he could step.

'Whenever Zanuck was making a picture, he did it at night and the rest of us were allowed to come and see him work,' he told me. 'I used to sit and absorb what he did. Because of that experience, I learned a great deal about cutting pictures.'

He also learned that if Warners were going to continue in business as a major concern they had to develop a stamp and a personality all their own. He chose to make it the studio that told things as they were. Not for Burbank the gloss of MGM—where, as he said, every room looked as though it had been floodlit—or the total escapism of Paramount.

The gangster series continued. *The Ruling Voice,* now virtually forgotten, followed by the much more memorable *Five Star Final,* starring Edward G. Robinson, and by Warren William in both *The Mouthpiece* and *The Match King,* confirmed that they were on to a

brilliant thing. A whole succession of James Cagney films like *Taxi,*
Hard To Handle and *Picture Snatcher* brought people rushing into
the cinemas.

'I was making so many pictures like that,' Wallis recalled for me,
'they used to call me "Murder Incorporated".'

But there were other pictures that went beyond guns being fired
and bad guys ending up in the gutters. Very often that became a
mere ingredient in films that showed the company was also demon-
strating a social conscience.

That was never more effectively evident than in the 1932 Paul
Muni picture *I Am A Fugitive From A Chain Gang,* a film that
threatened to have the whole Warner Bros output banned in the
Deep South and earned the gratitude of prison-reformers throughout the country.

It was based on the true story of a man wrongly convicted of a
hold-up and sent to work on a chain gang in Georgia, who then
escapes only to find himself constantly on the run.

The real convict was Robert E. Burns, who eventually found
refuge in New Jersey and dictated his story to his brother, a priest.
Muni's characterization was brilliant, and so was the direction of
Mervyn LeRoy, who decided it would be more effective to end the
picture with the convict still on the run.

In the final scene Muni disappears into the darkness after seeing
his wife for one last time—it turned out that the screen went dark
because the lights failed; if that was so it was one of the most
fortunate accidents ever to occur in a studio. 'How do you live?' she
asked him. 'I steal,' was his reply.

Films like *Fugitive* earned Warners a journalist's accolade which
it thereafter boasted proudly whenever the occasion arose, 'Combining Good Picture-making with Good Citizenship'.

Harry, however, was more interested in combining dividends
with more noughts on the balance sheet. It was about this time
that he coined a phrase that has since been credited to virtually
every other Hollywood mogul. When he was congratulated on the
great effect pictures like *Fugitive* were having on the American
conscience, he replied, 'We should leave messages to Western
Union.'

But Harry thought he had reason enough to feel cynical. His
whole life seemed to be crashing around him. His adored only son
Lewis developed blood-poisoning while on holiday in Havana. His
gums had become infected, and the treatment given to the 22-
year-old heir to the Warner empire only seemed to make things
worse.

Harry flew out to Cuba and managed to bring Lewis to New
York. But the poisoning had gone too far. It was an age away from

antibiotics, and the most effective cure was often prayer. This time it didn't work. Pneumonia set in, and before long Lewis was dead.

Harry was never the same again. For months he was inconsolable, and retreated into an impenetrable shell. When he did start communicating again it was in a totally irrational way.

Harry's son-in-law Milton Sperling told me how Harry's daughter Doris was woken up once in the middle of the night. Her father was standing by her bed. 'Come. Get dressed,' he said. 'We're going out.'

It was so late, she didn't know what to say. She was also too tired to argue with a man so clearly at that moment demented. Without speaking, he drove her to the Warners' New York office, at 44th Street, and walked through the darkened, forbiddingly lonely corridors.

In the elevator they stood silently looking at each other before getting out in front of the private suite.

Harry unlocked the door himself, an unusual circumstance, because there was always someone to do it for him during the day. But it was an unusual night.

'Sit down in my chair,' he ordered. 'You're going to take Lewis's place and learn the business.' For the next couple of hours he bombarded the eighteen-year-old girl with a mass of statistics that he thought illustrated the development of a movie from its initial purchase to the time the dollars and cents registered on the final accounting.

The poor girl was totally bewildered.

She was not the only one. Another was Adolph Zukor, head of Paramount. He told Sperling that about this time Harry called on him at his office uninvited, sat in front of his desk and for two hours did nothing but weep uncontrollably.

The effect of all this was to make Harry more than head of the studio. He now considered himself divine protector of the family. With Benjamin and Pearl living in retirement, their daughters married and living a typical Jewish suburban existence, he took it upon himself to supervise everything that the family did. If he didn't like the way Jack was taking his responsibilities as a father—and he didn't— he said so. In fact, he kept none of his reservations about his brother quiet.

Harry and Abe both dressed well but conservatively. Jack was the family dandy. His suits were the best that the Hollywood tailors could provide, and every trip to Europe meant orders for the cutters of Savile Row. He never left home without spats over his highly polished shoes, a *boutonnière* in his lapel and a kerchief in his breast-pocket.

'All this made him less trustworthy to his brothers,' Milton Sperling added.

As he sat behind his desk he sometimes looked more like a man playing a Mighty Würlitzer organ in a movie theatre than a mogul at the head of one of the great studios providing the very lifeblood of that theatre.

The desk, one executive told me, was always 'squeaky clean'. On one wall he had a huge map of the United States—constructed in such a way that Burbank seemed the capital of the country (not surprising, since that was what Jack believed it to be!) and the routes between New York and California, with Chicago on the way, were marked out by pictures of trains and aircraft.

It was a touch of flamboyance that irritated Harry enormously.

The two brothers who had once run a bicycle shop now acted as if they were riding a tandem—in opposite directions.

Jack would authorize expenditure on a film and Harry would try to block it, saying he was wasting family assets. His brother's answer was that if he hadn't spent the money, there wouldn't have been any assets in the first place.

Once Harry sent Jack an angry telegram:

SUGGEST WE SUE RAILROAD STOP YOU SAID FILM YOU WERE SENDING WAS WONDERFUL STOP RAIL-ROAD MUST BE TAMPERING WITH IT STOP WHEN IT ARRIVED HERE IT WAS TERRIBLE.

It was funnier than most things Harry did.

Jack, on the other hand, seemed to make jokes out of anything, even when he wasn't in a particularly good mood. If business was bad his mood seemed sunnier than ever. That was usually because he could turn down an application for a rise with a clear conscience. 'These are turbulent times,' he would reply. 'Turbulent times.' When he wasn't on quite such firm ground the pussy-cat mogul would turn into something closer to the martinet.

You couldn't argue with Jack Warner successfully even if you wanted to. An executive determined to get his own way would just as likely be greeted with a twist of the cigar, a puff of smoke and a point of an index finger.

'Whose name on the front of the building?' he'd ask, and there could be but one answer: 'Yours, chief.'

People got to know the expression. After a couple of sessions with a recalcitrant employee he only had to say, 'Whose name . . .' and there was no need to finish the sentence. After a time he stopped bothering to. 'Whose name . . .?' was enough.

If he tried to give the impression of being overwhelmed with his responsibilities—of which Harry and a dozen other executives waiting in the wings would have been delighted to relieve him—he would bring out the treasured line 'Uneasy lies the head that wears the toilet seat.'

If story conferences got so long that Jack lost the drift he would hold up his arms to bring the conversation to an abrupt end. 'OK, boys,' he would say, 'look, I'm from the Bon Ton Woollen Underwear Company and haven't a clue what you are saying.'

Any idea had to be made as clear to him as it would to an unworldly representative of the mythical underwear firm. The phrase became so well known that before long Bill Orr had a card printed that read: 'The Bon Ton Woollen Underwear Company. Jack Warner, President.'

Jack thought it was all terribly amusing. Whether an Italian journalist interviewing him around this time thought the same thing is a matter for speculation. After the chat the reporter bade Jack 'Arrivederci'. 'Yeh,' replied Warner, 'and a dirty river to you, too.'

Quite frequently young actresses with no noticeable star potential received the great man's personal attention—and still without any sexual involvement.

Among them was a girl born Gretchen Young. Neither Jack nor Mervyn LeRoy, who was asked to take her under his wing, liked the name very much, and Mervyn suggested she change it to Loretta.

She had a number of small parts, but none of them was sufficiently big to make it damaging for the studio for her to travel to work by bus. And she couldn't afford a car.

She got so fed up with using public transport that she asked Jack if the studio would lend her the money to buy a car. He told her he would think about it.

Eventually the answer came at one of the big show-biz extravaganzas so beloved of Hollywood in the 1930s. She was sitting in what today would be called a motorcade, inching its way along Jefferson Avenue towards the famous Shrine Auditorium.

At her side were two of the biggest stars of the era, Alice White and Grant Withers—who were as surprised as the assembled crowd to see the figure of Jack Warner jump on to the running-board and call to Loretta, 'You can have your car, kid. Pay me back when you can.'

There was no suggestion that the offer was in the form of anything but a loan. 'In those days,' she told me, 'if he had given me the money, there would have been strings attached.'

Plenty of other people in the United States would have been equally content to get such an offer. The Depression and Prohibition continued, and the slough of despair in the country got deeper—all of which continued to be represented in Warner films.

If anyone offered a change of national mood it was the Democratic candidate for the Presidency, Franklin D. Roosevelt, whom the brothers, to everyone's surprise—and probably also to their own—decided to back, following his highly successful term as Governor of New York.

Harry probably had good reason to back Roosevelt.

Earlier that year there had been an investigation into allegations that he had been manipulating Warner shares. What he had been doing was taking advantage of the inside knowledge he had of his own company's finances. He sold shares at an average of 54 dollars a certificate and then bought them back again for just over 20. There was nothing wrong with that according to the law of the day, but it struck a number of senators that it wasn't very nice.

In facing the music Harry was acting as the spokesman for his brothers, although he declined to be the fall guy. They were all in the mire together. The brothers admitted making a profit of 7 million dollars in their own share deals during 1930—not a popular thing to do while the Depression wrapped itself around America like a racoon coat.

The suggestion was that they sold the shares, knowing that the earnings of the company were falling. On the contrary, said Harry, they were selling shares simply to raise money for their company. And it certainly needed it.

Warners lost nearly 8 million dollars in 1932. And yet as writs came tumbling in—and as the cheques once more took a week to clear—the studio would still announce grandiose plans for sixty films in the coming year, some of which would come off; others being merely products of some salesman's imagination. In an attempt to gain the enthusiasm of exhibitors they drew up posters and publicity material for films they had no intention of ever making—and what was more, based on stories that had never been written. Sometimes they were on firmer ground—listing films they were planning to make, but with stars whom they had no thoughts of featuring.

They revealed too that they were hiring Greta Garbo to play the lead in *The Match King*.

For the moment it all looked good at the conventions and in Press releases, but their creditors were getting worried. Finally a group of them decided to call in a receiver.

It was a brief but bitter fight. A group of shareholders agreed that they wanted the brothers out, and to put the running of the company into other hands.

The Warners drummed up majority support and were able to breathe again, but it left a nasty taste in the mouth, particularly in Hoover Government circles.

Perhaps a new administration would forget what had happened. The brothers may have had some doubts about the new President, but they thought it wise to celebrate his inauguration. They organized a special train from Los Angeles to Washington to take their stars to the capital for the occasion.

Among those making the trip were William Powell, George Brent, Douglas Fairbanks junior, James Cagney, Kay Francis, Ruby Keeler, Loretta Young, Ginger Rogers and a girl whom Warner was to call 'an explosive little broad with a sharp left', Bette Davis.

Roosevelt himself saw the value of having the media behind him, and as his campaign drew to its close in 1932 he had bid for the support of the most potent medium of them all, the movies. He did so by offering Jack Warner a job.

'Would you like to be an Ambassador?' he repeated after California declared for the Governor. 'Thank you, Mr President,' Jack replied. 'I am very flattered. But I think I can do more for foreign relations by making a good picture about America now and then.'

Roosevelt's campaign song had been 'Happy Days Are Here Again'. Not many people believed it, but they were prepared to accept that they might be around the corner.

Warners took that as a signal to show it on the screen. They brought back the musical.

CHAPTER 8

FOOTLIGHTS PARADE

In all our battles, I was always very fond of you.
*Olivia de Havilland in a speech at a tribute dinner to
Jack L. Warner*

When the talkies first turned Warner Bros into a major studio it seemed obvious that all the important new films would be musicals. After all, there was no better way of using sound; no more certain way of publicizing a movie than having people going out of a theatre whistling a song they had heard during the show.

But they didn't do musicals well enough. *The Jazz Singer* was a huge success, *The Singing Fool* even bigger. But if Al Jolson was their biggest asset, they used him badly. The man who had taken Broadway by storm, dominating an audience by singing brash songs from the runway stretching from the back of the Winter Garden Theatre to the stage at the front, was suddenly locked into a formula. He was either Mammy's boy or Sonny Boy's dad—always crying.

It turned into a monster for himself—*Say It With Songs,* which followed *The Singing Fool,* was a disaster, and a millstone around the necks of Warners.

But Jack still worshipped Jolson, and had encouraged him to make two more pictures in 1930, *Big Boy,* an entertaining story about a Black jockey, and *Mammy,* with music by Irving Berlin. Both did quite well. However, Jolson was, with one other entertainer, virtually the only star still singing in Warner films.

The other performer was the central attraction of a Jerome Kern show which became one of the very first Broadway musicals to be transferred to the screen, *Sally.* Marilyn Miller was not only brought in to repeat her New York success but, conveniently for Jack, to break one of his principal rules. She was sleeping with him.

The news didn't exactly enchant Irma. It also caused an extreme attack of apoplexy in Harry, who saw it as rocking the Burbank studios and doing no end of harm to the family. The eldest of the brothers called a family conference and arranged for himself to read the Jewish version of the Riot Act.

His shouts seemed to reverberate throughout the San Fernando Valley, but they didn't get into the newspapers. In those days it took only a fatherly hand on the shoulders of the Warner publicity corps for the message to be received loud and clear.

The newspapers—not a little bit influenced by the Warners' friend, Willian Randolph Hearst—weren't about to cut off the hand that fed them so generously all the year round, and agreed to say nothing about it.

However, Jack wasn't going to allow his brother to dictate to him, showed Harry some of the rushes of *Sally* and promptly announced Miss Miller was going to make more pictures for him. She followed *Sally* with the alliteratively named *Sunny*—she had had a success on Broadway in that too—filmed the same year, and then with *Her Majesty, Love,* a huge flop twelve months later.

Almost overnight, Warners decided to kill off the whole concept of screen musicals. But then they met Busby Berkeley, and largely through Hal Wallis, decided they could live up to the studio motto and really combine entertainment with a social conscience.

It had actually been Zanuck who had signed Berkeley to a seven-year contract. He had seen what Busby could do after experiencing *Whoopie*, the film he made for Sam Goldwyn in 1933. It was a move shrewd enough to bring in the dividends the moment he was put to work with his first Warner film, *42nd Street.*

The story wasn't that exciting. The dialogue was full of lines that became clichés so quickly that so-called sophisticates would line up simply for a chance to laugh when Warner Baxter as the musical-show director tells his ingénue understudy, Ruby Keeler, 'You are going out a youngster. But you've got to come back a star.'

The film did just that—for the moderately talented Miss Keeler herself; for Mr Berkeley; and for Warner Bros musicals.

Of course, what it also did was create a new kind of film, with huge sets supposedly showing action on theatre stages which to cope with it all had to be a mile and a half deep and carry an inexhaustible supply of water—to say nothing of streets, parks and plenty of brick-built skyscrapers.

If cinema audiences did wonder about the feasibility of such things, it just made them all the more enthusiastic. The film did so well that Mr Berkeley was told to repeat the exercise, which he did with *Gold Diggers of 1933*. It was a very loose follow-on to the 1929 *Gold Diggers of Broadway,* which had featured one of the best-known songs of the period, 'Painting The Clouds With Sunshine'.

As in the previous film, it told the story of the love-affairs of three girls—this time, Joan Blondell, Aline MacMahon and Ruby Keeler.

Warren William, Guy Kibbee and Dick Powell (at the start of a virtual career as Warners' perennial juvenile) were for good or ill the men in their lives.

Once more it was Busby Berkeley's escapist routines that set the tone of the picture, using the sexiest girls seen in a show since Florenz Ziegfeld first opened his Follies. He seemed to use an aerial kaleidoscope to make girls blossom from flowers or dive in and out of water like performing seals, defying both gravity and records for endurance.

It must have been made during the Hays Office's long summer vacation. 'The Pettin' In The Park' number had another batch of girls showing most of what they had under their skirts (as fine a set of suspendered thighs as had ever been exposed on celluloid) and then, for no apparent reason at all, had them escaping from a rainstorm before completely stripping down behind a translucent curtain. They were only seen in silhouette, but Busby Berkeley's imagination was the only one that needed to work anything out.

That number has gone down into Hollywood folklore. So has the one in which an orchestra of girl violinists, each in white tiered and hooped dresses, danced down a spiral staircase. When the lights went out it was clear that each of the violins had been ringed by a neon tube, and the girls had been wired up to each other. The studio resounded with the chuckles of men contemplating the effects of pulling the wrong wire and sending one girl flying on to the top of another like a house of cards.

But that would have been one routine Mr Berkeley had not planned. He was not known for his tolerance when things went other than the way he had orchestrated them, and when everything did collapse, girls fell down, and the staircase shook abominably his language was the sort to which no young maiden should ever have been exposed. He was not easily satisfied when told that it was simply a matter of California experiencing another of its frequent minor earthquakes.

The set was rebuilt, the girls brushed down, the electricians called in, and the filming of the number completed to a superb finale—all the neon-lit violins combining to form a shape which, from Busby Berkeley's overhead camera, became a giant-sized fiddle.

Berkeley planned every number in advance with a mathematical precision. He then cut his scenes in the camera, leaving very little for the cutting-room where more traditional editing was done.

The cost of the films in which his routines were featured was immense—up to half a million dollars. They brought Jack Warner out in a rash every time he saw one, but he trusted Hal Wallis, and loved the way he could see an interesting routine on screen become a marvellous publicity gimmick when the film was released.

Gold Diggers of 1933 was heralded on Broadway by a parade of neon-violin-playing young ladies marching down the Great White Way. The *New York Sun* looked forward to the event with eagerness. 'It promises to be another of those dignified Warner openings,' said its reporter.

Berkeley himself was unrepentant about the extravagance that he was plainly engendering. He said years later, 'My idea was to give them something they'd never seen before. For instance, I knew they'd never done a water ballet with a hundred girls before, so I told them to build me a tank.'

In its way, the film was seen as a signal that those happy days really were, if not here again, on their way. It opened with a shot of girls (what else!) dressed up in what were made to appear to be large silver dollars, singing *We're In The Money*. In front of the line and singing the song was a certain Ginger Rogers, who was about to go on to bigger things at RKO with Fred Astaire.

If it all seemed nice escapist stuff, Hal Wallis insisted that audiences should be shaken back into reality. He ordered that the musical numbers should also include one that showed the problems of America in all its misery.

The result was *My Forgotten Man,* sung by a slinkily clad Joan Blondell to the accompaniment of the marching feet of soldiers on a huge multidecked bridge, who later turn into a crowd of unshaven workless standing in a breadline. It was a telling moment that really did bring the escapism of the most lavish film musical to date into line with all the horrors of Depression America.

Harry Warner still needed some convincing about the realism of those breadlines and soup kitchens. 'Those guys look horrible,' he said. 'Who the hell wants to see a man with a dirty face?'

Abe could have told him—and probably did. The film was a smash, filled the Warner theatres for years, and is still a cult movie.

It might not have become one without its publicity. The best films in the world could easily have been confined to dust-trap vaults had there been no one there to sell them from the start.

And that was where Warners' publicity outfit, perhaps the strongest in the business, came into play. Every week seven thousand newspapers were sent details of the studio's plans, together with specialized newsletters like *The Woman's Page,* or general feature material headed *Studio Highlight Starlights*. All could be lifted directly on to a newspaper's centre spread. The colour offered by the musicals made them certain winners, particularly to America's small-town papers.

Of course, it wasn't just the Berkeley sets that made the Warner musicals sensational for their time. His was, certainly, the innovative genius, but his ideas had to have a springboard. That usually came from the men who wrote the songs—and in particular a couple of writers newly in from New York, Harry Warren and Al Dubin.

Some of the songs they wrote were like the output of any generation of songwriters, potboilers that became big hits or genuine works of art that were remembered only by the men who wrote them—and sometimes not even then.

Other Warren-Dubin songs (Warren wrote the music, Dubin the lyrics) like 'I Only Have Eyes For You' or the song that over the past half-century has come to symbolize the best-known street in the world, 'The Lullaby of Broadway', were to become as familiar to the generation of the 1980s as they were to that of fifty years before.

Harry Warren told me on one occasion, 'I am not sure Berkeley could have operated without the songwriter going into action first. I remember him pacing the floor waiting for either Al or me to appear with the material.'

Jack Warner appreciated the work of the two men, but what he could not grasp was that it sometimes took a little longer to write a number than it would have taken him to sing it.

Harry Warren recalled how Warner once asked him how long it really did take to write a song. 'About three weeks,' said Warren insouciantly.

Warner was aghast. 'Three weeks!' he screamed. 'Three weeks to write one lousy song!'

'No,' said Warren. 'Three weeks to write one good song.'

The message must have gone home, because he stayed on the Warner payroll for more than ten years.

The songwriters formed their own community at Warner Bros, as did the screenplay writers, the directors, the cameramen and the people in the wardrobe department. Jack worried about this from time to time, but in his more lenient moods—and to be fair, they were frequent—he encouraged them to enjoy themselves. If the men were happy, he thought, they wrote happy music, and that was the kind that not only seemed to make better musical films but in turn sold more records and sheet music for the burgeoning Warner Bros publishing empire.

Sometimes his patience was more sorely tried, as when Sammy Fain arrived on the lot for the first time and crashed into a fire hydrant. Jack was being shaved in his private barber shop at the time—his pride and joy this, by now with his own barber, rather than using the man who serviced the actors—when he heard the crash. 'You'd better make up for this, young man,' he said, shaving-soap all over his face.

Fain did, with a song called 'By a Waterfall' sung by Dick Powell in the James Cagney film *Footlights Parade*. That picture gave Cagney a chance to break away from his gangster image. It was a

Warner Bros concession, although the company preferred doing the things for which it was justly celebrated, particularly the 'social conscience' films.

Among the most stirring of these was *Wild Boys Of The Road* (renamed as films so frequently were in those days for impressionable British viewers, *Dangerous Age*). It was a story straight out of the Depression, with language and sets that said as much about the times as a string of Press clippings or a contemporary newsreel.

A gang of boys in search of work become involved with a posse of uniformed officers.

Of course, they are taken away and of course they get ordered off to reform school by a judge. But the man looks humane. He is also made to look like President Roosevelt—a cunning move on Jack Warner's part, that; he still believed that the President would one day be useful to Warner Bros, and the eagle symbol of the National Relief Agency is plain to see in the background.

After sentencing the boys he allows one of them to speak: 'You send us to gaol because you don't want to see us. You want to forget us. But you can't do it.'

The heart of the law is softened. The boys are told to go home, and assured that the judge shared their hope that they would soon find work. Happy days would soon be here again!

As far as the Warners were concerned, the box-office told them they had arrived for good.

John Wayne was making Westerns—*Ride Him, Cowboy, The Man From Monterey,* and *The Telegraph Trail.* Joan Blondell was practically a one-woman movie factory, churning out as many films as she could physically make.

Many of the films were being justly praised by the critics, although some newspapermen made Jack's hair stand on end by what he considered to be unjustified carping. However, he didn't worry about it; he was too busy fighting some of his actors to bother with critics. The rows with his stars were becoming a part of Jack's daily routine, and if he didn't love every slanging moment of them, his opponents might have got a lot further than some of them did.

There was no more persistent sparring partner than Cagney, although sometimes Jack's tactics were not of the soundest. He didn't mind arguing about his stars in their presence—which he might have thought was reasonable enough, since they wouldn't have understood what he was saying. He and Harry were happy to argue for hours about an actor's pay claim—in Yiddish.

What he didn't realize was that Cagney, the 'feisty Irishman', as Frank Sinatra was to describe him, grew up in Yorkville, New York, which had quite as many Jewish families as Catholics. He learned Yiddish with the best of them when he was still at school.

71

Jack and Harry were on this occasion screaming at each other in the language when Jack, turning white, looked towards a Cagney barely able to contain his laughter.

'*Shveig,*' Jack whispered to his brother, '*der goy vershtait Yiddish.* (Quiet, the Gentile understands Yiddish.')

He also understood, in English, when Warners suspended him for refusing to make pictures which he said were exhausting him. And he wanted more money. Being on suspension meant that the period an actor was off work was added to the time of his contract, which was usually seven years.

Cagney was asking for 4,000 dollars a week, instead of the 1,600 weekly he had been earning while making his last 1932 film *Winner Takes All.* When Jack refused he and his wife got into their car and drove off to New York.

'I'm through with movies for good,' he told reporters, and added that he was going to study medicine.

Jack was beside himself when he heard the news. He knew perfectly well that his contracted star had no intention of doing anything of the kind. 'We are going to find out if the people who work for us are employees or whether they do as they please,' he declared.

That word 'employee' had always stuck in stars' throats, but Jack and the other studio bosses were not having it any other way. They reckoned that contracts were two-way documents. While the actors believed they were being exploited by the studios, the moguls could fairly point out that if they themselves broke any agreements the unions would call an all-out strike.

The problems were not confined to Warner Bros. At Paramount Adolph Zukor was trying to restrain Marlene Dietrich and her patron Josef von Sternberg from leaving the studio in the lurch.

Ann Dvorak—who had appeared with James Cagney in *The Crowd Roars,* and done well in her own right in *Love Is A Racket*—was telling Warners that she too was going to be difficult. She and her lawyer announced she was staying on in Berlin until a new deal was worked out.

All this meant Jack Warner was going to stick in his heels, if not on his own and his studio's behalf, then for the whole of the film industry. When Cagney offered to do a deal to make no more than three films at the existing rate and then negotiate new terms, Jack would not budge.

In a series of interviews the name James Cagney was emblazoned across the front pages of newspapers throughout America. 'Life is long and applause is short,' he said in one. And in another he commented, 'I feel that I have given the best years of my life working for inadequate compensation. A player should be in a position to demand what he is worth, so long as he is worth it. When his box-office value drops his earnings should be lopped off accordingly.'

Warner would have accepted the sentiments in that last sentence, but not the previous one. There would be no deal.

Cagney's lawyer, Arthur Sherman, thought he had discovered a way out of the row with the studio. An 'essential clause' was missing. Most contracts had provision for firing a star without notice. James's did not—so it was plain, Sherman said, that he could not be suspended without thirty days' notice.

It was a matter affecting the whole of Hollywood, and Jack saw his obligations to his fellow studio heads—to say nothing of desperately needing their support. He called a meeting of the Motion Picture Producers Association.

They passed a resolution affirming that no 'striking' actor—the term placed the performers in a suitable pigeonhole—would ever be employed by a rival studio. By taking away alternative work from an actor, they were thereby depriving him of anywhere to go.

The Cagney row was finally settled with his getting 3,000 dollars a week and the promise of further increases up to 1935. It meant that Jack would no longer have to look for alternatives when a role that he had been particularly tailoring for Cagney came up.

That had happened all too recently for his liking. When Cagney had been unable to make *20,000 Years In Sing Sing* Jack had to borrow Spencer Tracy to do it instead.

But Tracy was a good name, and Warners had to admit they were proud to have it on their own list of stars, if only for one picture. And they could afford him.

In fact, Warners emerged from the Depression very well indeed, except that just when things appeared to be at their best, a fire ravaged a major part of the Burbank lot. Among the things lost was a host of early Vitagraph pictures.

In later years Bob Hope was to joke, 'Warner Bros either had a good picture or a good fire.' There could be no suggestion of arson this time, although Irma continued to think Jack had lit a fuse under their marriage. Finally in July 1932 she decided she had had enough and sued for divorce.

The man who had spent so long lecturing staff about the immorality of using the casting couch had gone from one affair to another, sometimes with ladies who would have taken off their clothes for virtually anyone at the drop of a five-dollar bill. When Jack left the marital home Irma charged desertion, and a property settlement was drawn up covering both her and their son, the eighteen-year-old Jack Junior.

Relations were somewhat strained between the two Jacks, but

73

between Irma and her former husband there was a void that could not be bridged. The chasm was so deep that when Jack came to write his own autobiography he didn't even mention his former wife's existence. Consequently, Jack Junior wasn't mentioned either.

What he did say was that he fell in love with a beautiful lady called Ann, who subsequently became his wife. As he wrote the story, neither of them were then married, so why shouldn't they go to the altar together?

There were a number of people who could have answered that question.

Jack kept fairly quiet about Ann's background too, neglecting to point out that she had been married as well, to Don Alvarado.

It wasn't difficult to see what Jack saw in Ann, petite, with dark Latin eyes, a mouth and nose that made a whole succession of artists want to paint her, and a figure that was enchanting. But that didn't make things any easier for him in the bosom of his family.

The divorce came at about the same time as the death of Pearl. The matriarch of the family had asked no more than that she should do her duty as a Jewish mother and to enjoy the fruits of the labours of her sons. It wasn't a good moment to initiate a huge family row, particularly so as not to upset old Benjamin Warner, but Jack was left in no doubt how the family felt.

Irma had been Jewish, maternal and houseproud—the three things that families like the Warners believed were most important in a woman joining their clan. Her brother, 'Doc', was still a close family friend (and, incidentally, features a number of times in Jack's book).

Ann was maternal, too—she had a daughter—but she was also Catholic and very, very pretty. If the women in the Warner family could accept the former (and it was difficult) they were totally unable to forgive the latter. The Warner sisters were not beautiful.

Jack's divorce and subsequent marriage brought a rift in the family that never healed. But where his father, sisters and brother Abe would before long accept Jack's actions as done and irrevocable, Harry treated it all as a personal insult.

Harry saw himself as the heir-in-waiting to the head of the family, the now ailing Ben. It was his duty to maintain what he believed were Warner family standards, and now with his own son dead and Abe childless, he believed it incumbent on Jack to show a sense of responsibility in that direction too.

The tirades—in Yiddish—in which Harry berated his brother for marrying 'the shickseh' became another subject for hot gossip at Burbank.

Jack expected Ann to move into the house he and Irma had lived in on Angelo Drive, a quiet green avenue sufficiently far away from the hubbub of Sunset Boulevard to make it one of the most sought-after residential roads in Beverly Hills.

It was a large house, built in the colonial style, and at first Ann said she would be happy to live there. Before long, however, she had changed her mind. It wasn't the conventional reluctance of one woman to step over the threshold of a home built by another. More, it was simply a question of taste. Ann had her own ideas about what she liked.

She decided to furnish the house with European antiques. Before she did so she studied the subject, so that she knew what she was buying. She learnt architecture too, and insisted on one room being panelled in the style she saw in a British stately home. Jack bid for the panelling, and the stately home exported it to Hollywood, where Jack had the room remodelled to fit the panels, instead of the other way round. For years afterwards, however, there could be heard the alarming sound of wood popping and cracking as it tried painfully to get used to the drier Los Angeles climate.

All this, however, produced results which delighted hundreds of dinner guests in the years that followed. One of whom was a certain Mr Samuel Goldwyn.

Sam, together with the other rival Hollywood moguls, was a priority show-off guest. Before drinks that night he was invited into the Warners' 'back-yard' for drinks.

Mrs Jean Negulesco, wife of one of the studio's leading directors at the time, delighted in telling me about that evening when Goldwyn came across the sundial that formed the centrepiece of the Warner lawn.

'What's that?' he asked.

'Oh, it's a sundial,' she answered.

'A what?'

'A sundial,' she said. 'You see, every day the sun casts a shadow from the piece of metal at the top. Since the shadow changes all through the day, you can tell what time it is.'

'My!' said Sam. 'What will they think of next!'

That garden never did satisfy Ann. Which provided a few problems for Jack, who had become an ardent tennis player—quite good, although never quite as competent as he thought he was.

He liked the idea of playing with the top tennis names in the country, most of whom were fascinated to be invited to the home of such an important figure in Hollywood, and who could never be sure when it might be necessary to capitalize on that friendship.

Any Wimbledon refugee who had such an idea had two choices—either to lose or not to play too well. Those who didn't weren't invited again.

One of Jack's favourite 'opponents' was his casting director Solly

Biano, a small man but a brilliant athlete, who knew what he had to do to come back again and again.

It was Jack's personal secretary, Bill Schaefer, who regularly had to work out a list of ten or twelve players for the next scheduled tennis party, a job quite as important to his boss as identifying the complete cast of his next production.

Tennis was very much a social game. Above all, it was considered a game for ladies and gentlemen, and Jack, ever conscious of his roots, regarded it as his final passport to respectability.

All that, however, didn't necessarily impress Ann. When she decided she wanted the garden remade she bravely informed him he wouldn't be able to play tennis for three months.

Ann was a perfectionist. After bringing a team of gardeners in to rebuild the whole layout she decided she didn't like it and they had to start all over again. A set of steps was moved fourteen times and the stonemasons responsible stayed on the payroll for eighteen months.

They didn't argue. It was good business.

The house itself was so luxurious that it became the talking point in Hollywood society. It was dubbed alternatively the 'Ivory Tower' and 'San Simeonette', after the William Randolph Hearst castle.

Photoplay magazine listed both the house and the entertaining that went on there as the film capital's 'most spectacular'. If you were in the Warner social group, Jack and his wife were the most charming people in America.

There were some people Jack wouldn't have in his house. In the 1930s the famous mobster Bugsy Siegel had moved into Los Angeles to take up his pitch at the head of the California racket business. He made it clear that to cement that position he would like to be invited to the best parties.

When Jack heard about it he told everyone that he wouldn't allow the racketeer into his house. 'I wasn't going to wake up one morning,' he said, 'and see the front page saying "Movie Tycoon machine-gunned by Opposition Mob".'

As he said it he realized that might have been a difficult proposition. 'Of course, I wouldn't be able to read about it if I were machine-gunned, would I? Anyway, I wouldn't have him in my house.'

Jack was very good at eating his words. A short while later Siegel came to a Warner party.

But for other people the relationship with Warner Bros continued to be one long battle in the courts. Sometimes, they were huge business concerns. Frequently—including an on-going battle over their denial of films to private exhibitors which opened up the whole issue of studios owning theatres—they involved the Federal courts.

Jack seemed to enjoy them all. The legal battles which angered him were the ones with his stars; people he believed he had nurtured, who now were so ungrateful that they had the audacity to ask for more money once their names had taken off and become gilt-edged investments. Sometimes they just complained about being overworked—or not given the right parts.

CHAPTER 9

WOMEN ARE LIKE THAT

He was always great fun to be with. Never a bore.

Milton Sperling

It was very much the age of the star. They weren't all young and glamorous either, although Jack was inclined to dismiss anyone with a facial blemish as totally unsuitable for the movies. A wart, a mole or the slightest inconsistency in skin pigmentation was enough to ensure an actor's dismissal.

He didn't have that problem with George Arliss, whose statue he was proud to report he had seen in the British Houses of Parliament! What he had spotted in fact was a sculpture of Disraeli, but since Arliss had played the famous Prime Minister favourite of Queen Victoria, it seemed a reasonable mistake.

He played Disraeli twice for Warner Bros—a very successful silent version in 1921 and a talkie remake eight years later, which really didn't quite take off. However, Arliss was firmly entrenched as a Warner staple, and he was also slowly but steadily helping to create yet another studio trademark—the biographical film. He was to go on to play in turn Alexander Hamilton, Voltaire, the first of the Rothschilds (in *House of Rothschild*), Cardinal Richelieu and the Duke of Wellington (in *The Iron Duke*).

Arliss was reliable, extravagant and had a huge following. He would also take credit for another Warner Bros phenomenon, one Miss Bette Davis.

Bette had made a few pictures for Columbia and Universal, but Arliss would always say that he recommended her for her start at Warner Bros, *The Man Who Played God*. In this she played the girl befriended by Arliss, a concert pianist whose career is ruined when he is deafened by an exploding bomb.

After he signed her to a five-year contract—with yearly options to follow—Jack Warner was to think of Miss Davis as something of an exploding bomb herself.

Under her contract she was given a clutch of parts which she said did nothing whatever for her career, although she was left with no alternative but to play them. Virtually from the beginning, she and Jack were in a state of undeclared war— she begging for roles which she thought were more suitable for her, he decreeing that she did what she was told.

The studio certainly took advantage of her in their publicity. When they sent round posters for *Ex Lady,* they showed a soulful, bare-shouldered Bette, under the legend, 'We daren't tell you how daring it is.'

No more daring than fighting her was going to prove to be.

In fairness it shouldn't be forgotten that some of the films of which she complained, such as *The Working Man* and *Bureau of Missing Persons,* had to be weighed against *20,000 Years In Sing Sing, Cabin In The Cotton* and *The Rich Are Always With Us.*

Satan Met A Lady hadn't been her cup of coffee at all, and Jack's offer of the part of a lumberjack in another picture was insulting.

It was one thing to make her a star, quite another to expect her to be for ever after grateful and agree to make whatever film he had in mind.

The test came in 1932, when Pandro S. Berman wanted her to play the lead in RKO's *Of Human Bondage.* She desperately wanted to accept. Jack kept saying no. He wouldn't release her.

Until, that is, RKO came up with the kind of offer even Warner Bros couldn't refuse.

Bette recalled that when Jack finally relented he told her, 'Go hang yourself!'

She was paid exceedingly well for her services; all of which went to Warner Bros. Bette herself received no more than her regular Warner salary. Such were the practices of the film industry at the time—which Bette thought were very unfair indeed.

She was never more incensed than a year later, when she heard that Jack was doing everything in his power to prevent her being nominated for an Oscar for the role. He thought that if she were to get an Award it should be for a Warner picture. More significantly, getting one would only serve to swell her head, and prove how right she had been in insisting on the part in the first place.

The word was passed, and the nominating committee decided it was politic not to cross a big studio boss. She didn't get a nomination.

It was just the beginning of eighteen years of conflict between the two fixtures of Burbank, Jack and his most unyielding star. He honestly believed she had gained as much out of Warner Bros as they had got from her. She thought the studio was exploiting her—and, worse still, giving her dreadful roles.

To Jack her actions were not just crass disloyalty, they were also the epitome of stupidity and ingratitude. Here he had made an unknown actress into a star of international repute, had taken George Arliss's advice and given the youngster whose option was about to be dropped by Universal a new chance, and allowed what she once described to me as a 'very young innocent-looking Yankee girl' the perks and excitement that went with it, and here she was, flinging it all back in his face.

She had even just won her first Oscar, for *Dangerous,* which most people considered a consolation prize for what hadn't happened in 1935. Jack believed it only made Bette too cocky by half. But it wasn't so much the lingering row over the Oscar that made her decide to try to rid herself of her Warner Bros obligations as a picture called *The Golden Arrow,* in which she played an heiress, trying to fight off a whole gang of spongers. She not only hated the picture, she finally declared there would be no more like it.

When he said he had optioned a new novel called *Gone With The Wind* with the part of a girl called Scarlett O'Hara just made to measure for Bette's talents and personality she stormed out of his office crying, 'I bet it's a pip'.

She then was summarily suspended.

Other stars were content simply to make an appointment to see Jack, demand their suspension be lifted, perhaps crawl a little, and then suggest roles in films they were itching to play.

Bette, suspended and unable to work for Warner Bros, rashly accepted an offer from Ludovic Toeplitz—he had produced *The Private Life of Henry VIII* for Alexander Korda—to make two films in London, one with Douglass Montgomery, the other with Maurice Chevalier. It was highly illegal.

With her new husband, Harmon Nelson, she took off for Canada, from whence they boarded the *Duchess of Bedford* for England. It would be a second honeymoon—and a test of the law.

If Warner Bros chose to catch up with her, could Bette possibly win? Her lawyers thought that she could, once she had left American soil.

Jack and Ann were on honeymoon too—and in London. Which proved to be very convenient indeed, because once he discovered what was afoot he initiated legal proceedings in the Law Courts in the Strand.

And there, in the stone-floored, slightly dusty Gothic majesty of the second highest court in the land, Bette Davis saw the biggest drama of her still young life enacted, without going before a movie camera even once.

It was a very high-blown affair, with both sides represented by the cream of the British Bar. For Warner Bros was perhaps the best-known barrister in the country, Sir Patrick Hastings, KC, a member of the last Labour Government. Representing Bette was coincidentally a man who would ten years later be Lord Chancellor in the next Labour administration, Sir William Jowitt.

Originally, the then Mr Norman Birkett was to appear for Warner Bros, because Sir Patrick had been away on holiday. But Hastings came back for the hearing, and both men—each of them highly eminent—sat in court on the studio's behalf.

Jack loved it all before either a word was said or anyone could prejudge the outcome. The wigs, the gowns, the smells. He was mentally taking notes and planning the next picture he could make that would use this setting.

Even the 'billing' for the hearing was a publicist's dream—Warner Bros v. Nelson. Bette was being sued under her married name. The case was heard by the Vacation Judge, Mr Justice Branson.

William Randolph Hearst—whose protégée Marion Davies had been given a succession of roles beyond her talents as a *quid pro quo* for all the nice things the Hearst newspaper chain was saying about Warner films—came to London to hold a watching brief on Jack's behalf. His papers had already decided that Bette was a naughty schoolgirl who deserved to have her bottom smacked.

It was the kind of moral support Jack thought he liked to have around him at important and exciting moments. Not that he for a minute thought he would lose. At times like this there was an almost messianic certainty in his bones that God was with him.

He spent hours in consultation, not with Sir Patrick himself, who didn't like to be involved in such detail, but with junior counsel and with the solicitors instructing him.

Most people saw the case as a big Hollywood occasion, transported by a quirk of fate to the British capital, so that naturally Sir Patrick was regarded as the star of the piece. When he opened the case he struck the note which indicated the degree of paternal concern which the studio wanted to show was its main objective in pursuing the matter.

'I can't help but think, My Lord, that this is the action of a very naughty young lady.' The court echoed to the polite titters of the public gallery.

Miss Davis, he said, had alleged that working for Warner Bros amounted to 'slavery'.

'This slavery has a silver lining,' said Sir Patrick, 'because the slave was, to say the least, well remunerated.'

Her contract had until 1942 to run, by when she would get £600 (2,400 dollars) a week. 'If anyone,' said Sir Patrick (more titters in the gallery, and among his bewigged colleagues) 'wants to put me into perpetual servitude on that basis of remuneration, I shall be prepared to consider it.'

To the regulars in the King's Bench Division courtroom—the reporters, the ushers and those who sought vicarious thrills by enjoying the troubles of less fortunate beings, the case was not just merely light relief. It was high-quality entertainment with a star-studded cast.

'What this young lady is seeking to do,' continued Sir Patrick, 'is in effect to tear up her contract and say that whether she is right or wrong, the court will not grant an injunction against her.'

He said that she was demanding more money, which Bette always denied; she maintained it was better parts she was after, not more cash.

Eventually Jack's big moment came. Savouring every moment of it, and speaking—as one paper reported at the time— in his 'perfect Pittsburgh accent', he told the judge how maligned he believed he had been by his employees. Making Bette Davis a star had cost the studio a great deal of money and hard work, he said.

Casual visitors to the court that day might have noted that it seemed like money well spent.

Jack didn't allow himself to be totally carried away by the surroundings. It was a good opportunity to state his case, to say how badly treated the studios so frequently were by their 'employees'.

Next to be called was a 'character witness', Mr Alexander Korda; it was a nice touch, since it had been his man who started it all by trying to take Bette away from Warner Bros.

His heart was beating for Jack and his brothers. If a star walked out during the making of a picture, the financial loss would be vast, he said. But he added, 'No actress is indispensable in the film industry.'

It was now time for the defence to present its own case.

Sir William thought he had the answer to it all:

'If a producer transfers an actress against her will it would be hard on her. An actress doesn't always know her will or what she wants to do.'

The laughter in the court showed just how much most of the people there were enjoying it all.

Bette Davis, he said, really had been subjected to slavery, whether it was the kind most people had in mind or not. 'Slavery is no less slavery because the bars are gilded,' he said, not quite totally making his point.

And he referred to the option clause that Warners had inserted in the very contract his client was now fighting so passionately.

'Even if she decides to wait until 1942,' said Sir William, 'and not work for anyone else, there is a clause whereby the period will never have to come to an end. It is therefore a life sentence.'

He added, this time persuasively, 'She wouldn't even be allowed to become an assistant in a hairdresser's shop in the wilds of Africa—if they have hairdressing establishments there. . . . She cannot allow her husband to take a snapshot of her in the back garden because that is an appearance of a kind.

'She would not be allowed to set up a ball or some party in aid of a charity and she had to ask permission for her name to be used.

'If the producer chooses to order her to play in the chorus, she is bound to do it. There are penalties for absence. If she were to become a mother, the employers would have the option of terminating her contract.' And then he added succinctly, 'There is no evidence that this lady walked out in the middle of a film.'

Bette herself didn't go into the witness-box. In fact, there were no witnesses at all called by her side—a situation that disappointed the assembled public and so annoyed Sir Patrick—denied what he anticipated would be one of the golden moments of his career—that he pulled off his wig and threw it the length of the courtroom.

He needn't have worried. The court found in Warners' favour and said that Bette had to go back to work.

It wasn't just Jack and his brothers who drank a celebratory glass of champagne after the proceedings had ended and Bette's fate had been sealed. Jack was immediately on the line to California, and the sounds of relief from the Warner executives—who had got to their offices in the middle of the night to take the prearranged booked call—were audible over 5,500 miles of radio static.

It was a message that spelt reprieve to the entire studio contract system. Even more important, it showed that a court all those miles away from Hollywood could impose jurisdiction on a wayward young actress whom most of the producers' community had regarded as too conceited by half.

In London itself Gaumont British studios held a celebration party. If the effect of the court action could be important to people in Hollywood, it was totally binding to those closer to home. The court's judgment had given a bright green light to the British studios for continuing their own contract system.

The case was vitally important not merely to the film industry on both sides of the Atlantic. It has since been regarded as a leading case in the British law of contract.

None of this, of course, gave much pleasure to Bette. 'If I had won,' she said afterwards, 'lots of people would just walk out, as 75 per cent of all contracts are just like mine.'

Reporters found her at the tiny but picturesque seaside hotel at Rottingdean, near Brighton, where she had taken refuge. She said that she didn't know how to cope with a situation that had left her 'broken-hearted'. She said, 'This means my career to me, and though to go back is the only thing to do, I can never see myself eating humble pie.'

Humble pie, however, was a taste she had to get used to. She was saddled with court costs that amounted to more than 100,000 dollars. As a gesture of reconciliation, Jack said the studio would pay if she went back to work. Like a good girl, she was on the next available ship to New York, and soon after returning to California was driving through the Burbank entrance.

For the moment the fight was in a state of truce—although *The New York Times* said that Bette was 'much chastened' by her experience and knew 'what it meant to be alone in the world without the protecting arm of a publicity man to shield her from cruel reporters'.

Jack meanwhile stayed behind and had his first meeting with Sir Patrick outside the courtroom. It was intended as a courtesy call. After the two men had shaken hands, and Jack had done the right thing in praising Sir Patrick's brilliant stewardship of his case, the wily counsel said he had a favour to ask.

'There is a young man here, my son-in-law, actually, who is very keen to work in the cinema.' He then shuffled around in his drawer and pulled out a photograph. 'Do you think you could give him what I think is called a screen test?'

Jack was polite but evasive—the kind of evasiveness he had learned in twenty years in the film business, the sort that made people not realize he was being evasive at all.

Then Sir Patrick reached into his drawer again. This time he produced a very bulky document. It was not a brief, not a dusty tome of case histories.

'Do you think you could read this some time, Mr Warner?' he asked.

The leading King's Counsel of his day had written the definitive script and was hoping that Warner Bros would make it into a movie. The script was buried under a mountain of lesser prose and never became a film. But Jack was to dine out on the story for the rest of his life.

Life wasn't all nice and sweet between Jack and Bette thereafter. On one celebrated occasion, when yet again they were arguing over script suggestions and ideas in his office, Jack saw her out with a playful kick in the butt.

'What's that for?' she asked, realizing that he wasn't deliberately trying to exert some kind of physical pressure.

'That,' he said, 'is for tomorrow.'

But 'tomorrow' she made *Marked Woman*, about a girl working in a clip joint who has a double-cross branded on her cheek.

Much against Jack's wishes (to say nothing of those of Hal Wallis), she insisted on the most lifelike scar possible being inflicted by the makeup department.

The film seemed as real as her makeup. Even more important, she liked it too. It seemed as though Jack had got the message. It was easier to try to keep Bette happy by giving her parts she liked than by arguing.

Besides, he had other people to argue with.

CHAPTER 10

HARD TO HANDLE

The studio motto should have been: 'When not in use, turn off the juice'.

Darryl F. Zanuck

One of Harry's great contributions to the studios was his profound belief that if Warner Bros stood still they were practically walking backward. It was due to his foresight that Warners had opened their German office—only to lose it very soon afterwards to Adolf Hitler.

Now they were moving into Britain, too. The British film industry had had a chequered life, producing the odd acclaimed success like Hitchcock's *Blackmail,* the first British talkie, but very rarely did it manage to export its films overseas. Even in Britain itself the expression 'an English picture' was something rather less than a recommendation.

The film market in the country, however, did have a factor well worth commending, much as did the idea of Warners owning their own theatres. There was a quota system imposed by the Government that decreed that a certain number of films should always be British-made, but which did not mean that the pictures should be British-owned. And that was why Warner Bros had decided to establish their own British studios at Teddington in 1931. They put their own man Irving Asher in control, and announced that in the first year, they would make fifteen feature pictures—plus another twelve in French, which would solve another overseas marketing problem that had been worrying the brothers for some time.

Jack Warner promised that the films would be shown in the United States as well as in England, and that they would feature some of Warners' top stars, including the home-grown George Arliss. But these were fairly empty words. More than a hundred films were to be shot at the studios, but few of them were ever seen outside of Britain.

The only performers who later crossed the Atlantic from Teddington were Ida Lupino and Edmund Gwenn. There was also a young Australian called Errol Flynn, but that was still a little time away, and another story completely.

The brothers kept an eye on what was happening in London, but not a very closely focused one. They rarely bothered to see what the Teddington studios were putting out, taking the view that what they didn't see they were hardly likely to grieve about—providing the figures were large and black in the account books, which they usually were.

Jack for his part often said that he couldn't understand the plummy accents that were as much a characteristic of the average British movie as the white ties and tails which seemed to crop up in virtually every one of them.

No, he was much more concerned with what was going on at Burbank, which was as ever his own domain. When he decided that quality was being sacrificed for the sake of quantity, he made no bones about making a statement to the Press declaring, 'We have discontinued mass production.'

He went on to explain: 'Six months ago, we had nineteen pictures in production at the same time. This is entirely impossible, and we have come to realize that worthwhile films cannot be produced under such conditions.'

That scared the life out of some Warner employees, but Jack promised, 'We have stopped worrying about overheads—that a director's salary is going on for twelve or fourteen weeks while he remains idle.'

The words looked good in print. But they were anything but true. He was still demanding his pound of flesh, and taking every opportunity to avoid paying for it when it wasn't offered on the kind of plate he considered suitable.

One by one directors and actors who were thought to be less than essential were slated for projects everyone at the studio knew they would never take. When they refused they were put on suspension. It was to be another Warner characteristic. Director Irving Rapper told me, 'I was to have more suspensions than the Golden Gate Bridge.'

And if they were not suspended they were laid off. Most of the Warner contracts had clauses allowing the studio not to pay their employees for up to four weeks a year.

But there were developments that helped to improve the standard of film-making. One of them came at the suggestion of George Arliss, who insisted—with some reason—that a stage play succeeded, as much as anything else, because of the degree of planning that went into its production. For a reason which no one could satisfactorily explain, nobody ever thought of demanding rehearsals for movies.

'Formerly, we gave a director the script of his picture and told him to go ahead,' Jack declared. 'Now we permit him from four to six weeks in which to rehearse his principals. That is the only way to improve the quality of motion pictures.'

The idea of even four weeks doing nothing but rehearsing was not to last, but it was a step in a new direction. From then on the cameras wouldn't begin to turn until a scene was considered suitably rehearsed.

Sometimes Jack wished he had taken similar precautions before signing contracts—and he wasn't thinking about Bette Davis. There was the case, for instance, of a singer called Walter Woolfe, who sued the company 'for failing to exhibit his vocal powers'. The company answered that Woolfe didn't come up to their standards. Compared with the interminable arguments with Miss Davis, he was small fry indeed.

There was even trouble with the nation's coalminers when Paul Muni made the 1935 film *Black Fury*. He himself played a miner involved with a racketeering organization aimed at the takeover of the underground men's union. The union complained bitterly about being maligned by the capitalist studio bosses.

They didn't take the matter to court either, but Jack would have been happy if they had.

Even if Harry did regard it all as part of the business of running a company, and Abe would undoubtedly have been much happier in charge of a dress and shirt manufacturing operation, where such things didn't often happen, Jack regarded litigation as a lot more fun than making movies. When he himself went into the witness-stand he was back on the vaudeville boards once more.

Once he had to face a composer named Irving Gielow who wanted 550,000 dollars because he said two of his songs had been used in the film *Flirtation Walk* without payment. And then Henry Armstrong and Richard Gerard, the composers of the song 'Sweet Adeline', the international anthem of the over-inebriated, said that their tune had been used without permission in Warner films, and demanded 250,000 dollars compensation. Needless to say, they didn't get it.

There was also the continuing matter of Mr James Cagney, dubbed by Jack 'the professional againster'. In 1936 he claimed he was overworked. He said that his contract stipulated that he shouldn't have to make more than four films a year, but in the previous two years he had made ten. The court agreed he was overworked, particularly after it heard that the studio had been in breach of its contract by a technicality. Cagney was always supposed to get top billing, and yet a suburban cinema showing *Ceiling Zero* had put Pat O'Brien's name above his. Jack appealed and won. But Warners agreed to pay him much more money in the future. For *Boy Meets Girl* he would get all of 150,000 dollars.

Then there was the matter of the Poles.

The Polish Government decided that *The Life of Jimmy Dolan,* in which Douglas Fairbanks junior starred as a boxer, was insulting to the Polish nation, because one of the disreputable characters in the movie bore the name Pulaski. This name also happened to be that of a Polish national hero, so the Government took offence and banned all Warner films. They also added to the list any products bearing the imprints of First National and Vitaphone. Then, when they heard that another film, *How Many More Knights?,* had a gangster called Koscluszco, they were firmly convinced that it was all part of a vicious Warner Bros plot. Harry said something to the effect that it was more likely another symptom of Polish antisemitism, and decided not to worry too much.

It was a time when writs flew in and out of the Burbank offices almost as frequently as copies of *Variety* and *Photoplay.* People didn't like the way they were portrayed on the screen and sued. Others said that their ideas were being plagiarized, and did the same.

The Rothschild clan didn't sue when they saw *The House of Rothschild,* but admitted that there were internal family differences about it just the same. The rival house of Baring Brothers, on the other hand, were somewhat less sanguine. They decided they were distinctly offended by the way their ancestors had been shown to be idiots on the screen, and threatened legal proceedings, which they didn't follow through.

Even if they had have done, it is doubtful if it would have worried those other brothers, the Warners, very much. They were much more concerned with what they had planned for the future.

One of Hal Wallis's favourite stories is of the time he asked Jack if he had yet ploughed through a somewhat intimidating-looking book.

'Read it?' said Jack. 'Hell, I couldn't even lift it.'

Jack Warner never read a book. But when Wallis boiled the thousand pages of *Anthony Adverse* down to a one-sheet synopsis he decided he could 'lift' the story and make a movie out of it. The result was a massive box-office hit in 1935, starring Fredric March, Claude Rains, the newly imported Edmund Gwenn and a beautiful, fragile little thing who was later to prove that her looks belied her strength, Olivia de Havilland.

It was the start of what was to be a lengthy golden age for Warner Bros: expensive, highly prestigious films made by people with equally golden talents.

Jack himself took a great deal of the credit for the studio's output;

89

and frequently quite justifiably. He had antennae that tweaked like a water-diviner's rod at the approach of new film subjects he knew Warners could make better than anyone else. When he heard there was a Broadway play that might make a good movie he was on the first train across country so that he could see it for himself.

Hollywood lore being what it is, there were people who were convinced Jack believed that *A Midsummer Night's Dream* was a new play worth signing up. The astonishing thing is that Warners rushed in to make Shakespeare's most lyrical tale where other studios feared not merely to tread, but even to tip-toe.

It wasn't a total success—there was no way that audiences wouldn't wonder whether there was a gun hidden under the ass's head worn by James Cagney as Bottom. There were others expecting big, funny things from Joe E. Brown. But it was a cinema landmark, nevertheless.

Olivia de Havilland was a lovely-looking Hermia, but few found her Shakespearean debut to be more than an opportunity to enjoy her beauty.

Jack had doubts about the whole enterprise, but once more was talked into it by Hal Wallis, who wanted the Warner company to break out of what he feared was becoming its stereotyped image. Rightly, he thought it one thing to have a reputation for doing a certain kind of film brilliantly, quite another not to try new paths.

Within a week Warner himself was telling everyone at the studio about the brilliant idea he had had to make a lot of money out of culture. He had become totally infected by Wallis's excitement, and had almost convinced himself that it was his own idea.

It was Hal's plan to use the sprawling acres surrounding the Hollywood Bowl for the setting, and to import the one man whom he believed could transfer the project to the screen, Max Reinhardt.

It would be Reinhardt's first film, if he could be persuaded to leave his magnificent Austrian schloss, Leopoldskron, for the unknown pastures of Hollywood. Persuaded he was—by an offer of riches even he had never known before.

If the picture had been not so ambitious, and sold to an expectant public with rather less ballyhoo, then it might have worked. As it was, the Warner publicity machine plugged it as though it were a new Busby Berkeley spectacular, and incredulous cinema audiences who accepted the studio's blandishments decided that, as they thought, they didn't like Shakespeare.

Moreover, the film was fraught with difficulties from the start. Mickey Rooney, playing Puck, broke a leg and had to spend most of his time on the film being wheeled through the lot on a specially made trolley.

What worried both Jack and Wallis most, however, was the

patently obvious fact that Reinhardt was still a novice behind a camera. They selected the Teutonic William Dieterle, who had studied under Reinhardt, to assist him. They thought that the two men spoke the same language. Why no one thought of importing someone who spoke Shakespeare's language—perhaps from the theatre at Stratford-upon-Avon—is another matter.

Jack, as always, saw all the rushes after they were brought to his home each evening. He didn't like the experience one little bit.

It wasn't just his innate sense of Philistinism, either. The film, he decided, looked too dark.

Cameraman Ernest Haller so much wanted to capture the idea of the *Dream* being set in a forest that in addition to the Bowl he used two vast Burbank sound-stages to create the effect. Real trees were felled specially for the film and brought to the studio. The trouble was that they were so tall and overpowering that they couldn't be seen at all. Haller was replaced by Hal Mohr, who not only changed the lighting effects dramatically, but together with Anton Grot, the set-designer, chopped the trees down by a third, brought in leaves from a real forest and sprayed them with silver paint. Other leaves and moss were imported for the sound-stage floor, which then became unbearably pulpy overnight.

But the problems were overcome. The film was made and, in parts, looked beautiful.

When Harry and Abe saw the box-office returns they turned on Jack, who vented his spleen on Hal Wallis. He never wanted to make the goddamned picture in the first place, he said, choosing to forget how he had quite willingly been caught up in Hal Wallis's previous enthusiasm. It was easy to be right when other people didn't know you had been wrong.

Wallis was frequently in the middle of these exercises of spontaneous dissent. He had the idea to star Paul Muni in *The Story of Louis Pasteur*.

Jack treated the whole project as though it were simply a story about dairy-farming.

'Who wants to see a movie about a man who makes milk pure?' he demanded.

Wallis was insistent, so Jack had to think of new reasons for saying no. 'We don't want a period piece,' he said. 'And we don't want to hide Paul behind a beard. Why the hell should we pay him a fortune if no one will know who he is?'

When Hal Wallis finally talked him into the idea of a film that had, he said, tremendous pathos and drama that would lend itself superbly to Muni's acting skills, he accepted the undertaking, but reluctantly.

Through the length of the production he referred to Muni as

'the milkman'. He only stopped the name-calling when audience reaction proved that Hal Wallis had been right.

Two years later he was bathing in the satisfaction of seeing another Wallis-Muni production received in the same way. *The Life of Emile Zola* was, in fact, an even greater success—for Muni, for the studio, and for director William Dieterle.

For the first time Warner Bros in 1937 won an Oscar for the best picture of the year. Muni himself was nominated, but didn't win, although Awards went to Max Steiner, for the best musical score; to Heinz Herald and Geza Herczeg, for best original story; to Anton Grot, for best art-direction; and to Nathan Levinson for best sound-recording—a just reward for the man who had helped put Warners' first radio station on the air.

Even though Muni did fail to win an Oscar, it was his picture all the way, fighting with all his power the injustice that sent Alfred Dreyfus to Devil's Island.

Jack wasn't sure about that film either. Once more there were rows with Wallis about the wisdom of making a picture about a Frenchman. But he was wrong again.

The French Government decided that these films were so good for their national prestige that they deserved some signal honour.

Would M. Warner be prepared to accept the Légion d'Honneur? M. Warner, who now made sure that 'Jack L. Warner in charge of production' was featured in the movie's publicity, took the first available ship.

The citation said that the award was made because of Jack L Warner's services to 'the glory of France, of science, of men of good will throughout the world and to the enduring art of the cinema'. Jack L. Warner couldn't have put it any better himself.

But the Zola film had its blemishes, and the same people who in retrospect cheered so loudly the French writer's stand had good cause to point the 'J'Accuse' finger at Warner Bros.

Astonishing as it may now seem, not once was the real cause of Dreyfus's condemnation mentioned. No one spoke of antisemitism. No one even said that the maligned French officer was a Jew.

That was typical of the way Jack Warner now saw his role in America in general, and in Hollywood in particular. The studio that had been built up as much as anything by Harry's rout of the Jew-baiting Wall Street aristocracy was extraordinarily sensitive about its origins.

Jack was embarrassed by the notion that anyone might think that he was wearing his Judaism on his sleeve, and his directive was that Jewish stories were strictly verboten. He felt much the same way about Jewish actors—Aryan good looks made better box office.

The exceptions, Muni himself and Edward G. Robinson, merely proved his rule.

If Jack felt secure in business the one thing that unnerved him still were the very Jewish roots that caused so much of the friction with his elder brother.

When Julius and Philip Epstein were signed to write the script of a Kay Francis-George Brent picture, *Living on Velvet,* in 1934 Jack told them, 'Don't think I'm putting any pressure on you, any pressure at all. But if you want to change your names, now is the time to do it—before the credits go on the film.'

They said 'No, thank you', and one of the most respected names in film-writing was preserved for posterity. But how different would the career of Edward G. Robinson have been had he continued to be known as Emanuel Goldenberg? Or if Paul Muni had remained Muni Weisenfreund?

With actors, changing your name seemed—to use a phrase Jack would have appreciated, for his language never adapted to outside pressures—kosher. It wasn't just their backgrounds that Muni and Robinson had in common. Both admitted that their work was virtually interchangeable. (Not that they liked each other. In his book Robinson was to write 'I disliked Muni and Muni detested me.')

And Muni could be difficult. There were also times when it seemed that there was a personal vendetta between him and Jack.

Harry also occasionally joined in. Both brothers would find excuses for not liking him, even if it only concerned the title of the films he was making with them. It was through Harry that Muni's film *America Kneels* became *The World Changes.*

The president of the studio said of the original title, 'It sounds like everybody in the country is either a Catholic or a goddamned queer.'

That had been merely part of a continuing story.

Black Fury didn't just upset the Poles. Jack didn't like that film's original title either. He sent a memo forcibly addressed to 'All Departments'. It read: 'The new and final title for the picture now known as *Black Hell* will be *Black Fury.* Delete *Hell,* add *Fury.*'

Paul Muni could have been forgiven for thinking that characterized his relationship with the Warners, although Jack saw his value and accepted that he was the obvious heir to George Arliss's crown as the biographical king of the studio.

On one of his more indulgent days he called the star to his art deco office and asked him to think of new biographical subjects he would like to play. Muni had no doubts about the answer. He wanted to play Beethoven. He had already done a great deal of research into the composer's life, and he knew he could do it justice.

'Fine,' said Jack, patting Paul on the back and promising to call up Hal Wallis and ask him to make the necessary arrangements.

He did call Hal, and asked him to organize Warners' stable of writers on dreaming up some new biographical subjects. 'Anything,' he said, 'but Beethoven.' In his own inimical phraseology, he let Wallis know that 'Nobody wants to see a movie about a blind composer.' Fortunately, he didn't call him a songwriter.

Jack once more was the arbiter of the nation's tastes, and wasn't going to allow his own knowledge of history to disturb the facts. He still wasn't sure that the kind of pictures Muni made would always be good box office. He was bolstered in his opinion by a letter from an anxious exhibitor. 'Please,' he wrote, 'for heaven's sake, don't send us any more pictures where the leading guy writes with a feather.'

Jack agreed, and then added the injunction to his producers: 'No one makes any money doing pictures about those guys in three-cornered hats.'

But Paul Muni stayed on the Warner books, and proved that occasionally Jack Warner did break his own rules. Another exception, of course, was Al Jolson, who could still do no wrong in Jack's eyes, even when a film like *The Singing Kid* did nothing to enhance his reputation. To Jack, Jolson was still the King, and when he came to Warner Bros it was Al who held court.

Jack would do anything to keep him there, even though he detected a waning of the great man's popularity; not helped, it must be added, by the Busby Berkeley vogue of musicals featuring Al's wife Ruby Keeler. If Jolson could have taken a fall-off in his own popularity—he certainly didn't need the money; like the Warner brothers he had handled the Wall Street crash as deftly as a routine on stage at the Winter Garden, by getting out early—he wasn't prepared to let Ruby be a beneficiary.

It was Jack who had the answer to this little local difficulty. He suggested that Al and Ruby should make a picture together. The result was one of the best that Jolson ever made—*Go Into Your Dance,* in true Warner tradition, originally called *Casino de Paree* (which became its British title) and which was to make a lot of money for the studio.

But although all the publicity stressed that Al and Ruby were now a professional as well as a private partnership, no one had any doubt that Jolson was the star of the family.

Jack begged him to repeat the success with a sequel. Al, however, saw too many risks on the horizon. He said no, and Jack sat behind his desk, puffing a cigar, a disappointed man.

In fact, Jack was now convinced that the musical as a genre was finished. And that meant work for one of his aides who had the job of summoning members of the music department and firing them summarily. Choreographers were dismissed. Songwriters had to pack their bags. Only a very few remained to provide a skeleton staff for the odd musical inserts. Jack was unhappy about losing a part of the set-up he enjoyed most, but that was the movie business.

There were, however, not many things that disappointed Jack L. Warner in the mid- and late 1930s.

Business was thriving. People seemed to like the Warner films and the Warner actors, and the shareholders felt that the disasters caused by the financial crash had now passed. Big dividends were plainly on the way. Where there was discord it was usually through more of Jack's rows with his stars. He wasn't unique among the Hollywood moguls in this, of course, although usually they kept their problems very much to themselves—as though involving any-one else would mean opening up a family quarrel.

This tradition, however, was firmly scotched in 1935 with the celebrated case of Mary Astor's diaries. Miss Astor, who had been Warner's principal glamour star when she appeared opposite John Barrymore in *Don Juan,* meticulously wrote up practically every-thing that happened to her, particularly details of her love life.

Her affair with the distinguished screen writer George S. Kauf-man was particularly graphically described. It was in the volume which fell into the hands of her husband, Dr Franklyn Thorpe, at the time he was suing for divorce.

The pages were read in open court, and consequently, the Press had more fun than at any time since Colonel Lindbergh crossed the Atlantic. Newspapers published details of Miss Astor's Top Ten Lovers—not a few top Hollywood names figured in the list—and what they didn't publish was compensated by innuendo.

What had begun as a personal matter, and then as a subject of considerable public entertainment, now suddenly threatened to do as much harm to the motion-picture industry as the Fatty Arbuckle scandal a decade earlier—when the obese silent-screen star had been unjustly brought down by the death of a young girl, raped at a party in his house.

One by one the names of the top stars of all the major studios were being paraded about in a series of conversations that at any moment were likely to be published in the newspapers and film magazines. And then to make things worse for all concerned, Miss Astor's lawyers announced they were going to publish the diaries in full, just so that the innuendoes would stop.

But fortunately for the studios, the judge decided that that would be inadmissible: since the diaries were incomplete, they couldn't be introduced as evidence. The moguls breathed a collective sigh of relief. They knew that, diaries or no diaries, people never stopped talking about Hollywood. For the world outside, it was still fairy-land.

For those inside, there were still elements that justified calling it a dream factory.

CHAPTER 11

THANK YOUR LUCKY STARS

That night at the dinner for Jack, it was the first
standing ovation I really meant.

Loretta Young

The trouble with being in the film business, the brothers Warner
might well have said, was that you needed actors.

To be fair, Abe had no special feelings on the subject. A good
name brought the customers into the company's ever-spiralling
theatre empire, and that pleased him, but stars didn't seem to show
too much temperament when they were projected thirty feet high
on to a screen in Baltimore or Brooklyn. At least, not the sort that
caused him any pain.

Jack and Harry, however, saw them rather more life-size. Harry
believed they were part of a conspiracy initiated by Jack to bring
him to an early grave. In his more charitable moments, he took it no
further than to suggest that his younger brother was using his wiles
to drum him out of the business. He was convinced that there was a
scheme afoot to go broke, and then immediately start up all over
again.

Harry was the business brains of the operation, but there was a
fairly strong argument for saying that an infusion of paranoia had
got him where he was. If anyone was persecuting him, he felt it to be
Jack, who was having so much fun with all those actors—to say
nothing of the actresses whom Harry was convinced were taking
their clothes off for him three times a day.

Milton Sperling told me, 'He would say to Jack: "I put bread in
your mouth and made your fortune. But you're just a playboy." '

Jack didn't see it quite that way. He could well argue that if he
didn't have stars to bother with his pictures would be a lot less
troublesome and a lot less expensive (which would please Harry a
great deal, too). Of course, nobody would go to see them either.

When the rows in the art-deco office seemed to be going against
him there was one name to invoke which in his mind spelled perfec-

tion. 'Remember,' he'd say, 'it was a dog that saved the studio. Why can't they all be like Rin Tin Tin?'

At the same time, when things were going well, he loved being with stars more than any other people. Watching an actor at work, he was vicariously performing himself—hence his continuing adoration for Al Jolson, whom he would have kept busy at Warner Bros, simply for the thrill of having him around. When Al decided he didn't want to make the two films still outstanding on his contract Jack was a miserable man.

Other stars pleased him less easily—even the 'uncomplicated' and frequently considered uncomplaining ones like Edward G. Robinson, who finally decided he had had enough of the gangster image. It had, he believed, been sculpted a little too precisely for him.

As far as the studio was concerned, it was a successful formula, too successful to discard simply because Edward G. was himself getting bored with it. Moreover Jack, who believed that success was his exclusive title, wouldn't compromise that situation by lending him to other studios. As Robinson said in his book *All My Yesterdays,* 'If the ensuing picture was a hit, it would mean that Warners were not so bright and clever as the new guy.' When Columbia wanted to borrow him Jack personally phoned Harry Cohn, that studio's iron dictator, and told him, 'You're nuts. Edward G. Robinson is box-office poison.'

Cohn was more astute than Jack was prepared to believe. Doubtless figuring that Warners wouldn't hold on to anyone who didn't bring them dividends, he kept pressing, and finally did a deal to borrow him for *The Whole Town's Talking,* co-starring Jean Arthur.

Somewhat bitterly, Robinson wrote in his incisive book, 'The financial details of this bit of big business have never been revealed to me, but if there were any monies involved beyond the salary Warners were paying me, you can be absolutely certain they did not accrue to me. It was not uncommon for the studios in those days to make money on our flesh.'

Hollywood was indeed very much something of the slave market Bette Davis had alluded to in London, even if the cells were padded and perfumed and the inmates allowed every day the sort of luxuries most prisoners would not have anticipated outside of the condemned cell, a few hours before the walk to the scaffold.

Edward G. Robinson need have had no doubts that the monies paid to Warners by Columbia—a studio frequently referred to as being on 'Poverty Row'—were substantially in excess of his own contract, while every penny was indeed paid not to the star himself but to his employers. As far as the studios were concerned, it was merely a commercial undertaking, a form of compensation for the times when they reckoned their human investments were not being sufficiently realized.

In 1937 Jack decided that Edward G. was sufficiently important to him to justify a certain amount of pampering. With a script under his arm, he pretended that he had merely come to inquire about his 'very dear friend's' health, but his ever-open face gave him away.

As Edward G. wrote, Jack wasn't really interested in the new Robinson patio. He had a deal he desperately wanted to get under way.

Before doing so, he emphasized how different Mr Robinson was from the stars giving him headaches, like Bette and 'young Livvy'—Olivia de Havilland. 'At that point,' Robinson wrote, Jack 'nearly sobbed—and by God he was sincere about it.'

He said how he appreciated that Edward G. was a 'perfectionist . . . he made it sound like some dread disease'.

Jack told him, 'We'll have many more happy years together.'

'What happy years?' Edward G. asked.

'The years we'll be associated together from now on, Eddie. You shall have everything you want.'

'For my last picture?'

'What last picture?'

'There is only one more picture left on my contract.'

'Formality,' said Jack, not anxious to get into that one again. A red danger signal was flashing for him. 'Formality,' he repeated. 'Just tell your agent what you want and it's yours.'

Then came the rub. 'Within reason, of course. After all, we're both reasonable men.'

That had to be accepted as a compliment, although it was sometimes doubtful whether Jack's definition of reasonable was one that anyone else would like to have pinned on himself.

Jack wanted Edward G. to make a picture about a boxer—he'd be the manager, not the fighter, he was assured. The movie was to be called *Kid Galahad*.

They had a deal, the picture was made, and became a huge success, but not before Jack and Eddie Robinson got themselves into a political tussle. Warners were worried that the man they had championed so vociferously four years before, Franklin D. Roosevelt, was becoming too left-wing by far, so would the actor kindly not be so forthcoming in his praise of the pinko President? And why was Eddie involved with the Anti-Nazi League? It was just a communist front.

Robinson almost threw his employer off the premises, but contented himself with a message on just what the Nazis were threatening to do—and already doing—to civilization. Spain was just the beginning.

In the end Jack decided that it was better to have a good actor who was a little too left-wing for his sensitivities than to allow him to go elsewhere.

Robinson did try one thing, and lost. He wanted his contract to be minus the then obligatory clause that said the employee wouldn't do anything that 'might subject you or the studio to low esteem'. Jack wouldn't budge. It would have been surprising had he done so. That one sentence was enough to make an agreement invalid as far as the studio was concerned, practically any time they chose to invoke it.

And how they would all have liked to try! The only thing hindering them was again that matter of the value of actors. It was very difficult indeed to make a movie without them.

The contract system was a two-way affair, despite all that the stars said about it. It not only gave the actors work—or, at least, money—on a fairly regular basis, but just as there were Bette Davises trying to be released from commitments to what they saw as 'slavery', so there were a number of lesser beings who hadn't lived up to early promise, yet were on the books for the length of their agreements. Providing they kept their noses tidy, it was no easier for the studios to get rid of them than it would have been for the actors to pack up and work elsewhere.

Jack regarded it as a betrayal of the trust he had put in his actors in the first place. Taking a fairly indifferent role after a triumph seemed to him to be no more than part of the job of being a star. 'Who put them where they are?' Jack would ask his legal department, pointing for once not at the name over the studios but at a poster for the current box-office hit. He genuinely felt hurt, and he regarded it as much more serious an offence when the 'guilty party' had been discovered and nurtured at Burbank, rather than one who had come there after having made his name at some other studio. When in later years Joan Crawford or Gary Cooper didn't like the work they were offered, he believed they were much more entitled to make that choice for themselves than were Cagney or Bette Davis.

Why was it that when so many leading actors were once established they decided that they would be better off elsewhere? It was partly vanity—a deep-seated belief that they were supremely important and irreplaceable. It was partly a conviction that they were being exploited; and, despite the fact that the contract system did offer them security, it couldn't be denied that it was hard when documents signed at a time that a performer was a nobody still held after they had become superstars.

It was also a fact that Jack, like all the other moguls, saw himself as a universal provider who, like both Chairman Mao and the

Japanese business tycoons twenty and thirty years afterwards, thought he deserved constant thanks.

He wasn't a lover of yes-men, yet when he twisted and flicked that cigar and said, 'Whose . . .?' that had to be the end of the argument. The name Warner Bros was not just over the studio entrance now, but emblazoned on the water-tower on the lot overlooking Universal and the Disney studios. In his more articulate moments, he would add, 'Whose name on the water-tower?' and then you knew he knew he was unbeatable. Which didn't endear him any the more to people who would laugh with him to his face and about him behind his back—like Humphrey Bogart and Errol Flynn. And sometimes they weren't laughing.

Bogart's story was far from typical, although his relationship with Jack was distinctly in the studio mould.

He began as a bit player, and eventually reached stardom only via a whole series of supporting roles that accounted for ten years of his life. Jack didn't forget that time, either. 'That sonofabitch took ten years off of my life,' he said every time Bogart's name was mentioned, as if he were reciting a speech in a play, or a verse that automatically continued on from the one heard before.

Bogart himself always considered that somewhat ungenerous. His success at Warners, he once told writer Charles Hamblett, came from 'licking assholes'.

Jack, on the other hand, put it somewhat more delicately. Bogey, he said, was a 'great apple polisher', by which we can assume he meant he usually said the right things at the right time in the right place. What he said at other times at other places didn't take very long to get out. He thought Jack, in particular, was too content to keep him in the also-featuring spots. He seemed to like him only as a tuxedo-wearing nightclub boss-cum-racketeer or a shyster lawyer.

Bogart's first Warner film was *Big City Blues,* and was followed by *Three On A Match,* both in 1932. Nothing much happened for him until 1936, when he repeated his stage role as Duke Mantee in *The Petrified Forest,* largely at the insistence of co-star Leslie Howard.

George Raft had turned down the part—which was one of his contributions to the war of attrition between the actors and Warners—and for the first time Bogart established himself as a tough performer to be reckoned with. Nevertheless, as the killer he was still playing second fiddle (or more accurately, firing second shotgun) to Leslie Howard and Bette Davis. It was a situation that would not be resolved until *High Sierra* in 1941.

After *The Petrified Forest,* his was a face most people who went to the movies recognized. His roles with James Cagney in *The Roaring Twenties* and *Angels With Dirty Faces* established a coterie of

101

Bogart fans, but the cult days were still in the future, and Bogie around the Warner lot was a frustrated figure.

When he went into the art-deco office Jack usually greeted him with an offer of a great cigar, a terrible joke and a pat on the back.

Bogart, of course, contributed to Warner's gangster cycle, which was still very good business indeed. Indirectly it helped its 'good citizenship' identity too, although without always realizing it.

A group of army officers happened to be visiting the studios on one occasion—one of the moments which Jack accepted as proof that his outfit was much more than a mere movie factory—when a gangster film was being shot. They were amazed at how the actors were able to use machine-guns without them ever becoming jammed. That didn't happen in the Army—and yet they used the same weapons.

'Our guns *have* to work,' said Jack. 'We can't afford for them not to do so.' The soldiers were introduced to the Warner gun expert, who explained the modifications he had fitted to the arms. Within a few weeks all the Army's guns were changed in just the same way.

Bogie, to be fair, wouldn't have been impressed. He would have much preferred simply to burn down the studio—which in 1935 he and Errol Flynn tried to do. Errol was at Burbank making *The Charge of the Light Brigade* at the same time as Bogart was struggling with the part of Duke Mantee. With a can of kerosene and a box of matches, they actually started a fire on one of the sound-stages.

For all Bob Hope's humour, Warners employed men to fight their fires with the same kind of loyalty as those they took on as senior executives. They were in the business of smelling out the merest suggestion of trouble. There would, in the not too distant future, be occasions when their function would be somewhat different, but when Bogart and Flynn got busy the firemen were not too far away. They were already on the scene, their hoses gushing, before a single prop could be more than slightly singed.

Years later, Bogart was slightly uneasy about those things. 'A lovely man,' he was to say of Jack Warner. It was not a sentiment he allowed to cross his lips too often in the early days.

As for Flynn, he and Jack were in a state of undeclared war virtually from the time of his arrival in Burbank in 1935, soon after he came to the country, until his contract ended. That was when he claimed 300 dollars for a camel-hair coat which he said had been stolen at the studio. 'No one could remember him ever having that coat,' Jack frequently repeated. The claim was needless to say paid, but it rankled with Jack for years afterwards.

Jack always believed he could talk to Errol. He planned well in advance just how he would dress him down when the Australian-born star came into his office, but by the time Errol had walked down the steps and promenaded along the carpet leading to the desk he was slapping him on the back and telling him stories.

Arguing with Errol just wasn't feasible, because he had sufficient charm to make a bearded lady in the circus feel like the winner of the Miss Universe contest. If Jack were to suggest that his openly lascivious behaviour was doing no little harm to the studio's reputation Errol would merely shrug his shoulders, praise Jack's taste in drinks, consume half a bottle of whisky and say, 'You know, sport, I wish I understood women the way you do. I also wish I had half of your appeal to them.

'Now that girl I had last night, for instance. She was quite beautiful. I had her in the sack in twenty minutes, but all she kept saying was that she thought the most dignified, handsome man in Hollywood was Jack Warner. What *is* it that you have, Chief?'

Who could argue with sentiments like that? The sincerity with which those choice words were uttered had to be totally disarming.

Flynn began his Warner Hollywood career as the corpse in a film called *The Case of The Curious Bride*, and followed this walk-on (or rather lay-on) role with something equally inauspicious called *Don't Bet On Blondes*. No one was betting on Flynn either, except as a rather good tennis-player and as a Don Juan of some note.

Things could very easily have stayed that way if Mike Curtiz, who had by now established himself as one of the studio's most innovative directors, hadn't been searching for a star to play the title role in *Captain Blood*. Robert Donat had been prepared for the part, but at the last moment he and Jack had a row over the transatlantic telephone—a rare thing to do in 1935—and so the director had to find someone else.

It was Curtiz who, after testing a succession of fairly important Warner stars and coming to the conclusion that none of them was right, landed on Flynn. One day, in the midst of a search that would later be dwarfed only by the trek for a Scarlett O'Hara, Curtiz could contain himself no longer. He ran through the second-floor corridor leading to Jack's office and, without knocking, burst in as though he were announcing that the place was on fire. In a way it was.

'I zink zo I have zee best man for zee part,' the Hungarian revealed. 'Errol Fleen. He's a very good-looking young man, JL, and I zink you should let me make a test from heem.'

Jack's reply was laconic to the point of desperation. He could never understand why, with the whole world wanting to get into pictures, it was so difficult to find a square peg to fit an equally square hole.

'Make a test,' he said. 'You've made one of everyone else.'

Hal Wallis was the first to see the result. He liked Flynn, but hated his outfit. He personally tore the lace from his cuffs and shirt-front.

'They make you look like a cissy,' he declared. It was not the sort of thing one said lightly to Errol Flynn. But at that stage the senior people at Warners didn't really have any idea at all about what it was they were going to say to him. What they did know was that they liked the way he looked on screen—and that they weren't too sure about his behaviour off it.

He had hardly got started before Jack was personally calling him into his office ready to administer a severe dose of chastisement. 'Look here, Flynn,' he said, in a posture he had been rehearsing ever since he first instructed Bill Schaefer, his secretary, to call the young actor to the presence. 'One thing I have to tell you. No one drinks at Warner Bros. You may go.'

Both Jack and Harry had ulcers now, and it seemed only just that they should share the benefits they bestowed with as many other people as possible.

The reason for his outburst was that Errol had collapsed on the set of *Captain Blood*. Everyone assumed he was no more seriously ill than any drunk falling down in the middle of The Bowery. Jack decided he had to put his foot down while there was still time. It was another two days before the studio's doctors diagnosed an attack of the blackwater fever Errol had picked up in the South Pacific.

Nevertheless, Jack had one of his hunches—the kind that frequently told him whether a movie was going to be good or bad, and which now indicated that there was likely to be trouble with Mr Flynn before very long. How right he was!

It was Jack's hunch, too, to put Errol in *The Charge of the Light Brigade*, a film which confused the Crimean War with the North West Frontier in India but had a great deal of adventure, and the opportunity for women in the cinema audiences all over the world to swoon at Errol Flynn, dressed in what appeared to be an immaculate black uniform.

He looked magnificent in a picture that has become more famous for a line uttered off camera than any that were picked up by the microphones—the one about the empty horses.

Flynn, on the other hand, was much better behaved on screen than off. For the cameras he was handsome, charming and heroic. Off screen, Curtiz was calling him either a 'bum' or his favourite expletive, 'sohn of a beetch'.

He was always late, and rarely remembered his lines. Curtiz in one frenzied outburst declared, 'I picked you up from a corpse and made you into a hero. And now from a hero I'll put you back to a corpse and you'll be a bum again.'

Jack, who had as many sources of information as the FBI, heard about it all and wondered again whether it wouldn't have been a lot easier treading the boards in vaudeville. His son, Jack Junior, told me, 'My father used to say, "Any actor you helped today is going to screw you tomorrow".'

It didn't take too much intuition on Jack's part to realize that Errol's behaviour was already 'screwing' Warner Bros. He was delaying production every day.

Irving Rapper, before his period as one of Warners' most influential directors, was working on the picture as a dialogue coach.

'I remember,' he told me, 'Jack coming on the set and saying to Curtiz, "Good heavens, Mike, what the hell are you doing? It's taking much too long. Let's get some footage." '

The dialogue seems remarkably restrained for Jack Warner in one of his less easy moods. It was to get more salty as the episode went on. Not satisfied with Curtiz's ability to persuade Errol to come to heel, he went to the company manager, a tough-talking Irishman called Jack Sullivan. 'Can't you push Mike around a little bit?' he asked.

'Can I help it,' asked Sullivan, 'if all the time he wants to fuck around?'

Curtiz heard: 'Honest to God, Jack,' he said, 'I don't fuck.'

The director was made the recipient of Jack's goodwill, and there were times when he exuded kindness as frequently and as fulsomely as other moguls were reputed to spit venom.

About this time some thirty elderly actors whose usefulness to the studio most thought was completely exhausted were told that their contracts were being renewed. In their heydays, in the silent era, they had earned perhaps as much as 30,000 dollars a year. Now they could have expected to have been put out to grass. Jack, Rapper recalls, simply told them, 'If you're prepared to work with Mike Curtiz, the contract is yours.'

There were times when Jack would despair of Curtiz almost as much as he would of Errol. The Hungarian's fractured English made Sam Goldwyn sound like an Oxford graduate, or at least an Ivy Leaguer. It was during the making of *Light Brigade* that he called over one of his unit directors, 'You are a genius, but over here it stinks a bit.'

Curtiz himself sometimes worried about what he saw as Jack's interference. 'Don't call me back,' he said, walking out of the art-deco office, 'until you're not ready.'

But Errol was at the root of the trouble, and Jack knew it. It was also a mutual problem. While the Warners saw Errol's potential as a box-office money-spinner, they had to be prepared to take his somewhat less than professional behaviour as part of the deal. Flynn for his part saw no obligation to like Jack, on whom he proceeded to shower every invective he knew, frequently with the prefix 'Jew'. If Jack had never been particularly aware of his Jewish background before, Errol would have reminded him in full measure—had he heard him.

Jack's greatest worry, which had been transferred to him by an incessant barrage from Harry, was the effect of Errol's behaviour on the studio's corporate image. When Flynn and the delicious French actress Lili Damita seemed to be having an interminable affair Jack issued an ultimatum: they either married immediately or were seen to end the relationship. Errol, faced with the alternative of giving up the stimulating but fiery affair or losing out to *that* clause, chose marriage—and a few more expletives directed at Jack Warner.

But Jack wasn't always the winner. When the itchy feet which were always part of Errol's makeup got the better of him there was nothing that the threat of ending a contract could do to ease the sensation.

The Spanish Civil War of 1936 filled Errol with dreams of achieving in real life what the Warner script department were planning for him on camera. Jack knew nothing about it, but Errol headed for Spain posing as a war correspondent, narrowly missed getting killed, and came back just before a suspension notice could take effect.

While other Warner artists quarrelled with Jack simply over the parts they were given, Errol was content to have his rows on a more personal basis. Providing the money was right—and he could charm his way towards receiving an adequate number of noughts on a cheque as easily as he could get a girl into his bed—he didn't worry about the parts he was given.

It wouldn't be long before he and another young Warner performer, the pretty Ida Lupino, would decide that Jack was at the root of all their troubles, and reflect their displeasure by standing on one of the Hollywood Hills overlooking the San Fernando Valley and throwing rocks down on to the Burbank studios.

There were stormy battles between Errol and Jack to come. For the moment the brothers Warner were deciding they had more important wars to fight.

CHAPTER 12

THE HORN BLOWS AT MIDNIGHT

Jack Warner was a coward.

Milton Sperling

'Don't pay attention to bad reviews,' Jack would say in his more sanguine moments. 'Today's newspaper is tomorrow's toilet paper.'

It was an axiom that was to be borrowed by generations of producers trying to ward off criticisms from studio heads—and perversely by not a few newspaper editors endeavouring to knock images of glory from the heads of conceited writers. Jack used it as a defence mechanism at a time when he considered he made all the important decisions at the studio. Frequently, however, he deputed the responsibility to Hal Wallis.

It was through Wallis that Jack made his contacts, and when there were rows brewing with Flynn or Bette Davis he had usually been the initial buffer. His office adjoined Jack's, and if he needed the personal Warner say-so, he was in a position to influence that decision the way he generally wanted it to go.

Warners paid Wallis a fortune—enough for him to amass vast estates—to do the work and to take responsibility, just as he paid other people to fulfil other individual roles.

To the shareholders, however, it was Harry who carried the final can. Hal Wallis would propose. Jack would suppose—that it was all right to make films, how much to spend on them, and who should be hired, but it was Harry who disposed in the end the long-term policy. Once that policy had been decided, it was Jack who had to see it through to the end of production.

That did not stop the mistakes being made, or people having fun at his expense.

In the early 1930s Jack had taken the plunge and signed a former New York cop called Phil Regan, whom he thought would be a great singing star. Sammy Fain, now one of Warners' top music men, had been specifically asked to write a song for Regan, who turned out to be less than perfect. That was when Jack had the idea to bring in Rudy Vallee instead.

Now, other people faced with such a situation would simply pull themselves up to their full strength, admit they were wrong and tell the artist concerned that the role wasn't theirs after all. Not Jack. He couldn't bring himself to cancel the man's part, any more than he could fire an executive. He decided it should be Fain's task, even though he was employed simply as a songwriter.

'We're giving the number to Rudy Vallee,' said Jack.

'But I've already sold it to Regan,' a disturbed Sammy Fain replied.

'So unsell it to him,' Jack thundered, and ended the subject.

The only way to do that, Fain decided, was to play the tune in a key he knew Regan couldn't manage, at a speed that made him sound like an undertaker's assistant. Poor Mr Regan said that Fain would have to get himself another boy, and Rudy Vallee had the top role in a now forgotten movie called *Sweet Music*.

For years Regan had to content himself with a series of walk-on roles with barely a line of dialogue to string together. Julius Epstein felt sorry for him. He gave him a line to recite.

In *Sweet Adeline*, Regan had to rush over to Irene Dunne after she fell off a swing.

'Quick,' he was made to say, 'get a doctor.'

Epstein thought he needed more chances to expand his dialogue talents. So in a whole succession of films, he wrote lines specially for him. In one film he was heard to say, 'Thank God, you're here, Doctor.' In another, it was 'How is she, Doctor?' And that was all.

'Jack never noticed!' Julius Epstein told me. Nor, apparently, did Regan, who was glad to say anything at all. In any case, the real target for the fun and games was Jack himself.

There would be more serious bouts to follow, for writers were to prove as difficult characters for the brothers Warner to swallow as any actor.

That, however, was a crisis still to come. Jack's battle with the actors was an on-going one, but for a time as 1936 got into swing (using the term in its musical as well as its metaphorical sense) the battle lines were being drawn with the songwriters—men who, unlike Sammy Fain, were not so willing to have their roles altered.

The big row had broken in December 1935 via Warners' own music-publishing company—set up so that the company could exploit to the full all the numbers being whistled and hummed by people leaving cinemas showing Warner musicals.

The brothers believed they still were riding the crest of the musical wave, and didn't think they were obliged to let anyone else share the loot—after all, the Warner songwriters had to be content with their salaries; their royalties at first went straight to the studios who owned the copyrights.

In December 1935 Warners chose to break away from what was always considered the tunesmiths' 'trade union', the American Society of Composers, Authors and Publishers (ASCAP).

Warners had divided their musical interests among eleven different companies, and they were withdrawing from ASCAP, not as the General Manager of the society, Edward C. Mills, declared, 'solely and selfishly in the interests of themselves', but entirely from motives of 'self preservation'. ASCAP had 'utterly failed to obtain adequate payments for the use of music by radio'.

A company statement said, 'As things stand today, the society has disposed of its rights to radio for the next five years on a basis which would render it impossible to keep our music publishing companies alive if they retained their memberships.'

As a result, it was forbidden to broadcast any of the big Warner film themes. That was, of course, as much a two-way matter as any Hollywood contract. The radio network wanted to broadcast the music, but the music companies needed to have the tunes played if it were going to sell records or sheet music.

One answer was for Warners to come to an agreement with a group of independent broadcasting companies, allowing them rights to broadcast the tunes for three months.

Variety saw the row in its own inimitable way: WB NIXES ASCAP OK'S ETHER; WEBBS PIX BEEF. Or in English, 'Warner Bros says no to ASCAP's agreement over broadcasts. Row between picture companies and radio networks.'

The row was also a case of internecine warfare between Warners and the other music companies, most of whom resented the fact that the studio had bought the rights to songs that had no connection with films made at Burbank.

For instance, Paul Whiteman couldn't play *Rhapsody In Blue* on the air, though it had been featured in *The King of Jazz*, a Universal film. Abe Lyman, a famous bandleader of his day, suddenly found himself unable to use his signature tune, *California, Here I Come*. Even more ironically, MGM were barred from publicizing the music from what they expected (they were right) would be their great film success of the coming year, *Rose Marie*. Warners owned that, too.

The Warner answer was equally effective. ASCAP had done very well out of them too, since although they owned the radio and publishing rights to Irving Berlin's score for the Al Jolson film *Mammy*, they had had to pay ASCAP 5,000 dollars to use the music in the picture itself.

In real terms, the row amounted simply to money. Warners

calculated they owned the rights to between 25 and 40 per cent of all the music broadcast—there was no way of being more accurate, which was one of the problems—and yet it never received more than 10 per cent of all the royalties collected from the radio networks by ASCAP. The works of Romberg and Kern, as well as other products of the genius of George Gershwin, were affected by the row, and consequently suddenly denied exposure on the air-waves.

The fight lasted until August 1936. By then both sides decided it was in their interests to kiss and make up. Warners agreed to withdraw a suit they were planning to bring, demanding 4 million dollars compensation. It was total capitulation. ASCAP announced that Warners were back in the fold and the dispute was over, 'as though it had never happened'.

It wouldn't be long before the publishing companies would for a long time be Warners' only real stake in the music industry. Once more they were becoming disheartened with the film musical, and although Jack would continue to develop his Jolsonesque accent, not even Al Jolson himself could get a job in a Warner movie.

The real writing on the wall for the musical was the fate of Busby Berkeley, who had graduated to becoming a director for the company, but who according to Hal Wallis treated every scene as though it were a musical number. The year after the problems with ASCAP were settled Berkeley was fired.

He was making *Garden of the Moon* and up to his eyes in memos from Wallis, who not only hated the photography and the clothes but also Berkeley's ideas of casting. Pat O'Brien had the lead, but the director initially wanted Edward G. Robinson singing and dancing. Wallis told him to think again. What Eddie Robinson thought of the idea is not on record.

The affair followed on a road crash in which Berkeley's car had piled into another. Three people were killed. Afterwards Berkeley admitted he had been drunk. Largely through the genius of the ace trial lawyer, Jerry Giesler—who was to get Warners out of a few nasty scrapes with Errol Flynn before long—Berkeley was acquitted. But the die was cast. After *Garden of the Moon* he was told he had to go.

People were beginning to wonder whether the studio's biggest strength was not its capacity to deal with contemporary issues—even if they weren't always on the front pages. Both Jack and Hal Wallis thought that it was.

They Won't Forget, based on the case of Leo Frank, a factory superintendent lynched after being charged with raping a fifteen-year-old girl in the Deep South, had the stamp 'Warner Bros' all over it.

The magnificent Mervyn LeRoy film exposed the whole issue of racial prejudice. Claude Rains was brilliant as the prosecuting attorney desperate to get a conviction. And yet in retrospect perhaps the most notable performance was by the actress playing the rape victim—the debut of the girl supposedly found behind the bar of a Hollywood soda fountain, Lana Turner. The sweater she wore in that film is still spoken about today.

It was not one of Jack's more glorious moments.

'Nice pair of tits,' he said. 'But who needs 'em? Let her go!' The studio didn't take up her option and the 'Sweater Queen', as she was dubbed before the draught from the door slammed in her face had gone, went to MGM and a niche in Hollywood folklore.

It was also Mervyn LeRoy's last film for Warners. He too went to MGM, but he told me he never stopped missing Jack. He was probably the only director who was given total carte blanche at Warners, subject only to Jack's personal whims.

'I'd be working on a set and just know that he was around, trying to hide behind a prop or a piece of scenery. I'd say, "All right, Jack, I know you're there."'

Perhaps that was Warners' real contribution to the films of the late 1930s. People always knew they were there.

They of course had their critics. But there was always one staunch supporter who knew about every film the studio was making, saw as many as he humanly could, and loved every one of them—Benjamin Warner. In 1937 he died, playing cards with some old friends in Youngstown. His body was brought back to California and buried next to that of Pearl.

Jack, who always gave the impression of being a hedonist with little time for sentiment, was distraught. Harry and Abe took the old man's death as further reason to be aware of their family responsibilities, but showed little emotion. To Jack, Ben's death was recognition that the man who had made him his favourite was gone, and the way to show his appreciation of the fact was to mourn. He was so unhappy that studio executives decided it was politic not to interrupt the mourning with mere business conversation.

The family was contracting. Of the brothers, Milton was already dead, and David, who had a serious brain disease, died soon after his father. The most popular surviving member of the family was the Brothers' sister Rose. Jack Junior told me she was 'everyone's idea of a favourite aunt'.

But if the family was no longer as big, the studio grew apace.

And not just at Burbank. Warners were still very busy making that other staple of the film programme, the short. The old Vitaphone studios in Flatbush, Brooklyn, were making nearly all of these—some 140 every year—mostly using top bands, singers and vaudeville acts.

The only shorts made in Hollywood were the studio's ever-increasing cartoon output—which was taking a long time to worry Walt Disney—and the occasional historical piece in colour.

The smallest set was one that was used over and over again, mostly for screen tests.

On one of the studio walls was an announcement that Jack devised, and which he intended to be taken very seriously:

ATTENTION
To inspire you in your work, the following artists were tested on this stage and have received Hollywood contracts: Dick Powell, Pat O'Brien, Humphrey Bogart, Allen Jenkins. . . .

There were other names too. The fact that Humphrey Bogart was neither singled out nor first in the list gives some idea of his importance at the time.

But it was Burbank that gave Warners a position that was still near the top in Hollywood at the time—even if MGM probably still gave them a long run for their money.

In 1938 Edward G. Robinson made *A Slight Case of Murder* and *The Amazing Dr Clitterhouse*, Humphrey Bogart was on alternate sides of the law in *Racket Busters* and *Crime School*, and Bette Davis had never been better served, either.

To be fair, it didn't always seem that way. She hoped desperately to play the part she had dismissed in that moment of frustration as a 'pip', Scarlett O'Hara in *Gone With The Wind*. Warners had at first turned down the screen rights to the book and then, when they changed their minds, were beaten to it by David O. Selznick, and the distribution deal he had with his father-in-law Louis B. Mayer.

Selznick wanted Davis for the Scarlett role. He also wanted Errol Flynn. Bette said no to any such idea, and Selznick, who wanted both or neither, began the celebrated search that led to Vivien Leigh.

'Oh, if only I could have played it with Gable!' she wrote in *Mother Goddam*.

Gone With The Wind, of course, has to be written down as one of the *big* Warner mistakes. Jack was the first studio head to be offered the film rights, and he could have had them for 50,000 dollars. 'No story is worth that sort of money,' he said, and rejected the idea flat, without trying to bring the price down.

If Bette couldn't get what is now regarded as the most famous role in the history of the cinema, there were certain compensations on the way. Jack saw her as a natural to star in the picture which he anticipated would be his studio's answer to *Gone With The Wind*, *Jezebel*. Or rather, he took Hal Wallis's view that she would be. Wallis produced the movie and William Wyler directed: with Bette improvising dialogue she thought sounded better than the words provided by Clements Ripley.

She was a Southern belle spitting as much fire as any Scarlett and being just as downright rude to her lover (Henry Fonda) as Vivien Leigh was to the assorted young men seeking her hand in *GWTW*. It won her her second Oscar in three years.

Thereafter she wasn't so pleased with the things going on at Warner Bros. Hal offered her more parts. She made appointments to see Jack to say that she wasn't going to take them. Inevitably, she was put back on suspension, where she stayed until he offered her another part opposite Errol Flynn. She took the role, but that didn't mean she had stopped fighting Jack.

The film she said yes to was *The Sisters*, which had first been planned for Kay Francis. It was about turn-of-the-century life in San Francisco before the earthquake—which would be the picture's impressive finale. She was the eldest of three sisters (Anita Louise and Jane Bryan were the others), and Flynn was a newspaperman who entered their lives and stayed there.

After his huge success in *Charge of the Light Brigade*, Jack wanted Errol to have over-the-title billing. Bette's name would be below that of the film. That was what she objected to.

It was due to Bette Davis's own persistence that she followed her triumphs in *Jezebel* and *The Sisters* with *Dark Victory*. She had found the story herself, and tried in vain to get Warners to make the picture.

Jack was adamant. 'Who the hell wants to see someone dying from a brain tumour?' he told Hal Wallis, convinced that would have to be the end of the matter. It wasn't. The demand went on and on like rain hammering on a glass roof.

Finally Jack succumbed. 'To keep peace in the family,' he told her, 'I'll buy it for you. Just get off my back.'

Even George Brent as the doctor was brilliant. The tears rolled down the faces of the audience, and the money rolled through the box offices.

To Bette it provided a chance to play the sort of part she liked best—'a real person'. The movie also had a secret ingredient for success. It was a perfect woman's picture. Once Jack realized how successful it was he ordered the studio's credit-writers to include the card, 'Jack Warner in charge of production.'

His reluctance to go along with the picture at the beginning was wholly consistent with his usual thinking. He always insisted on happy endings for his films, and there had to be very good reasons for breaking that law.

Above all, he was against showing sickness in pictures unless there was money in it. He was never ill himself, and when he did feel off colour he wouldn't let anyone know about it. That was how it had to be in the pictures too. If a woman had to have a baby in a Warner film he was much happier to see her have it in the back of a taxi than in a hospital room.

There were different reasons for arguments over Bette's 1940 film, *The Letter*.

Jack was as usual involved in the minutest details, and that involvement seemed to grow in direct proportion to the amount of temper being lost. When it involved a vast number of 'takes' of Bette in the film—she and the producer, William Wyler, were having a widely publicized affair at the time—most of the studio seemed to be involved on Warner's side.

Hal Wallis and Jack were together in trying to find ways of curbing Wyler's enthusiasms for over-shooting scenes. In *The Letter* one scene was shot no fewer than thirty-two times. By the time it was all complete there *was* something perfect to show in the day's rushes. 'So you see,' said Wyler, justifying himself, 'why I shot it so many times.'

'No,' said Wallis. 'We used the first one.'

One of Bette Davis's greatest roles after this was in *The Little Foxes*, which wasn't made at Warners at all.

Against his better judgment (to say nothing of his determination to hold on to all his assets whenever he could) Jack Warner agreed to lend her to Sam Goldwyn. There was, however, a method in this seemingly inconsistent madness. Hal Wallis had decided that the only person who could play the lead in *Sergeant York*, the story of the hillbilly Bible-puncher who rounds up more prisoners in one episode in the First World War than in the whole history of warfare, was Gary Cooper. Cooper 'belonged' to Sam Goldwyn, so there was no choice but to lend Bette for *Little Foxes* in exchange.

Sergeant York was worth the trouble—except that the real sergeant, who came to New York for the première, found Jack's salty language unpalatable and literally told him to cut it out or get out. Jack had to agree that a little cussin' wasn't worth losing the publicity value of having the real man along with them for the event.

Another dispute was over the case of Olivia de Havilland, who had also wanted to be loaned to Selznick for *Gone With The Wind,* not for the part of Scarlett, but for the somewhat saccharine-sweet Melanie, who married Ashley (Leslie Howard).

Selznick wanted her too, and so badly that Jack was determined he shouldn't have her. Olivia, who looked as breakable as a piece of Dresden porcelain in her recent Warner film *The Great Garrick*, to say nothing of her roles opposite Errol in both *Captain Blood* and *The Charge of the Light Brigade*, was in real life made of much stronger stuff.

She said she wanted to play Melanie, and Jack said no. 'If I let you go,' he said, 'you'll be difficult.'

Not an unreasonable deduction, as she was to admit. However, he promised to consider the idea and while he was considering it 'Livvy' went behind his back and registered an appeal with Ann Warner, which, as she said forty years later, was 'not the sort of thing you did when you were twenty-two years of age'.

Ann agreed to have dinner with her at the Beverly Hills Brown Derby. The move worked. Jack said yes to a loan-out, and then regretted it for ever after. But in relenting he wasn't acting entirely selflessly. It was a convenient way of getting another *quid pro quo*. In exchange he acquired the services of Jimmy Stewart, whom he wanted for *No Time For Comedy*, with Rosalind Russell.

The day work on the Melanie role finished Olivia was back at Burbank playing Bette Davis's lady-in-waiting in *Elizabeth and Essex*.

Her name was below the title. As she said years later, 'I spent all my time curtseying to Bette Davis and watched my name do the same.'

Jack believed he had reason to grumble. He banned Olivia from attending the world première of GWTW at Atlanta. (Not that she took any notice: she went just the same.)

For that piece of disobedience he had the perfect revenge.

He told her on a Friday that she was being loaned out to Columbia, and sent her a script with twenty pages of dialogue. 'You have to know it all by Monday morning,' he said.

Only Errol Flynn would have dared match that for audacity. He and Olivia were in love with each other, but Errol was still married to Lili Damita, and the risk of compromising situations was something neither Olivia nor the studio fancied. So there was no affair between them.

That didn't mean that she could be ignored.

Errol therefore found her a more than suitable candidate for one of his practical jokes. Out on location in the desert one day, he hid a dead snake in a pair of the panties she was about to wear in her next scene. Jack heard about it and immediately tried to complain, but it ended in the inevitable ribald laughter.

He didn't want to spoil their relationship in the film he was convinced would be the biggest thing to come out of Hollywood in 1939, *The Adventures of Robin Hood*. And that was precisely what it was—magnificent colour, superb action, precise direction from Michael Curtiz, and Errol Flynn in the title role. Olivia as Maid Marian was magnificent.

Inevitably, once more Errol made both Curtiz and Jack feel that there had to be easier ways of earning a few million dollars. William

Keighley was originally retained to direct the picture, but Errol took it upon himself to tell Hal Wallis, 'It's no good, sport, I can't make anything of a part that sends me to sleep.'

Curtiz made sure he did nothing of the kind. 'Here we go,' Errol said, when he heard the news that his old sparring partner was taking over. 'I think we're ready for some fun.'

He was, but there were others working on the *Robin Hood* lot who saw things slightly differently.

The film was shot in the midst of a hotter than usual Californian summer. Hundreds of extras were bolted into the heaviest armour ever worn in a Hollywood film, and were finding it difficult to stay conscious, let alone ride, fence and fall off drawbridges. And yet they had to hang around, the sun beating down on their highly reflective portable ovens, until Errol decided to turn up, frequently as much as two hours late.

Once everything came to a halt because the star decided it was a good time to ask for a rise. He sat in his dressing-room and awaited the conclusion of new, satisfactory terms— followed by four thousand extras demanding more money too. Of course, they all got it.

Jack, who had taken as personal an interest in this production as in anything else, came to the set hourly, and thought he was either about to burst a blood-vessel or develop a new ulcer.

About halfway through Ann Warner was confiding her worries to the backroom boys working on the picture. She and Jack had just bought a home at Juan-les-Pins, a place where they thought they could escape both the hassle of studio politics and the ever-continuing rows with Harry.

'All I hear all day is about the rows with Flynn,' Ann told Irving Rapper. 'I can't wait to get Jack off to France.'

The *New York Times*'s Frank S. Nugent no doubt would have said it was all worth the effort. He said that *Robin Hood* as a picture was 'a richly produced, bravely bedecked, romantic and colourful show'. It 'leaps boldly to the forefront of this year's best and can be calculated to rejoice the eights, rejuvenate the eighties and delight those in between'.

A much less well remembered picture of the year was in its way much more important. *Confessions of a Nazi Spy* was both of topical interest—the first inmates of the concentration camps had been released, and come to America with horrifying tales of early Nazi atrocities—and harked back to the first film Warners ever made, *My Four Years In Germany*.

If it seemed to be a perfect fit for the Warner Bros mould, it was also the cause of tremendous soul-searching in the Burbank executive offices. Neither Jack nor Harry really wanted to make it. They

116

were concerned it would make them too vulnerable to the sneers of the American right wing, to say nothing of the hard core of antisemitism lingering in its midst. They still held to the belief that staying out of that kind of limelight and not making trouble was the safest way to keep in business.

However, Jack was talked out of his reservations, and once talked out set about making the most thorough exposé of the Nazi spy network in America anyone had yet imagined. With the blessing of President Roosevelt, he sent a writer named Milton Krims to work with Leon G. Turrou, the special investigator appointed by the FBI to discover the extent to which Nazi secret agents had infiltrated American life on the eastern seaboard.

Krims found his way into meetings of both the undercover operations and those which American democracy allowed to be in the open—like the German-American Bund, where under the bald eagle and portraits of George Washington Nazis in brown uniforms strutted and saluted the swastika and the name Adolf Hitler.

J. Edgar Hoover did not, however, know of these activities. When he found out he fired Turrou, who was also writing a series of newspaper articles on the subject.

The result was a brilliant indictment of the Nazis and a huge row for Warner Bros, with a storm of protests against Edward G. Robinson's magnificent portrayal of Turrou and of the whole concept of Warners' attack on an officially 'friendly' nation like Germany.

The German consul protested. Businessmen who were successfully engaged in commercial undertakings with Germany took fright.

So too did Jack and Ann Warner. Shortly before the film was released they both received a series of threats of imminent kidnap and 'execution' if the company went ahead with showing the movie. At the same time they were told that the theatre where the première was to be held would be blown up.

On that first night in Hollywood there seemed to be almost as many police in the crowds outside the theatre as there were movie fans, but they were not needed. Neither was there any evidence that the personal threats against the Warners were likely to be carried out.

Nevertheless, the opponents of the picture kept trying to show that they were the ones being abused. In a brave gesture, the German-American Bund sued for half a million dollars, and then withdrew their action when the man who headed their complaint was jailed for misappropriation of their own finances.

After the film was made Jack again doubted whether it had been worth while. People stayed away from the cinemas—even those run by Warners themselves—in their hundreds of thousands. The film was pronounced a gilt-edged flop. The cinema-going hordes of Americans either didn't believe what it was suggesting or if they did believe it, they didn't care.

Either way, it was not a recipe for success for Warner Bros.

CHAPTER 13

HIS BROTHER'S KEEPER

He was a pussy cat.

Mervyn LeRoy

The only link between the brothers Warner was their business. Now that Ben was dead, Harry and Abe were merely Jack's partners. Jack and Abe may have considered themselves distant friends, but no more. It was relatively easy to be friendly with the big, burly Abe: he almost never came to California.

Florida was much more to Abe's liking. He was running racehorses, and the theatres were running themselves. He also had real-estate interests that fascinated him a lot more than movies. Occasionally he would invite Jack and Ann—a singular gesture, because no one else in the family wanted to include her in their arrangements—to spend a weekend with him in Miami Beach. They usually accepted—it was far away from Hollywood and its pressures, and gave Jack an opportunity to be with his brother. Sometimes Jack would take his masseur Abdul and secretary Bill Schaefer too (Schaefer to this day is a little upset he was not invited to use Abe's pool until it was almost time to go home).

As for Harry, it seemed as though he searched for excuses to fight Jack almost as readily as he still looked for old nails.

When a carpenter named Chris Nyby did some work at Harry's house in Hollywood Warner was so pleased he offered him any favour he wanted.

'Yes,' said Nyby. 'I'd like to work in the studio's cutting department.'

The next day he was there—until Jack spotted him.

'I'm Chris Nyby,' he said. 'Mr Harry Warner put me here.'

Jack turned to an aide and in a moment of bravery said, 'Lay him off.'

Word of this was swift in reaching Harry, who probably thought he had found the perfect revenge for the way his wishes had been countermanded in the case of Hal Wallis all those years before. 'Put him back,' he ordered.

The human shuttlecock flew over the studio net four times. Ultimately, Nyby stayed— and became a director.

Those who only saw the tough 'mogul' side of the face that Jack offered people involved with him in business deals found it difficult to imagine that there could be a more humane facet to his nature. In some ways he was like the harsh landlord who for the sake of what he considered to be good business puts a poor widow on the street, and then organizes a collection to buy her a new rent-free house.

If he believed that an employee had personal problems he regarded it as his own sacred duty to try to help; financially or simply by using influence, a commodity with which he was blessed in abundance.

When in the late 1930s Jack made one of his frequent trips to Europe he added to his itinerary a personal errand on behalf of Mike Curtiz. The director's mother and two brothers were still in Hungary, and the director desperately wanted to get them out of the country and into America before it was too late—no easy task on either side of the world. Jack was able to see the authorities in both countries and arrange exit and entry permits.

It was about the same time that Jack had had a message passed to him by one of Mussolini's henchmen. Il Duce himself, said the man, was willing to put up a million dollars if Warner Bros would make a film in Italy about the life of Michelangelo.

The first intimation of the offer had come from William Dieterle, the director who had been specializing in the Muni biographies, and who now never did anything without being sure that his stars—the astrological kind—were on his side.

Michelangelo, he and the stars believed, would be another perfect vehicle for Muni. Jack could only agree, and went to Italy, where the true story leaked out.

Mussolini would put up only half a million dollars, still a considerable sum. But there would have to be kickbacks in the region of 10 per cent for the henchmen.

Jack told them he had easier ways of eating spaghetti. 'Arrivederci,' said the principal negotiator. It was, of course, another heaven-sent opportunity to wish the man, 'A dirty river to you, too.'

It was written down to experience. Dieterle meanwhile said he was as grateful as he knew his colleague Mr Curtiz had been.

There were other people who would say that Jack's kindnesses were typical of him. When May Robson, an old silent-screen actress, celebrated her seventy-fifth birthday Jack stopped production to host a luncheon in her honour, and presented her with a huge diamond ring.

'Tears welled in her eyes,' a *New York Times* reporter noted.

They undoubtedly came in torrents into the eyes of another long-standing Warner actress, Kay Francis. She was a year away from completing her seven-year contract with the studio, still earning 4,000 dollars a week, the studio's most expensive star.

But Jack took a dislike to the lady who never went on suspension—because she never broke any of the Warner rules. Quite without apparent reason, he made an announcement to the Press that she would spend the remaining months of her contract working in 'B' pictures. She didn't say so at the time, but before she died Miss Francis revealed that it broke her heart.

It was another typical gesture on the part of a man who once he had taken a dislike for anyone working for him proceeded to treat that dislike almost as a death sentence—even if it would take a long time before that sentence was carried out.

Years later he would treat the veteran and previously loyal producer Henry Blanke much the same as the way he operated with Miss Francis. Jack decided he wanted to get rid of Blanke, but his contract was so solid that Jack had to put up with him sitting around with no work to do until the document said he was free to lay him off.

Harry complained that Jack's attitude to his own son showed much the same coldness. Harry used to try to persuade Jack to allow Jack Junior to sit in on production meetings, to get him ready for the day when, as the sole surviving male representative of the next generation of Warners, he would take over the empire. But Jack senior wasn't interested. More than that, he was opposed to any such notion.

To his way of thinking, his relationship with the junior Jack Warner was not close enough, nor was his son aggressive enough, for such a role. In this he may have felt an obligation to Ann. Since Jack Junior was the product of his first marriage, he totally and wrongheadedly believed he should sever every connection with that union.

Meanwhile, growing up with Jack as a father was rather more difficult than having him as an employer. He behaved as a strict but reasonably benevolent father to Ann's daughter Joy, and showed no more but certainly no less devotion to their joint daughter Barbara. They weren't able to gratify every possible desire simply by smiling sweetly at their father, but they lacked for nothing either. By most definitions, he appeared to love them, if not as much as he loved the Warner Bros studio.

On the other hand, the girls were allowed to pick up scripts and tell their father what they thought of them. If he didn't like what they said, they would get the same sort of answer available to people at the studio.

Jack Junior, who was clever but sensitive, knew that he wasn't loved as much as his half-sisters. 'I don't know if I felt deprived,' he told me. 'I think every son of a successful man is made to feel he has a lot to live up to, and that is never easy.'

However, he was led to understand that he had a future in the business. While still at school, he would work in the studio's production department. Later he was involved in the organization of film crews, budgets and other forms of logistical planning. It was as though he were there to watch how the studio ticked in readiness for something that was understood if never specified. The only things with which he was never concerned were scripts and casting.

As the 1930s melted into a new decade, he could have felt that this was going to be every bit as much his territory as that of his father and uncles. Jack senior, however, gave no indication that he wanted to treat him as anything special.

But then, it could have been argued, Jack had more pressing matters on his mind—like an annual turnover of what continued to be some sixty feature films a year, half of them 'B' films under the jurisdiction of Bryan—Brynie—Foy, who had seemingly done the impossible; carved his own kingdom out of the Warners' domain.

They could afford it. Profits were multiplying to the length of long-distance telephone numbers; from just over 600,000 dollars in 1935 to between 4 and 5 million three years later. Yet if profits came from progress, there were disappointments ahead for those who waxed nostalgic. The company finally decided to close their Brooklyn studios, the ones where it had all began, and which saw the beginning of the Vitaphone age with *Don Juan*.

What was making things hum for Warners was the huge success of their theatrical operations. By 1938 they owned so many theatres, and the moviegoing habit was so entrenched—people would go as regularly, and some might say as religiously, as they once went to church—that they could have stayed in business making nothing more expensive than 'B' movies.

At that juncture the issue of whether studios should be allowed to own theatres at all came up again in a Federal court case. Warners, together with Twentieth Century-Fox, were the main defendants in the action, although all the other film companies were to a lesser degree involved also.

The decision to make the move—against what was described as a 'flagrant violation' of the Sherman Anti-Trust Law—caused a flurry of excitement in the industry. *The New York Times* said, 'The producers are alarmed; the [independent] exhibitors delighted and the public, by and large, mystified.' As well the public might have been. All they knew was that they paid their ten cents and had a long evening's entertainment, two films, a short, a newsreel and a trailer for what was coming the following week, and the one after that. Sometimes they even had a stage show.

Private exhibitors were also given a chance to rent the producers' films—but not usually until at least five weeks after they had been shown at the company theatres. Then they had to agree to rent 'blocks' of films; some great, some good and some terrible, the 'turkeys' of show-business parlance. What was more, the independents would have to agree to pay 30 per cent of their take to the studios, who only took 17·5 per cent from their own cinemas.

It all seemed wrong. Nobody could understand how they were allowed to get away with it. Yet the matter was shelved once again, helped possibly by the cross-examination of a Warner executive named Joseph Bernhard. Bernhard was asked if it were true that the company had six theatres in Washington, DC, itself. 'Yes,' he said, 'and if the Attorney General's office keeps increasing the size of its department, it may be necessary to open a seventh.'

Almost as a gesture of defiance, the company built one of its biggest theatres to date, in London's Leicester Square. They took over the site of the once famous Daly's Music Hall, and called the new building—inevitably—the Warner.

At the same time the company was increasing its output in Britain, with Irving Asher doing his best to find another Errol Flynn, or perhaps an Ian Hunter, who was also a Teddington find. Mostly, however, they were still making films which Asher and everyone else knew would probably never be seen outside the British Isles, starring names who meant precisely nothing to men and women who had never been in a music hall or repertory theatre.

Warners made great play over the signing of the comedian Max Miller—typified by his catch-phrase 'There'll never be another'—but it was a time when English comics, whose style was so very different from the Americans, offered the only real alternative to Hollywood. Nobody pretended the films were any good, but they fulfilled the quota obligations and represented a stake in the British market.

Jack wasn't so concerned about that. 'It's Harry's affair,' he answered when as expected shareholders complained about the spreading of Warners' resources abroad. He twisted and flicked his cigar and said, 'Let him worry about it.' Indeed, when Harry had expenditure in London to occupy himself with there was little time for him to worry about what was happening at Burbank. Which in 1940 was quite a lot.

A youngster called Ronald Reagan was making a sequel to his successful *Brother Rat* of two years previously. James Cagney was in *The Fighting 69th*, while *The Sea Hawk* had Errol Flynn teamed with Flora Robson.

Bette Davis began the new decade with *All This And Heaven, Too*.

If it was the year of anyone at all, 1940 was that of Edward G. Robinson, who not only outshone most of the competition but was also taking on, virtually single-handed, the remainder of Warners' reputation as the studio that worried about things.

A year earlier Paul Muni had decided he had had enough of what he considered Jack's philistinism, and ended his association with the studio. His last film, *Juarez*, produced jointly by Hal Wallis and Henry Blanke, was a brilliant portrait of a Mexican national hero but a flop at the cinemas. People either knew nothing at all about Mexican history or cared even less about what they did know. Jack saw him off with few regrets.

Even when the film first went into production, he wished he had never started it. (And it was, while seeing Muni's makeup tests for the part, with Perc Westmore going through a whole spectrum of colours to make him look like an Indian, that Jack repeated his doubts about Louis Pasteur and uttered the now historic line: 'You mean we're paying him all this dough and no one will know who the guy is?') Muni still had seven pictures to make, but Jack and most of the other people at the studio had quite simply had enough of him. He kept saying he wanted to make *Beethoven*, and Jack kept saying he wasn't going to do so.

The final break came when he was slated to make *High Sierra*, in which he would play a mobster on the run. Muni said he would do it only if it 'eliminated all the gunplay'—to which Jack said, 'Then it'll make about as much money as *Juarez*. You think you're a great artist. OK, but art won't make us a bean. We haven't the European market any more.' Paul walked out in a huff and his Warner contract was pronounced at an end. At about the same time, incidentally, William Dieterle resigned too, for much the same reason.

Their departures made the studio question whether or not its policy of filming biographies made good sense. Hal Wallis believed that it still did. Jack was determined that it didn't, but didn't feel strongly enough to make an issue of the matter. When Wallis suggested that Robinson step into what had been automatically considered to be Muni's shoes, Jack said yes. Until, that is, he heard what Wallis had in mind.

He wanted to make a film of the life of Paul Ehrlich, the scientist who had found a cure for syphilis. When Jack heard of the notion he reacted much as he would to suggestions of filming do-it-yourself abortions.

'It was a big hassle,' Hal Wallis recalled. 'He didn't want to make it, and looked for any excuse not to do so.'

His trump card was the Hays Office. 'They'll never let us make it,' he thundered at Wallis. 'Just imagine them giving the OK to a film about syphilis! And even if we did, what would the Catholics say?'

It was Jack's favourite line of attack. Anything that was not all right by the Catholics was no good for him either. Someone once suggested that if he felt that strongly about it he should go to confession, but he was prepared to draw the line where it suited him.

As it so happened, the Catholics did not protest, and the Hays Office allowed it through—because, they said, it carried a message. *Dr Ehrlich's Magic Bullet* turned out to be one of the most successful films of the year. There were suggestions, of course, that people in search of vicarious thrills would flock to see the movie, but the evidence turned out to be that they went because of Robinson. He had never acted better in his life.

But no matter how satisfied most people were with *Dr Ehrlich*, the voters of the Motion Picture Academy decided otherwise. It didn't win a single Oscar.

But Eddie Robinson was firmly entrenched in the popularity stakes with the Warner family. Harry decided to make a film of the barmitzvah of his son Eddie Junior (Manny), a rare thing in those days. He would always say that Manny (who later became estranged from his father) was his godson.

Jack regarded Harry's journeys into film-making as little indulgences that kept him out of mischief. He himself was wondering whether they ought to be involved in the war that was sweeping Europe, and now beginning to impinge on America, too. There was a stirring of American realization—initiated by President Roosevelt—that they couldn't stay out of a new conflict for ever.

Jack knew this also. It was his decision to become the flag-bearer of American patriotism, once he thought he was sure that he knew what most Americans would consider patriotism to be.

However, the fight for the war that had not yet happened was highly controversial. The isolationists were still not merely influential, but determined to put their influence into practice.

In September 1941 they managed to institute Congressional proceedings against what they termed war propaganda in the movies. Warner Bros were at the top of their attack list.

Harry vehemently denied that his studio was making war-propaganda movies. *Confessions of a Nazi Spy* had simply been 'factual' (a word he found difficult in swallowing: he was convinced that the studio was now reaping the trouble it had so regrettably sown).

There was no truth in suggestions that making the movies was an attempt to 'incite people to go to war'. He also laughed at thoughts that either the Government was behind the making of these films or that a committee of film-producers sat down to decide which films should or should not be made—both allegations made during the hearing. 'On the contrary,' he said (absolutely accurately), 'there is the sharpest rivalry between the companies.'

But he did say that Warners were now banning Nazi newsreels which were designed to give the impression that Germany was a peace-loving country.

It was a row that was plainly ended by the Pearl Harbor raid.

Certainly the growing preoccupation of his countrymen with the possibility of a fifth column operating in the United States would have been an obvious topical subject to deal with, had it not been done by the studio just a year before. *Confessions of a Nazi Spy* was now made to measure for 1940. 'Re-release it,' said Jack. 'With a new ending,' said Hal Wallis.

On to the end of the picture—which so many people in 1939 had decided was unconvincing—Wallis therefore added newsreel shots and newspaper headlines showing the invasion of France, Belgium, Holland, Denmark and Norway. The last three countries, incidentally, had been among those refusing to allow the film to be shown, for fear of upsetting the Germans.

There was still no fortune to be made from the *Confessions* film, but Warners said they believed there was enough value in anti-Nazi subjects to set up a committee of a hundred 'outstanding persons' to try to reflect public taste and get to grips with the kind of subjects they would consider appealing.

Jack's true sentiments were conveyed in the briefings he gave at his favourite meeting-place, the private dining-room which he had converted to the best restaurant in Hollywood.

'The American people don't give a damn about Nazis and don't want to see any more films about them.'

But he could note that things were slipping out of his hands. Roosevelt was moving more firmly into gear, and it wasn't difficult to see that if the American people weren't exactly going out of their minds over Nazi infiltration at home, it was going to be difficult to stay totally aloof from what was happening in Europe. Emissaries from Washington made secret visits to Hollywood, asking help from what they all recognized as the best possible way of getting a message across.

The studios to a greater or lesser degree agreed to help. MGM produced *The International Storm* with James Stewart and Margaret Sullavan. Again no one went to see it, and Jack couldn't fail to make the point every time he and his producers discussed their 'contrbution' to the secret war effort.

For the moment the most popular movies were the ones that were essentially love or adventure stories; which got the patriotic message through, as if only incidentally—like *Wings of the Navy* with George Brent, John Payne and Olivia de Havilland.

Harry meanwhile had another war of his own to fight. Before he had had time to relax after his Congressional grilling he was once more called to give evidence—this time before a Federal court.

He took the witness stand against William Bioff of the International Alliance of Theatrical Stage Employees. He said he had paid 20,000 dollars 'extortion money' to Bioff in return for a promise of an end to strikes at the Warner studios.

Abe also said he had paid money to Bioff; 10,000 dollars more than his brother because, he alleged, he was afraid of 'bodily harm'.

It was then that the true facts came out. Other executives, including the heads of all the major studios, had paid a total of 626,000 dollars in order to prevent a whole series of strikes going back to 1935.

As a result of the threats, Harry recruited a team of bodyguards from among the studio gatemen. Once Bioff and an accomplice named George E. Brown were safely out of harm's way in gaol the bodyguards became Warner gatemen again, and the studio could start thinking about hostilities on the screen.

By the time 1941 had got into its stride the message was somewhat stronger—but frequently disguised in tales of what had happened in the last war that America had fought, like the classic *Sergeant York* starring Gary Cooper and Joan Leslie, a young lady who had just turned sixteen and was to cause Jack to pull out a few more strands of his rapidly thinning hair. It was a marvellous flag-waving exercise which not only made the draft boards happy, but also eased many doubts that the American bible belt may have had as to the justice of fighting.

More up to date was one of Ronald Reagan's better vehicles, *International Squadron*, the story of an American pilot who ferries bombers to Britain and becomes so convinced of the justice of the cause he is aiding that he finally joins the RAF.

If that weren't enough to help Britain's war effort, Jack personally negotiated a deal with the country's Crown Film Unit to make what turned out to be a love story with a difference called *Target for Tonight*. The love was reserved almost exclusively for a bomber called *F for Freddie*, and the picture, made on location in Britain, became a historic document.

It was still too early for Hollywood to decide either when there actually would be a war or, if one were declared, whether the public would want to see war films to the practical exclusion of everything else, so that there existed other options that had to be kept open.

There were a number of people in the Warner repertory company for whom uniforms did not automatically seem to be made to measure. Bette Davis, for instance—although excuses would be found to put even her in khaki before long. William Wyler directed her in Somerset Maugham's *The Letter*, a film that in Warner Bros folklore has become more famous for the number of rewrites and retakes she insisted on making than for the finished product.

Pat O'Brien for the moment seemed more at home in baseball gear than battledress, and so was ideal casting for *Knute Rockne —All American*, the story of the Notre Dame coach.

And there was still Humphrey Bogart, continuing to put in outstanding performances, but still either an also-ran in the cast list or a possible third or fourth choice for a role when everyone else had turned it down.

That happened in *High Sierra*, rejected by Paul Muni and then offered to George Raft, whose judgment of good film parts was becoming more and more suspect. Raft said 'No.' He told Irving Rapper when he showed him the script, 'Too many words, Irving, too many words.'

It was a decision that was as good for Bogart as it was bad for Raft.

Reluctantly, Jack agreed with Hal Wallis's suggestion that Bogart should get the role. He complained about it every time they met. Bogart spoke with a funny lisp, he said. His face was too ugly to get the women interested. But the film proved him wrong.

Jack finally conceded he had found a star of unexpected magnitude. He also knew he had bought himself another bundle of trouble, but the reviews of the film had to convince him that it was a wise move. Certainly he had a number of occasions to be grateful he didn't consign Bogie to the same out tray into which Clark Gable and Lana Turner had been placed.

Not that Jack Warner made many mistakes. With sales figures in 1940 showing an annual turnover of about 100 million dollars, it was obvious that Warner hadn't often got things wrong, and as if to prove that they knew what they were doing, a trainload of their most glittering personalities descended on Washington DC for the most expensive, undoubtedly most patriotic sales convention ever.

Two hundred exhibitors, five hundred top Warner salesmen, and what *The New York Times* described as a 'regiment of studio executives and a galaxy of the Brothers' most glamorous stars' turned up on Jack's specific instructions to show that the company knew what the country wanted. It was, said the paper, a 'Blitzkrieg'. There were to be others.

Cagney, too, was helping the company's shareholders, and most notably with *The Strawberry Blonde,* co-starring Olivia de Havilland, Jack Carson and a girl Jack reluctantly borrowed from Columbia—Rita Hayworth. The Hayworth part was ideal for Ann Sheridan, but the Oomph girl, as this most beautiful of the Warner women had by now been dubbed, was having her own spot of trouble with Jack, and was on suspension.

The Warner publicity department had dubbed her the 'Oomph Girl', and for once they were not far wrong. It was at their bidding that Orry-Kelly, Warner's costume-designer and one of the most respected in the field—he was so well known as a homosexual that the most prim stars never objected to his handling them in a state of almost complete undress while they talked to their boy-friends on the phone—designed for her what was proudly proclaimed the 'Oomph Gown'.

It went as far as was considered decent in 1940, and Jack made sure that the Press knew about it. Not only that, he also told them that he had added a solid gold bracelet and a new five-year contract for full measure. But that wasn't enough. Within a year Ann was saying that her 600-dollar-a-week salary was too low, and her agent explained, 'It will take two thousand dollars a week to get her to oomph any more.' Such was the power of publicity that even its practitioners began to believe it.

Six months later an undisclosed compromise was struck and she was back at work.

But even Jack had to realize that these were not the films that had to be given priority. It was by now not just the President who was getting into a war mood. Certainly people at the studio tried to encourage Jack to go back to thinking more seriously about war films. Among them was a young newcomer to the Warner lot who had found a script lying around the studio offices which he then took to Brynie Foy, by now firmly established as King of the B's. The discoverer was Vincent Sherman. The screenplay was *Underground*, by Charles Grayson.

Sherman persuaded Foy to make it. More significantly, he convinced him that he himself should be allowed to direct it. The film was made for 186,000 dollars, and ran three days over schedule.

Sherman was not the most popular man in the company, but he was luckier than he would have been had he been making a first feature. Jack was never too concerned about events on Foy's territory, except that he happened to be outside one of the studio's projection rooms just as Foy had run a first rough cut of the picture.

He was with Leon Schlesinger, who was in charge of the Warner cartoon output. Jack could resist an awful lot of things, but the opportunity of seeing a new movie bearing the company's name when faced with a 'hot' reel of film and a waiting projector was not one of them.

'OK,' he said to Schlesinger. 'Let's look at a couple of reels of this Foy thing. It's some goddamned Nazi picture.'

The two reels were run, then four, then six, until he had finally seen all fifteen of them. 'I think it's one of the most sensational films I've ever seen,' he said. *Underground,* starring Jeffrey Lynn and Karen Verne, was upgraded to an 'A' film, with Jack's name added to that of Hal Wallis as executive producer. Vincent Sherman became a fully fledged feature director, and Warner was thereafter convinced he ought to make war films. They didn't stop coming for the next four years.

He followed *Underground* with another Nazi subject, *All Through The Night,* starring Humphrey Bogart. Jack thought Sherman was too slow in getting anything of substance into the camera. Hal Wallis recalled for me seeing a memo that Jack had sent him: 'Friday's dailies were over before I could get my cigar lighted. That great, no director can be.'

Jack could never be accused of being unusually prescient where Bogart was concerned. When he assigned him to the picture he told Sherman, 'I'm going to give you this guy Bogart. See if you can get him to do something other than Duke Mantee.' It was true that not even the director would claim that *All Through The Night* proved anything very much, but it took a few dollars at the box office.

In truth, 1941 was a very good year for Warner Bros. It was after all the year of *The Maltese Falcon,* in which Bogart convinced Jack that he really was a brilliant performer, and just about the most valuable asset he had on the lot. If only they had hated each other a little less, things would have been a lot easier.

After all, by now Jack thought he had the full measure of Errol Flynn, with whom he hadn't had a serious row for almost a year. The last time had been when they made *The Sea Hawk,* when Errol as a galley slave had been caught by the whip wielded by David Kashner, who had been employed as the slave-master mainly because he knew how to make his thongs look as though they were really biting into the flesh of his 'victims', even when they were in fact breaking an inch or so away. And if anyone doubted his abilities, they only had to take a look at the recently made *Road To Singapore,* when he whipped a rose from the mouth of Dorothy Lamour without so much as a wince.

Michael Curtiz—perhaps betraying his true love for Errol—had told Mr Kashner to make it all look as realistic as possible. 'Don't be timid,' he instructed. 'Flynn may be a star outside, but here he is only a slave.'

Kashner took his instructions literally, and brought Errol's wig off with his first thrust. 'Do that once more,' said Flynn, standing up in his place, chains flying out of the way much more simply than they would have done in reality, 'and I'm off.' Jack himself had to come on the lot to soothe his star's furrowed brow.

Now, however, he had to worry more about Errol's drinking. Jack took a personal interest in it all. Every time that Flynn arrived on the set suffering rather too much from the previous night's intake of booze he was a threat to the smooth running of the studio. Jack decided he had personally to take charge.

When Errol arrived on the set of *Dive Bomber*—yet another contribution to the effort for the war that hadn't yet started—he was greeted with a continuous supply of black coffee.

It didn't seem to make him any better. In fact, he was distinctly worse for the intake. Alexis Smith, who co-starred with Errol in the film, explained to me, 'It turned out he had bribed the boys who gave him the coffee to lace it with brandy.'

Jack meanwhile wanted to know how it could have happened. When Errol didn't appear on the set he ordered the studio doctor down to investigate.

After an hour the doctor too was missing. First, a posse of Warner aides and then finally Jack himself went down to the dressing-room, banged on the doors, and demanded that the doctor appear. He did. Staggering out of the room, he winked at his employer, while in the background a distinctly fuzzy-looking Errol could be seen raising a glass. 'Here's to you, Chief,' he said as Jack flicked his cigar angrily in the star's direction.

The coffee boys were replaced. The dressing-room was searched from top to bottom. More than that, Jack installed a 'private eye' in the loft above the room. However, Errol's intelligence service was better than Jack's. He was perfectly behaved for the whole day that the detective was on the case. When it was time to leave he dressed, turned out the light—and then casually removed the ladder that took the hitherto self-satisfied detective to the loft.

That night the cries from the private eye were anything but private.

Jack's action was typical of the way he saw the responsibility of controlling the studio. He may have been, for most of the time, content to let Hal Wallis go on running the production end of things, but there was never any doubt that it was Jack who was the supreme head of the studios in Burbank—even if Harry wouldn't have liked to think of it in those terms.

In truth, the undoubted fact that Jack knew so much more about the running of the business was the source of a great deal of the friction between the brothers.

The huge salaries paid to Hollywood stars, for instance, were always the despair of the eldest brother, who could never understand why actors were rewarded quite so outrageously. He would have been even less content had he realized it was partly the fault of his own outfit.

It was Warner Bros which began a habit that was a long time a-dying—poaching stars from other studios when their contracts were due for renewal.

By having their salaries doubled, Kay Francis, William Powell and Ruth Chatterton had all been induced to move from Paramount to Warners. They were then followed by a series of musical-chairs moves by other stars between other studios, doubling and sometimes trebling money as they went.

Eventually the moguls had to get together and agree to respect each other's 'property', at the risk of them all losing out as they proceeded to dance in ever-decreasing circles.

It was also true that once an actor was retained by the studio Jack made it his business to be solicitous for his well-being, and that was the case irrespective of whether the man was very important or just beginning what may have seemed a promising career.

When Bill Orr (one day to become head of production himself, and Jack's step son-in-law) was signed on as an actor—his debut was in *Brother Rat,* handing a telegram to Ronald Reagan—he summoned up the courage to ask to see the top man.

He took his mother with him. Jack was captivating—and captivated by Mrs Orr. 'Never mind the kid,' he said. Let's sign the old lady.' Jack told her a string of stories, and the 'old lady'—in reality, still quite young—was convinced that her son was with a very nice organization indeed.

Harry was never sure he liked that kind of relationship with people, which was another reason why he decided to keep a closer watch on what was happening at Burbank. He hadn't yet decided to open a full-time office at the studios, but he was getting to enjoy spending more time at the place. He couldn't help like its atmosphere, the flattering of the stars who knew the value of a meal ticket when they saw one. More important, he was totally convinced that Jack was having a much better time from the film business than he ever got himself. So he would make occasional visits to California— and, to annoy his younger brother even more, surprise ones at that.

Nevertheless, it was all a wonderland that never ceased to mystify him. He didn't understand the vastly more sophisticated machine that a collection of film lots had become over the past fifteen years. More than that, he didn't comprehend the ways of film people—and certainly they didn't understand him, a well-dressed, aloof middle-aged man who for no reason would bend down to pick up a nail he saw lying in the gutter.

His main problem, however, was that he didn't recognize people easily, even familiar faces that stared down from giant wall posters all over America. He knew he had seen them somewhere, but exactly where that was had him baffled. Sometimes he didn't know them at all.

Once as he walked through the studios with Ben Kalmenson (who was to become a vice-president of the company) he said, 'Look at that handsome young man. We should sign him up and give him a chance in pictures.' What this very presentable young man would be doing in a film studio if he wasn't already in the business didn't strike Harry as being at all relevant.

'I think he is already,' said Kalmenson. 'His name is Cary Grant.' The fact that Grant wasn't on the Warner books meant to Harry that he had never been near a movie camera in his life. He didn't know that the studio was in the process of signing him to play the lead in *Arsenic and Old Lace,* a picture that was taking a long time getting off the ground.

It was a moment to laugh, but occasionally Harry's blind spot got him into more embarrassing situations. Once at a film-industry charity function at the Mark Hopkins Hotel in San Francisco, surrounded by Warner executives, Harry spotted a young girl for whom he immediately had great plans.

He left his hangers-on and approached her with all the delicacy of a kamikaze pilot about to go into action. 'Look here,' he said, 'I'm too old to make a pass at you. But you know you ought to be in pictures.'

'Oh, thank you, sir,' said the girl.

Harry was about to pursue the matter, give his card and sign a letter of introduction to the Burbank casting department, when Irving Rapper managed to get him away. 'What are you doing?' Harry asked irritably. 'What is it?'

'Mr Warner,' Rapper replied. 'I think you ought to know that that young lady is Shirley Temple.'

'We became friends after that,' Rapper told me. 'Harry later even signed a letter that got me out of the Army. I went round telling people that the wrong Warner likes me.'

Most of Rapper's suspensions came from refusing to make films he simply didn't want to make.

'How dare you make a slave of me!' he told Jack in desperation at one session in the art-deco office. 'You ought to be grateful that I'm trying to save you so much money by not making the films.'

Years later Jack told him, 'I wish I'd have listened to you. I might have saved a few bucks.'

Out of the studio Jack was always a totally different man. The first rough cut of most of the Warner films was by now done by Jack himself, sitting in the projection theatre he had had built at his home on Angelo Drive. He would sit with his director on one side; his secretary, Bill Schaefer (to whom he would give a flow of instructions), on the other. After the film he would give his companions a drink and say, 'I want to show you what I've done with the gardens.'

Said Irving Rapper, 'I saw enough of those gardens to know every inch of them.'

To those who only saw Jack on those occasions, he was plainly the nicest man in Hollywood. George Raft once told me, 'JL was a gentleman in the living-room. But at the studio he made the place seem like Alcatraz.'

CHAPTER 14

CONFLICT

It was affable arrogance.

Julius Epstein

Warner Bros began the Second World War with *The New York Times* once again pinning the accolade on the studio for combining good citizenship with good picture-making. To which Julius Epstein, enjoying the liberality of Jack's catering enterprises, added, 'and great pickled herring'.

The truth of the matter was that Jack was a lot happier with the pickled herring than he was with some of the studio output. Just as he had with the Légion d'Honneur after *Pasteur* and *Zola*, he accepted the 'good citizenship' tag, but constantly battled with Wallis and others about the films that made him seem to everyone (except those who really knew him) to be a Hollywood liberal.

'Let's keep away from the controversial stuff,' he'd say as he munched that great pickled herring—and the best chopped liver in California—and told another outrageous story about Mrs Roosevelt.

Visitors to Hollywood knew that the Warner dining-room had to be as important a place to visit as the sets where Bette Davis and Errol Flynn were performing. Jack, needless to say, encouraged them in that belief. It was, after all, where he was the undoubted star.

He held court from a high-backed chair that was in every way his throne. The rest of the furnishings, the exquisite Chippendale chairs, the superbly hung curtains, were chosen by Ann, and Jack therefore treated them as nothing less than perfection. Most people had to agree. In fact, those who sat around the table at Jack's invitation—they paid a weekly fee of 10 dollars to cover the food they consumed, although even in 1942 it was worth four or five times that—had to agree with everything he said.

It was one of the most entertaining daily performances to be seen in what was the entertainment capital. Jack's jokes were getting cornier by the hour, but there was still a sense of excitement in being part of them.

The dining-room, just a few feet from the art-deco office, was the haunt of Jack's favoured producers, business buddies, and the directors currently working on projects at the Warner lot. There was no better demonstration of one's status with Jack than where you were placed at the lunch table. There were about fourteen seats at either side, and the most favoured executives were always the ones closest to him. If an old-timer was spotted at the bottom of the table, close by the salt, it was a sure sign he was in trouble.

The room was usually not open to Warners' stars. Had they been there they would have cramped Jack's style. He would always have been afraid that they were laughing at him rather than with him as he puffed and twisted his Havana and mentioned for the five-thousandth time the weight of that toilet seat. He knew too that people paid to act were quite capable of saying the nicest things while thinking just the opposite. Worse than that, however, was the fact that they would have been able to hear all the dreadful things he was saying about them—throwing to his lawyer at one moment a request to try to get out of a contract here, or to inveigle some other studio's 'property' to join them there.

It was in the dining-room that Jack (always a cute judge of character) could decide for himself who was with him and who was against. Not all of his favoured guests knew that. Most were content to allow the head waiter—imported from Paris with the chef—to recommend the *filet mignon* or the roast beef which would send them off to sleep for the rest of the afternoon.

The bonuses came when there were real celebrities to invite, like Madame Chiang Kai-shek, who arrived in America soon after Pearl Harbor on an aid-to-China fund-raising mission. She knew there was money in Hollywood, and the studios—with Jack at the helm—threw a huge money-making banquet on her behalf.

Jack decided to complete Madame Chiang's pleasure by inviting her to lunch in the dining-room. On that day a sprinkling of stars *were* present—Flynn, Robinson, the restored Ann Sheridan among them—together with the head of every department on the lot.

Madame Chiang made a gracious speech thanking Jack for the wonderful hospitality; praising the charm and beauty of the company's stars, the enterprise Warner Bros always showed in doing films that stirred the nation's conscience and the great contribution they were making, both to the war-effort and for her people.

The applause was deafening as the guest of honour sat down and Jack rose to reply. It was a moment that frequently sent regulars at the table hunting for glasses to polish or stains to remove from trouser-legs. This time they were not disappointed. Jack thanked Madame Chiang for her gracious words, looked her straight in her Chinese eyes and said, 'Gee, that reminds me. I forgot to take in my laundry!'

His guest did not forget Jack L. Warner. Of course, if Harry had known about it he would have bent over backward to apologize—had he been sure who the Chinese lady was. But he was not at the lunch. In fact he wasn't at any of Jack's lunches. The two brothers' secretaries had to regard it as a vital part of their duties to follow very carefully the movements of the Messrs Warner. Jack did not move towards the dining-room until he knew that Harry had vacated it, or vice versa.

If it had been as easy to escape from the problems of running the studio, Jack would have been a contented man. But as things were, there were new difficulties every day of the week—most of them, as before, concerning Mr Flynn, who was not only still drinking prodigiously and bringing women to his bed as though they were life-saving medications that had to be taken twice daily (and the way he saw it, they were), but breaking a rule that was becoming an obsession with Jack—punctuality.

During the shooting of *They Died With Their Boots On*, which featured one of Errol's best ever performances as General Custer making his last stand, Jack gave personal instructions to his gateman to inform him the precise moment Flynn drove into the studio.

In a way it was a gesture of revenge. Half-way through the picture (as usual, it was the time Errol knew he was beyond replacing) Flynn sat in his dressing-room and refused to leave. A bottle of brandy and another of vodka were his only company. The only person he would talk to, he said was Mr Jack Warner, who naturally arrived on the scene.

'I think I need some more money, chum,' Flynn said.

'Sure, Errol,' said Jack. 'Let's just get the picture over and we'll talk about it.' The Warner cigar was now twisting around of its own accord. There was so much sweat pouring off his forehead, it wouldn't have been any worse had he been sitting in front of an arc-light.

'No,' said Flynn, 'I think now.'

Normally anyone daring to ask Jack himself for a rise was never seen again. There were people he employed to deal with that problem for him. But at that moment he feared that the whole company were about to die with their boots on too.

'Sure, Errol,' he repeated. 'Let's do a deal now.'

They agreed a figure, shook hands, and Jack pounded Flynn on the back, smiling widely. 'The dirty sonofabitch.' he whispered under his breath.

Errol was lucky that Raoul Walsh, whom he called alternately 'Uncle' and 'the one-eyed bandit' (Walsh called Flynn, 'The Baron', a name Jack used for him too, in his more sanguine moments) directed the picture and looked after him like a kindergarten teacher pampering a child on his first day away from home.

Walsh described for me how he would try to beat the Warner wrath. He told Errol he would call for him on the way to the studio every morning.

'You're getting low on funds,' he told him. 'You've got to watch it. I'll pick you up at seven-thirty every morning and we'll get to the studio by eight. Then you can have a nap in your dressing-room and we'll get some coffee made and brought in to you.' The only trouble was that when Walsh called at 7.30 Errol was usually still naked in bed with a girl. The combined efforts of the director and Flynn's houseboy Alex managed, nevertheless, to get him to work on time.

The results were worth it, and for a time Errol was helping Warner Bros to stay at the top of all the Hollywood financial charts. *They Died With Their Boots On* was a great success. If only Errol had been able to keep his hands off the girls in the cast.

Since Errol was never satisfied with one new girl, he usually found reasons for them to introduce him to their friends. One of the girls who so obliged was Mickey June. She introduced him to one Peggy LaRue Satterlee, who a few months later charged Errol with statutory rape. She was under eighteen at the time. The complaint followed immediately on that by another minor, Betty Hansen.

The result was the most sensational scandal trial in Hollywood history, with both girls giving evidence of Errol first stripping them and then of having intercourse with them.

To Jack the charges were as much the rape of Warner Bros as of two girls who had seemingly not been unwilling to remove their skirts and blouses for Mr Flynn to fondle them. It was an affront to the studio that had patiently created Errol into an international superstar from what Michael Curtiz would have been very willing to point out once more had formerly been merely a corpse.

If its top star could have done such a thing, who would then be able to say that Warner Bros combined entertainment with good citizenship?

It was Jack's personal decision to call in Jerry Giesler, the top trial lawyer in Hollywood, who had a reputation for making cold-blooded murderers appear to be the innocent victims of a cruel society. He managed to create the same miracle on behalf of Errol Flynn, who was acquitted on both charges.

Jack heard the news in his office, called Errol a 'dirty sonofabitch' and sent Giesler a letter of congratulations. When he next saw Errol he slapped him on the shoulders and said, 'I always knew you were innocent. If there is anything I can ever do for you. . . '

If Jack was personally involved in practically everything to do with Errol Flynn—and he had to be, because Flynn knew precisely how to get him to do whatever he wanted—he tried and frequently succeeded in bowing out of other local difficulties.

In 1942 a piece of theatrical business which has become enshrined in Hollywood folklore threatened to bring the studio to a halt.

Casey Robinson, one of Hollywood's most gifted writers, had just produced a screenplay for a new Bette Davis film to be called *Now, Voyager*. It represented the principal introduction to American audiences of Paul Henreid. As an Austrian count—he was born Paul von Hernreid—he had fled Vienna when the Nazis moved in and appeared, under his real name, in *Goodbye Mr Chips* and *Night Train To Munich* in England.

Now, Voyager was giving him an opportunity of becoming much better known. It was a perfect part, except that he didn't like the bit in the script that required him to light a cigarette for Miss Davis. It involved a great deal of fumbling about, because he had to light one for himself at the same time.

The big row occurred because both Mr Henreid and Irving Rapper took credit for the solution to the problem. As the actors describes it, 'I thought it would be easier to do what my wife and I had done many times before. I put two cigarettes in my mouth, lit them both and gave one to Bette. When I told her she kept saying, "Show me, show me. It's fantastic." I called Hal Wallis on to the set and he said "It's great. It stays." '

Irving Rapper told me, on the other hand, 'Mr Wallis did not come on to the set at all. And it was my idea, not that of Henreid, who has gone on taking credit for it ever since.'

The lack of sympathy between star and director did not show in the finished picture, one of the most outstanding the studio ever produced. Jack hadn't wanted Bette to play the part of Charlotte, a spinster from Bette's own Yankee New England, but via Hal Wallis, she persuaded him to allow her to do so.

He was to write of this and other troubles with Bette: 'When you're dealing with talented people, I guess you have to expect some trouble and friction. You never hear a peep from the duds.'

Of course, Rapper was one of the causes of that trouble and friction. He might have been worse had Ann Warner not intervened yet again between Jack and one of his adversaries. It was during one of his many suspensions that she and the director met at the Copacabana night-club. Ann saw Rapper first, and ran towards him.

'You're not supposed to do that,' he said.

'Sometimes,' Ann replied, 'I wonder if Jack understands you—or me.'

In fact that lack of understanding brought the Warners to the point of separation at about this time. She left home, the Press reported, taking their children with them. But there was love between them too, and before long they were together again.

Nobody could deny, however, that Jack understood movies, and the people who could bring people into the theatres to see them. That was why he stood so much from Errol Flynn, and personally chose him to star in *Gentleman Jim*, about the famous Irish-American boxing hero, James J. Corbett, with Alexis Smith again co-starring.

Sometimes he made mistakes. *George Washington Slept Here* was one of them, even though it had Jack Benny, at the time America's favourite comedian, in the lead and Ann Sheridan playing opposite him, looking more beautiful than she had ever appeared before.

But the mistakes were interludes between the successes, and in 1943 there was a certain success called *Casablanca*.

CHAPTER 15

CASABLANCA

On reflection, now that we are at a time when we can't get anyone to make a single decision, I liked them very much indeed.

Julius Epstein

Casablanca was the picture that put together a succession of individual talents and turned the sum of the parts into a magnum of sparkling glory.

It was good for everybody connected with it. Marvellous for Warner Bros. Superb for Jack, who had given Hal Wallis the go-ahead to do what he liked with everything the studio could offer. Gratifying for Wallis himself that he had seen the potential of a play (which had never been produced) called *Everybody Goes To Rick's*. A stunning achievement for Michael Curtiz, who never equalled the quality of the direction he put into the picture. A great piece of writing from Julius and Philip Epstein (who with Curtiz and the studio won Oscars for what was voted the best film of the year).

Jack might not have agreed, but it wouldn't have happened without the actors: without Bogart as the armour-plated, soft-hearted Rick who runs his night-club in Vichy-controlled Casablanca, ostensibly happy to take the francs from whoever has them to spend, and Ingrid Bergman, who never looked lovelier or acted better as the girl he had met in Paris and who had seemingly deserted him for a patriot, Victor Laszlo (Paul Henreid).

Henreid himself, Claude Rains (as the police chief who appears no less happy to work for Berlin than he was for Paris), Peter Lorre, Sydney Greenstreet, S. Z. Sakall and Conrad Veidt (as the local Gestapo chief) all did exactly what everyone would have expected them to do.

And then there was *that* song, 'As Time Goes By'. Theme songs are usually forgotten, occasionally whistled as people leave the theatre. 'As Time Goes By' haunted those who heard it, and has stayed haunting them for the forty years that have passed since then.

In fact it was all so good that it might have been conjured by some magical spell. It looked so easy, especially since the ingredients were all there, and the only thing that had to be done was to shake them up.

It wasn't as easy as that. It wasn't easy at all.

Changing the title was the simplest thing to do. That was a blatant attempt at cashing in on the tremendous success of the recent movie *Algiers*. Hollywood was never beyond taking up a good idea simply because it had been someone else's.

Even Hal Wallis, who lovingly saw the whole thing through, from the first glance at a script to a traumatic night at the Oscar celebrations, will admit to not having anything to do with the greatest coup of all. It was released at precisely the moment Churchill, Roosevelt and Stalin met for their historic summit meeting—at Casablanca. No one at Warner Bros was that well in with the White House, to say nothing of Downing Street or the Kremlin. Until the meeting was under way, both the session itself and its destination were closely guarded secrets.

As for casting, who could imagine a better grouping than Bogart, Bergman and Henreid? But it wasn't all assured from the start. Casting presented horrendous problems.

When it came to finding an ending for the movie, Julius Epstein told me it was like a jigsaw puzzle. 'We threw the pieces up into the air and watched to see where they fell. That sort of thing happened a lot at other studios, but not at Warner Bros. We weren't sure how it was going to end until it was all finished.'

The decision was Wallis's although Jack had a bee in his bonnet that the best ending of all would be to show the summit meeting. He was politely talked out of that, which is fortunate, since the conference has been long forgotten by all but historians, while the film itself seems as fresh as ever.

Wallis wanted a cast that would demonstrate the bitter-sweet effect he sought for the story, which was another reason why the script took so long to manipulate, and why two endings were ultimately shot—until the world saw Bogart and Rains walking off in the fog at the 'beginning of a beautiful friendship'.

There was never any doubt in the minds of both Wallis and Jack that Ingrid Bergman would be fine for the female lead. But she was a David O. Selznick star, and as Wallis says in his autobiography *Starmaker,* Selznick was notoriously difficult about lending his stars. Finally a deal was done, 'swapping' Ingrid for the ubiquitous Olivia de Havilland, whom Selznick wanted for another picture.

Everyone was certain, too, that Bogart was right for the part of Rick—except that Bogie was about to be loaned to Columbia to make a picture called *Sahara* (which shows that the fashion for African place names in single-word film titles was unabated), in turn a *quid pro quo* for Columbia letting Warners have the services of Cary Grant for *Arsenic and Old Lace.*

Both stars were worrying about time schedules, Bogie because there was a risk of *Casablanca* narrowly defying geography and clashing with *Sahara* and Ingrid because she was anxious not to miss the chance of playing in *For Whom The Bell Tolls.*

Eventually they were both tied up. But the casting difficulties were not over.

Who was going to sing 'As Time Goes By'?

Hal Wallis wanted either Lena Horne or Ella Fitzgerald. Before he decided which, he changed his mind and opted for a male singer.

He chose Dooley Wilson, who had had a great success in the recent *Cabin In The Sky.* But Wilson was tied to Paramount. Warners bought his services for 3,500 dollars a week—which, incredibly, was 375 a week more than they were paying for Ingrid Bergman. Such is show business. But it was a good investment. Where would *Casablanca's* image be today without a 'Sam' to be ordered to 'play'—if not, strictly speaking, 'Play it again'?

Mind you, Max Steiner wasn't too happy with having to use someone else's music in the midst of his score, either 'As Time Goes By' or Wallis's instruction that he incorporate 'Perfidia' in one scene. However, everything played an essential, indispensable part in this story of the kind of love that comes twice and cruelly vanishes both times.

It had passion and patriotism, including Henreid's rendition of *La Marseillaise,* which was perhaps the most spirited heard since the days of the Revolution. Jack Warner, of course, loved it too. Particularly Mike Curtiz.

He later wrote that the director told him, 'Vell, Jock, the scenario isn't the exact truth, but ve haff the facts to prove it!' (How a man so successful at murdering the English language could create such masterpieces from its use is one of the mysteries of the art of motion pictures.)

Not only was the film one of the great successes of 1943, it was undoubtedly one of the most popular Academy Award winners ever. The film world assembled that night for the Oscar ceremonies showed that they were more than usually glad that *Casablanca* had won. And so was Jack.

It was a fairly historic evening. For the first time it was held at a theatre, the celebrated Graumann's Chinese, and not at a banqueting hall. Jack and his wife had seats by the aisle. Next to them were those occupied by Hal Wallis and his party. As it turned out, Jack had arranged his seating plan as part of a strategy that he put into effect the moment the winning film was announced from the stage.

As soon as the name *Casablanca* resounded through the loudspeakers, and almost before it could register long enough for the audience to begin their applause, Jack was jumping towards the stage, followed in what appeared to be an unseemly scramble by Hal Wallis.

As Hal explained to me, 'I had to clamber over the various legs that were in my way. But it should have been me that accepted the Oscar. It is always taken by the producer, and this was not a Jack L. Warner production. It was made under my complete supervision, a Hal Wallis production.'

The trade papers were full of the story the next day. Hal was reading the reactions of the Hollywood Press—all of it in his favour—when a package was delivered to his office from the Academy of Motion Picture Arts and Sciences. It was the Oscar inscribed with his name on it. (The awards presented on the big night are mere replicas.)

For Hal it was the beginning of the end of his time at Warner Bros. An atmosphere between Jack and himself developed and seemingly wouldn't go away, although for a time Wallis tried to carry on the four new pictures for which he was contracted that year.

At first Jack pretended nothing had changed. He continued to tell the same stories. He said nothing about the fracas to other people at the studio. The other Award winners were duly congratulated, either in person or at second hand.

Mike Curtiz had his share of praise at the evening itself. In a speech that was remarkable by even his standards, he told the assembled company, 'So many times I have a speech ready, but no dice. Always a bridesmaid, never a mother. Now I win, I have no speech.' What he had, however, was *Casablanca,* which said enough.

The only principals not present on the big night were the Epsteins, who had to have their congratulations from Jack decoded before they could make up their minds whether they were being lauded or fired. They were away in the east of the United States at the time of the Award ceremony, so there was no way that Jack could offer his congratulations in person. Instead he decided to send a telegram. But that wasn't so easy.

It was war-time, and civilian, non-emergency telegrams were banned. However, Jack wouldn't allow a moment like that to go unrecorded, so the message he sent read cryptically SORRY TO HEAR YOUR UNCLE DIED CONGRATULATIONS JACK L. WARNER.

The Epsteins undoubtedly deserved much credit for *Casablanca,* although hearing it from Julius now (Philip died in 1952) it sounds as though it were more a great deal of fun than a serious writing exercise.

Jack seems to have had as much fun as anyone. Unlike Harry, he knew who his actors were, and when they were available to make life happier for him he took full advantage of the fact.

Soon after *Casablanca,* the French Government in exile decided to show its appreciation by asking its ambassador in Washington to pay a personal visit to Burbank.

Jack was like a Paris poodle with two tails when he heard the news. In honour of the celebrity he gave one of his best lunches in the private dining-room, serving fillet steak and other luxuries that no one in wartime America was supposed to have seen for at least two years. Because he knew it would impress the envoy and his wife, he again opened the doors of his suite to his actors. Harry, whose Hollywood office adjoined the dining-room, thought it was the equivalent of putting the asylum in the hands of the inmates, but for once Jack won.

Graciously he welcomed his guests of honour and introduced the stars. 'Your Excellency,' he began, 'may I present Errol Flynn? . . . This lady, you know, of course . . . Miss Bette Davis (Bette hadn't heard so much courtesy from Jack for years). . . . And Miss Bergman, whom you liked so much in *Casablanca* . . .'

The Ambassador kissed Ingrid's hand. 'And this,' Jack added in a moment of *lèse-majesté,* 'this is the man who sang your song' (not the perfect way of describing *La Marseillaise*) '. . . Mr Paul Hemeroid.' Jack seemed to think it was funny. Paul Henreid didn't.

Henreid wasn't, however, sure how he felt about Warner Bros at the time. He had joined the company as a freelance to make *Now, Voyager* and been told he could have the Laszlo role in *Casablanca* if he went on contract. He decided the prize was worth the competition.

Jack, on the other hand, didn't really want to be tied to Henreid, when there was no suitable part for him to do. He followed his usual pattern, and came to the conclusion that there was no better way of saving money than by putting his actors on suspension—using the old Warner trick of offering parts he knew no decent actor could afford to accept. So on suspension Henreid went.

Some of the parts he turned down could have been good for him. He was offered the title role—opposite Bette Davis—in *Mr Skeffington,* which Claude Rains later did beautifully.

He says he doesn't regret it.

But he does feel sorry he rejected *Watch On The Rhine,* another Bette Davis picture, which won an Oscar for Paul Lukas, who did take the role.

He was, however, he told me, determined not to get a reputation for only being able to play Germans, and even had a clause to that effect inserted in his contract.

Now, on reflection, he says, 'I signed for Warners out of fear. The English had made me scared because they said I could be deported as an Austrian. I thought with the security of a contract that wouldn't happen.'

He also had a one-picture-a-year deal with RKO. It gave him time to write as well as act. The result was a script called *The Spanish Main*.

Jack rejected that instantly. 'If I want a pirate,' he said not unreasonably, 'I have Errol Flynn. You're supposed to be my gentleman.'

But he wasn't convinced that it was a role he had yet earned. 'I have made you a star. Don't forget you were a nobody before I found you.'

To back up his assertion he produced a selection of posters which showed his new star's billing.

'Jack,' said Henreid, 'I was a star before—in Vienna, in London and in New York. You hired me as a star. I don't think you are stupid enough to pay a star's salary to a nobody.'

The row was quickly brushed aside. 'I'll tell you what,' said Jack, 'I'd like to redo your dressing-room.' But Henreid said that it didn't need doing. Instead what he wanted was a 16-mm print of all his pictures.

'Done,' promised Jack. But it was a promise never kept.

Being an actor was a serious business at Warner Bros. A lot more so than being a member of the writing team. They seemed to spend most of their day visiting each other, talking over their work, or playing cards and telling jokes at the writers' table in the commissary.

'After all,' said Epstein, 'we weren't writing *War and Peace,* you know. None of us worked eight hours a day.' Which was a fact Jack found difficult to accept when he discovered what was going on a year or so later.

At present, however, he was basking in the glory those same writers had helped shower over him. So was Harry, who was now boasting that because he too was able to spend so much time at the studios, he was a close friend of every star on the lot, and the adviser to whom all his senior staff would come.

On one occasion the boast came as he was showing a party of Government VIPs around the lot. 'I know everybody,' said Harry, 'from the lowliest carpenter to our top stars.' When they reached the dining-room and opened the door producer Wolfgang Reinhardt came out. 'Hello, Mr Warner,' he said. 'Hello, Gang-wolf,' replied Harry.

The writers joked about that at their table for months.

146

Sometimes they suggested ideas themselves—usually to Irene Lee, who was one of Hal Wallis's assistants. It was either Miss Lee or Wallis himself who would decide which of the seventy-five to a hundred writers would work on which project.

The story editor was later Walter McEwan, who was to become one of Jack Warner's right-hand men.

Usually the writers worked on stories and saw them through to the time when their names appeared in the credits. Sometimes, however, other writers took over. Robert Buckner and Edmund Joseph had their names on *Yankee Doodle Dandy,* but it was actually the Epstein brothers who wrote the final script. 'Cagney didn't like the original,' Julius Epstein explains.

What *Casablanca* had done for the war effort in terms of promoting the Allied cause and stirring people's emotions to work for it *Yankee Doodle Dandy,* the supposed story of songwriter-actor-comedian George M. Cohan, did for American morale.

In black and white, it was one of the most colourful musicals of all time. James Cagney, who had always seen himself as essentially a song-and-dance man who had been condemned to playing tough guys, was finally given a pair of tap shoes to wear and a collection of songs to which he could step to his heart's content.

The old Cohan numbers *Give My Regards To Broadway* and *A Grand Old Flag,* to say nothing of *Yankee Doodle* itself, were sung and danced in a way that the man born on the Fourth of July (another falsification: Cohan loved to say that was his birth date, but it was actually 3 July) could thoroughly enjoy during his final illness.

Yankee Doodle was more than just something for the people at home to enjoy. The flags it waved were bigger and noisier than any previously paraded before a movie audience, and there were sufficient female tears prompted by it all to persuade a whole regiment of civilians to enlist—particularly as Cohan, clutching his newly awarded Medal of Merit, joins a parade of marching soldiers to sing *Over There.*

Cohan's music had a lot to do with it, but it was very much Cagney's film. Walter Huston was effective as Cohan's father, Rosemary De Camp played his mother, and Joan Leslie was his wife.

Joan was hopelessly too young for the part, but it was Jack's idea to give it to her. It was another one of his strategies; he believed she was going to be the big Warner glamour star of the future. With that thought in mind, he decided she needed to be encouraged, and more than that, to be nurtured. So she had to be given important roles. And even if she were only seventeen, making her up as an old lady now would give her no cause later on to make Bette Davis-type allegations of never being given anything decent to play. The psychology of that only partly worked.

He started watching over her like a cat with a single surviving kitten. He saw to it that she was seen at the best parties—but only with the sort of men who wouldn't spoil her image. Bogart was always very kind, but at one party things went ever so slightly awry. She was placed next to Errol Flynn. 'How do you do, Joan,' he said. 'I'm afraid we've never met.' It was an omission that was quite deliberate.

But now they were together the publicity department's cameras clicked and their flash bulbs exploded happily—which was more than Jack did when he heard about the meeting. He personally ordered all the pictures to be destroyed.

When she went on publicity tours to New York and other cities on the eastern seaboard Jack sent her away with the warning 'I don't want to see you smoking or drinking.'

'I don't do either,' she told him.

'Well,' he said, 'Just see that you don't.'

If that all seemed like a stern fatherly eye being kept on the girl, it was no more than Jack intended. Every time she had a birthday he brought the publicists along to see him presenting her with a gift—a watch on one occasion, and for her seventeenth birthday, celebrated on the set of *Yankee Doodle Dandy,* a gift that was in every way extra-special.

When all the cameramen were reported to be present Jack appeared on the set and clapped with everyone else as a shiny new car was wheeled through the lot. With a broad smile on his face and a chivalrous low bow, he presented Joan with the keys. 'Enjoy it,' he said, in the same sort of voice Al Jolson had used to encourage his mother to go to Coney Island with him in *The Jazz Singer.*

She almost collapsed with pure, unadulterated joy—all of which was captured by the cameras. As soon as the photographers had gone the keys were taken back and the car was wheeled away again.

'I never saw it any more,' she told me, still smarting forty years on from the disappointment only a seventeen-year-old could feel. 'But I suppose that was just part of the business,' she said—though it was a whole lot less satisfactory than the generosity he had shown a generation earlier to Loretta Young.

Jack probably saw it as an opportunity for him to demonstrate who was really boss at Warners. If Joan Leslie was an innocent victim, then she could tell all the others. He had recently had enough of rows with stars who thought they could do anything they liked. Stars such as George Raft, who announced he was on strike and would stay that way until Jack allowed him to go to work at Universal to make *Broadway*. For eight months he and Jack sat it

Showing appreciation to George Arliss. Harry, with his friend J. Edgar Hoover
looking on

Jack (*left*) and Harry (*right*) shelve their differences to welcome John Barrymore to Sunset Boulevard for *Beau Brummell*

Jack (*centre, back row*) on the set of *Don Juan*. Next to him is the director Alan Crosland. In the centre, smoking pipe, is the star, John Barrymore

Jack Warner with his idol, Al Jolson

Al Jolson in familiar pose (in *The Jazz Singer*)

Jack always believed in going down to where it all happened. Here he is with Mervyn LeRoy, Marion Davies and Hal Wallis

Paul Muni, just before becoming a 'Fugitive from a Chain Gang'

'Little Caesar' himself – Edward G. Robinson

Typically Busby Berkeley, in *Footlights Parade*

Play it, Sam – Dooley Wilson with Humphrey Bogart and Ingrid Bergman in *Casablanca*

This was Jack Warner's principal contribution to the war effort – *This is the Army*

out, looking at each other in one office or another. Finally he said Raft could go—just to rid himself of the problem.

He wasn't likely to have that difficulty with Cagney any more, however. The actor's contract had finally ended, and he announced that he was going into independent production with his brother William.

Almost as a gesture of reconciliation, Jack told the Press he was going to distribute the new Cagney films. It was a promise which it appeared would suit both of them. After all, when he had earned 362,500 dollars in 1942 from Warner films, becoming the highest-paid star in Hollywood, it was proof that his movies—none of them took less than a million dollars—were mutually satisfactory ventures.

Even so, it was a promise that was not instantly acted upon. Cagney would not make a Warner-released film until *White Heat* in 1949.

There were other ways in which the company thought it could make money in the early years of the War. By early 1943 it had firmly decided the time had come to enter the newsreel field, then a virtual licence to print money. No cinema dared offer a film pro-gramme without a newsreel, and why should Warners be excluded from what was clearly a very lucrative market? They decided not to exclude themselves.

It was also an opportunity for them to put to good use the still empty old Vitagraph studios in Brooklyn. However, it could not be organized simply with an announcement that the move was being made. It took a trip to Washington by Harry Warner to persuade Government officials not only to allow them censorship facilities—nothing could be shown without military approval—but also a release of sufficient cameramen to set the project in motion. Washington regarded it as too important an aid to fighting the War to object.

But the existing newsreel companies did object. They wanted to know how another organization in the field—there were four already, Paramount, Movietone, Universal and MGM's News of the Day—could possibly help the Government's plea to conserve film stock.

Jack characteristically alleged that the opposition were suffering from sour grapes. 'Public feeling and the feeling in high government circles', he declared, 'is that the present newsreels stink.'

The idea took a long time to gell, and it wasn't until the 1950s that Warners achieved their aim when they bought Pathé News. Harry was happy about that. 'We have a responsibility to inform the public,' he said.

While they were lecturing the rest of the industry about the quality of its newsreels, Harry took on the mantle of the resident Hollywood patriot. The other studios, he said, were not taking the War seriously enough.

Normally he would have been very happy to allow the opposition to neglect its duties, but now it was too good an opportunity to miss to show that Warner Bros were setting everyone else an example.

'If we failed to recognize that we have an obligation to inform as well as to entertain, there would be little justification for our existence,' he said.

He talked about 'a group of entertainment appeasers which is presently at work in the industry or being pressured by groups from the outside'. There had been an upsurge of escapist musicals from other studios, but it was the duty of Hollywood to explain what was going on.

'There are forces in this land who would like the people to live in darkness,' he declared. 'I take issue with them, because I have always felt that it's no one's assignment not to reason why, but to do or die.'

The cliché was just right for his audience, he felt. Probably more to the point, he knew that his studio had been geared for war films for longer than any of its competitors, and knew better than anyone else how to make them. Not only was he not frightened of the competition, it was a good way of patting himself on the back.

However, he was taken seriously, and he warmed to his theme. 'I wouldn't believe it, not for a single moment, if someone were to tell me that any mother who has a son with the victorious American forces in Africa can't wait for dinner to be finished so she can rush to the radio and hear anything but the latest news.'

It was not only good reading for the newspapers, it was also enough to bring an encouraging thump on the back from President Roosevelt. Visions of Medals of Merit and similar awards being pinned on his chest flashed before Harry's eyes, and Jack was hardly immune from such thoughts either.

It wasn't long before the expected call from the White House came. The President was very anxious to build up support among the public for the Soviet Union. If Warner Bros could help, Mr Roosevelt would be very grateful.

He also invited Jack to lunch, an event that caused something of a furore, because even the President was not spared some of the excesses of his lifestyle. When he went to Washington Jack insisted on taking his own silverwear with him, as though the knives and forks provided by the White House were somehow unclean. Mrs Roosevelt was livid when she heard about it.

The whole meeting was later to become saturated with controversy. White House staff were to say it never happened at all.

But for once the evidence appears to show that Jack was probably right. He did meet the President, and the decision to make *Mission To Moscow* did follow that meeting.

He was told, however, it was to be a highly confidential chat. With little preamble or room for small talk, Roosevelt spoke of the need of the Allies to get together, and for the nation to realize that they were making common cause. It was an appeal to the soul. The gratitude of the President—to say nothing of the way in which he could before long show that appreciation—prompted the brothers to go ahead and make *Mission To Moscow*.

It was based on a book by Joseph E. Davies, who for two years was America's Ambassador in the Soviet capital. Davies himself was featured in a prologue, in which he spoke of his true belief that the two countries had to get together.

Davies provided Warners with letters and diaries that were not featured in the original book, because, he said, he believed 'that a complete and frank portrayal of conditions and confidence between the two great peoples at this particular time may be of paramount service to the cause of the United Nations and to free men everywhere'.

The film after the prologue was pure drama, both on screen and in terms of what happened off it. The photographed story, starring Walter Huston in the principal role of Davies, assisted by a host of lookalikes—probably quite the most lifelike replicas ever featured in a film—ranged from Stalin's purges to Davies's visit to Winston Churchill.

Michael Curtiz directed it all with his customary lightness of touch. The story that followed the showing of the movie was a lot less delicately handled, and this time it was directed by Jack, with Harry acting as executive producer.

In fact, if Harry—who was now spending more and more time running his own real-estate empire and doing good philanthropic works—hadn't persuaded Jack to consider the value to the studio of abiding by the President's wishes the film would probably never have been made in the first place.

When the reactions came teeming in like rain in a thunderstorm both brothers wished that they hadn't—and, unusually, even Abe sent long memoranda saying how upset he was.

From all over the country came attacks on a studio which, the accusers said, had now shown itself in its true colours—all of which were various shades of red.

Bosley Crowther in *The New York Times* was the kindest of all about a film which he called 'clearly the most important picture on a political subject any American studio has ever made'. But, he said, the picture of Russia was too flattering by far. Not only that, it was an impertinence to go along with the Soviet party line that the Second World War was as much Trotsky's fault as that of Nazi Germany and Japan. The Russians were saying that Stalin's arch-rival (who had been murdered in Mexico on the leader's instructions three years earlier) had joined with the Axis Powers in trying to bring the overthrow of the Soviet state.

New York's Governor Thomas E. Dewey, shortly to oppose Roosevelt in the 1944 Presidential election, signed with Suzanne La Follette, the Secretary of an international commission of inquiry set up to look into Stalin's purges (Dewey was Chairman of the group, which had no backing whatever from Roosevelt's Administration), a long, angry diatribe to *The Times* protesting at the way the film accepted Russian intentions so passively.

The Hearst Press, no longer having a vested interest in Miss Marion Davies's screen career, joined the fray. They reprinted the Dewey letter. Jack dashed off a telegram to his old friend asking for a right to reply. Instead he got a gruff answer, which was simultaneously published in all the Hearst newspapers:

> Your film, Mr Warner [in *My First Hundred Years In Hollywood,* Warner says that Hearst had previously always called him 'Jack'] gives the 'other side of the case'—the Communist side—quite completely. My contention is that it is entirely essential—not only in the interest of fairness, but in the interests of free-dom—for an American newspaper to print the anti-Communist, the democratic side of the case.

The row thereafter snowballed. The eminent right-wing American writer Westbrook Pegler said the film should never have been made. Statements were made in Congress. Local politicians demanded that not just the film but all Warners' products should be boycotted by clean-living, decent Americans.

With few opportunities to put his side of a case which was difficult in the extreme to argue without weakening the country's position in the War, Jack kept quiet.

He tried to tell himself that it didn't matter, that today's newspapers were still tomorrow's toilet paper, but it wasn't easy.

Twenty years later he got it out of his system. Writing in his memoirs, he said that 'it hurt more than I cared to admit'. What hurt most of all was the fact that he hadn't been allowed to say that the picture had been made at Roosevelt's request.

He wrote with not a little bitterness:

> I did learn one lesson, I think. And it was this: There are some controversial subjects that are so explosive and so open to misin-terpretation by well-meaning supporters of one side or the other,

that it doesn't pay for anyone to be a hero or martyr. You're a dead pigeon either way. Unless of course, you do it under orders from the President of the United States. Even then you're just as dead.

The President made one other request to Jack Warner at this time—to try to use some influence with Charlie Chaplin, asking him not to address a Carnegie Hall rally called to support Russia's appeal for a Second Front. Although Roosevelt wanted *Mission To Moscow* made, he was not ready for a mission to a second front—yet.

Jack called to see Chaplin. They joked—or rather Jack, in his most pussy-cat mood, joked, while Charlie tried to explain why he was so keen on helping the Russians. Yet at the end of the afternoon it seemed that Jack had had his way. 'I promise,' the Warner memoirs recalled his saying, 'not to go.' But the next day he went. Chaplin was to write that he considered Jack's appeal to be a 'challenge'.

Jack, who for all his faults valued loyalty at the top of human attributes, regarded it as a snub. He vowed never to play tennis with Chaplin again. He did more than that. He never saw him again either.

He hadn't bargained with fighting with Charlie Chaplin as one of his contributions to the war effort, but then neither had he imagined that he would go into uniform. It was General 'Hap' Arnold, head of the Army Air Corps, who suggested that Jack would be more useful to the nation if he would enlist.

'I'll only do it if you make me a general,' he said, twisting the cigar in Arnold's direction. 'How about a lieutenant-colonel?' asked the General.

Jack thought about it, realized that it would be pretty good publicity, would make Harry as jealous as hell and would be one step up from 'the Major', Abe, and said yes.

The idea was that Jack should set up a military film unit, importing into it all the flair that he had given to Warner Bros. He had previously helped make training films, doing them somewhat better than he and Sam had managed to do in the previous conflict. One of the new batch, called *Winning Your Wings*, was so successful that it was followed by a massive number of young men volunteering to be pilots. He capped it with *Rear Gunner*.

Now, he was in business two ways—for the Government, and for his brothers and himself. For both organizations he wore the most expensive uniform—tailored by Eddie Schmidt, who made the best clothes for the best films in Hollywood—in the United States. His impeccably cut jacket, knife-creased trousers and brown Service cap, the like of which never saw action, went wherever he went at Burbank or at Culver City, where the unit set up operations. It was written down to the budget for the main film currently being made on the Warner lot, *Air Force*.

Jack was proud of the uniform. He wore it right until VJ Day. But he was prouder still of the rank that entitled him to do so. From then on he was called 'Colonel' by the people who worked for him—even those who up till then had been adopting the conventional American soubriquet of 'JL'.

He was happy, too, because it wasn't easy to argue with a colonel. His actors were all of a much lower rank, and they did what they were told or suffered penalties even a Hollywood mogul would never have contemplated (apart from in a beautiful dream).

But there were limits to his power.

His son Jack Junior had by now become a colonel too; and a full colonel at that, one who wore an eagle on his shoulder instead of a gold-coloured oak-leaf.

On his first leave home in the new rank he made one of his infrequent visits to his father. 'You'll have to salute me now,' said the son. 'He did not laugh,' the younger Jack recalled for me.

The same thing was to happen at Burbank.

It had not been a good day. Jack had earlier heard that the Army thought it would be an idea if, after two years in the Service, he had a training course abroad. He wasn't about to subject himself to anyone's training.

As he seethed with indignation at the suggestion a military delegation was on its way to the studio to discuss propaganda ideas. It was led by a full colonel whom Jack had never met before. Politely, he shook hands with the group.

'You should have saluted me,' said the colonel. That day Jack resigned his commission.

Nevertheless, he kept up his war with the Germans, and in so doing he helped contribute a very great deal to the morale not just of the families back home, but also of the American Serviceman.

Just as Jack was adjusting himself to the idea of being in civilian clothes, audiences around the world were watching a Warner film made entirely by men in military uniform. At the same time they were making a fortune for army charities.

This Is The Army was a love poem to America composed by Irving Berlin. The man who had become known as the song-writer laureate of the United States had devised a show as a reprise to his army career in the First World War. That had been spent writing a musical revue called *Yip Yip Yaphank,* a paean to Camp Yaphank, where Berlin himself was stationed.

The commanding officer had seen that he was less than enthusiastic about getting up early in the morning and sweeping out his barracks floor, and suggested that he might be more suitably employed putting on a show which would raise funds for the building of a small centre for soldiers' families.

Not only was the show a great success at Camp Yaphank, but it transferred to Broadway and made a lot of money for other army charities.

When the Second World War broke out Berlin immediately set to work writing a sequel. *This Is The Army* was the result, and became not only a Broadway sensation, but was played all over the world. There were special versions enacted in Britain—attended by the Royal Family and Winston Churchill—in Italy and in Japan.

It employed professional actors, singers and dancers who had been drafted into military service, and a few others too who showed they had talent. By the time the War ended more than 9 million dollars had been raised for army charities.

Of this, almost 2 million came from Warner Bros' filmed version of *TITA*, which starred Ronald Reagan, Joan Leslie and Frances Langford and a host of others with faces audiences were able to pick out through the movie like soft centres in a box of chocolates. Even world-heavyweight champion Joe Louis, in uniform as a sergeant, had a part in the film.

The studio paid half a million dollars—to the charities—for the screen rights. Uncharacteristically, the contract was signed by Abe Warner, but it was Jack's baby all the way through.

One of the reasons why Jack grabbed at the opportunity to get the screen rights to the show was that he heard that MGM were after it too. Any chance to score over Louis B. Mayer he took like a jealous child wanting another's toy.

The signal to start work meant that the film had to go ahead like any other military operation. Some three hundred men moved into billets near the studios. In charge of the operation was a major who was outranked only by Jack himself.

The dance director was Sergeant Bob Sidney. His protests at the major's demand that everyone go on an obstacle course were to no avail until a couple of dozen dancers came back with an assortment of broken ankles and strained ligaments.

Finally Mike Curtiz—he was not in uniform; the Hungarians had not managed to persuade him to join up—moved in. He told the major he could have soldiers or he could have dancers.

As far as he was concerned, he wanted dancers.

He was rather luckier with *This Is The Army* than he had been with another war film. For that other picture the Government lent him nine Air Force support planes, controlled by radio so that the filming from the ground would be sufficiently precise. Anxiously he watched the planes' progress in the viewfinder, and then decided they weren't doing it right. All he could think of doing was to jump up and down shouting, 'Back! Get Back! Back, I say' to the droning aeroplanes above. In *This Is The Army* they seemed to listen more closely to him.

But giving Jack the chance to produce the movie was equivalent to letting him personally hoist the Stars and Stripes on the White House lawn in the presence of the Roosevelts and the whole of Congress. That was one thing that he and Berlin had in common—a sense of superpatriotism that came from the fact that they both hailed from immigrant stock.

Although Jack himself had been born on the American continent, the fact that his parents, brothers and sisters came from Poland made him have a special sense of appreciation of the advantages of living in America. Berlin in this sense was the Warners writ large. He had been born in Siberia, and came to America at roughly the same time as the Warner family. He achieved fame and riches after spending his childhood in the New York slums—the Warners were millionaires by comparison—and as a result regarded America as God's gift to humanity. As a tribute to the country he wrote *God Bless America,* for years regarded as a second national anthem.

This Is The Army was to him a huge thank-you to his adopted country. To Jack and the other brothers, it was an opportunity to get in on an act they wished they had been the first to think of.

They left nothing to chance.

None of the 350 Servicemen in the cast drew more than their army salary. The Warner cast refused to take any money for their work either—those on contract salary did it as an extra job—and Casey Robinson, by now recognized as one of the studio's finest writers, provided a thoroughly entertaining script. It was able to avoid most of the clichés of revue films which were becoming a staple of Hollywood at the time—*Hollywood Canteen,* a little later on, produced by Warners had them all—and was marvellous to watch from the moment the opening credits faded from the screen.

The most important part of the film was just the ingredient which had been the most successful feature of the stage show—Berlin's music and lyrics. In addition to the rousing title song, there was the haunting barber-shop rhythm of 'I Left My Heart At The Stage Door Canteen', the ballad 'I'm Getting Tired So I Can Sleep' and two comedy numbers 'Poor Little Me, I'm On KP' and 'Oh, How I Hate To Get Up In The Morning.'

The latter, as Berlin himself told me, was a true cry from the heart. 'When I'm in love I write love songs,' he said. 'And I wrote "Oh, How I Hate To Get Up In The Morning" simply because I do hate to get up early.'

That number had been the hit not just of *This Is The Army* on stage, but also of *Yip Yip Yaphank*. And, just as he had in the live theatre, Berlin dressed up in his old ill-fitting First World War uniform, complete with Boy Scout-type hat, and warbled about his misery: 'Oh, how I'd love to murder the bugler, oh how I'd love to see him dead. And then I'd get that other pup, the one who wakes the bugler up. . . .'

Berlin never had a great voice. When he recorded the number on the film he was unfortunate enough to hear one electrician say to another, 'If the guy who wrote this song could hear the way this fellow's singing it, he'd turn over in his grave.'

The guy who wrote the song was happy enough with it in the film, and so were the Warners.

There were a number of other films that also flew the flag—if in different ways—Errol Flynn playing an Underground hero in *Edge of Darkness*; George Raft in *Background To Danger*; Raymond Massey's *Action In The North Atlantic*.

Warners were fighting the war on other fronts too. They had of course long lost their German division, and in 1944 the British studios at Teddington were rased to the ground by a direct hit from a flying-bomb. Among those who perished was the head of the studio, 'Doc' Solomons, Jack's close friend and former brother-in-law.

'Doc' had been at Warners since 1915, and had previously been one of the famous 'Flying Circus' pilots. Only a few nights before his death he had personally recorded the sound of a flying-bomb which was used on an American radio broadcast.

Needless to say, it didn't stop Warners making war films. They were good for business, besides helping the Allied cause.

Hollywood Canteen had a rough story-line, about a sailor (Dane Clark) who goes to the famous entertainment centre for American troops manned by the stars of the movie capital and wins a weekend with Joan Leslie. It was a good idea, because it would be very cheap to make—all those stars either on the Warner books already or more than willing to give their services for next to nothing to help win the War. Or so everyone thought.

But the Screen Actors Guild complained. They said that the amount paid to the guest stars amounted in total to half the regular fee earned by one contracted full-time Warner star.

Half-way through production of *Canteen,* they called a halt. The other studios said the Guild was right. This was hardly surprising: it was a wonderful opportunity to stem the competition. They said that they saw no reason to help Warner Bros out of their problems.

The result was that Warner Bros sued the Screen Actors Guild in the Los Angeles Superior Court. They said that the guild violated its

157

own contracts, especially the one that promised it would not operate a closed shop.

The studio said that between 750 and 1,000 extras were being denied work, and that a number of freelance actors who wanted the chance to demonstrate the work they were doing at the Canteen had been stopped in their tracks. What was more, the Canteen had been promised 250,000 dollars towards its funds, and now it wouldn't get it.

Warners claimed damages of 500,000 dollars.

The move worked. A compromise was arranged out of court and the film went on. Also for the first time, an inter-studio committee was set up to work out how future films of the kind would be made.

However, relations with the overall producers' organization, the Hays Office—otherwise known as the Motion Pictures Producers and Distributors of America—only grew worse as a result of what Jack decreed was their disloyalty. Early in December 1944 the studio resigned from the group.

Thank Your Lucky Stars was an easier film to make. Similarly, it was mainly a vast vaudeville show, which featured Bette Davis in her only singing role, performing 'They're Either Too Young Or Too Old' and Errol Flynn doing a song-and-dance number too, as a Cockney—but since it only featured Warner stars on contract, there were no problems.

More seriously, *Destination Tokyo, Watch On The Rhine, Adventure In Iraq* and Humphrey Bogart's *Passage to Marseilles* all, to one degree or another, continued the process, but they were not the only kind of films that people buying tickets at Warner theatres were able to enjoy in 1944.

There was the marvellous escapism of *Arsenic and Old Lace*—Cary Grant had made his picture finally—and a heavy-handed look-back to the era of Warner Bros biographies with Fredric March's *The Adventures of Mark Twain*. Paul Henreid meanwhile was allowed not to play a German. In *In Our Time* he was a Polish aristocrat.

Even the big musical made a comeback with *The Desert Song*, quite the worst version ever, with Dennis Morgan and Irene Manning. But this, caught in a rash of *Casablanca* fever, attempted to win the war of words against the Nazis in North Africa with a limp tale about collaboration in the desert.

One musical with no connection whatever with the War was an absolute labour of love for Jack, *Rhapsody In Blue,* supposedly the story of George Gershwin.

It was brought to Warners by Jesse Lasky, who had made the very first Hollywood film, *The Squaw Man,* and whose 'Famous Players' studio had become Paramount. Lasky was now an independent

158

producer, and *Rhapsody* was a follow-on to his bringing *Sergeant York* and *Mark Twain* to Warners.

It was *Rhapsody In Blue* that Jack loved—not because of Gershwin, or because he thought its fictional treatment made a particularly good story, but because it gave him a chance to again feature his old idol, Al Jolson.

Jolson had not yet recovered from lung surgery following an attack of malaria suffered while entertaining the troops. He looked old and weak—he was now just sixty—but he sang, danced and whistled *Swanee* as excitingly for an entirely new generation as he had on Broadway all those years before.

If an excuse could have been found to do nothing but let Jolson sing, Jack would have jumped at it. A year or so later he was to have an opportunity to do virtually just that, and turned it down. But that was another story. For the moment Jolson was singing and Jack was happy.

Nevertheless, the film wasn't really good enough. Astonishingly, the studio that had pioneered the very notion of film biographies found that what could have been the easiest form of that genre was the hardest to do. Like *Night and Day,* the equally unreal story of Cole Porter's life which the studio made the following year, it was saved only by its music. Robert Alda was no more convincing as Gershwin than was Cary Grant as Porter. Both films had Alexis Smith supplying the glamour.

Sometimes making the films at all was more difficult than getting people to go to see them. In October 1945 members of the Actors Guild picketed the studios during a strike, and no fewer than three hundred people were hurt in scuffles.

There were more serious injuries when cars proceeded to mow down men trying to prevent their moving through the gates.

The one principally blamed was Harry. He, however, indicated he was trying to be conciliatory. A huge sign was installed above the studio gates—'Warner Bros will agree to abide by whatever settlement is reached between the industry and the union—H. M. Warner, President.'

CHAPTER 16

THE GREAT RACE

One of Jack Warner's qualities was that he liked people
to stand up for themselves.

Bill Orr

Part of the art of running a studio was earnestly believing you knew
more about the business of making films than any of your rivals. In
1943 Warners had taken the plunge and rushed into a territory
where Louis B. Mayer had finally decided he was afraid to tread any
further.

They signed Joan Crawford to a six-year-contract.

Joan was still a big name, and as far as the public was concerned—none of the peculiarities which were to make her such
good copy and screen material after her death had yet leaked
out—was a great star. She had also convinced Jack that MGM had
fired her simply on a whim of Mr Mayer, who was behaving in one of
his more petulant moods.

It wasn't an easy transition. No matter how Jack tried to cosset
her, the trappings of stardom at Burbank seemed to be second-rate
after the glittering pampering she had been used to at the Metro
castle.

She was frequently unhappy, and when she was her language was
choice. It was replete with four-letter words, and when she wanted
to use longer ones it was only because they could be made to sound
even worse.

On one occasion the telephone in Jack's office vibrated with her
complaints of the 'f...ing cameraman', not knowing how to work
and how to get the best out of her beauty. (Bill Orr, who heard the
conversation, had some sympathy. 'It was true,' he told me. 'The
cameras were not getting any younger.'

She excoriated everyone—including Jack himself, who was blowing smoke-rings around the office, not for fun but because it was one
way to control his emotions.

'Yes, dear,' he said. 'No, Joan, dear. I'll see what I can do, darling.' After every promise came a new insult.

Orr couldn't understand why Jack was being so conciliatory. 'I have to be sure that she'll come into work tomorrow,' he replied.

It turned out to be sound judgment, for finally Joan turned up to make *Mildred Pierce* in 1945.

The story of the penniless waitress-turned-big-business-tycoon destroyed by the spoilt daughter (Ann Blyth) who marries her lover earned her an Oscar, and Warners a great way to see out the Second World War.

They were doing it without Hal Wallis. The loggerheads at which the two men had been in their relationship together ever since *Casablanca* ended up with a truck-load of horse manure.

The good feeling and mutual respect were destroyed by Jack's actions at the Oscar ceremony, with the result that every subsequent conversation between the two men—which before had been tempered with a smile and a drink—now became a strain. Jack demanded supervision of Wallis's work, and stopped sending him new ideas, but he wasn't planning to let him go.

Jack tried to persuade him to stay. But, as Hal told me, 'I said, "No. You have departed from our original agreement to such an extent that I don't think I'll be happy here." ' He gave a month's notice.

Once a decision had been made, however, Jack decided to make that month intolerable. He locked Wallis out of his office, with the result that he immediately installed a desk on the lawn outside. When Jack heard what was going on he instructed that a truck full of horse manure to be emptied alongside him.

Hal Wallis left California for New York, and Jack started giving a series of interviews to the Hollywood gossip-writers, condemning Hal both as a man and as a producer. He told *The New York Times* that Wallis had 'breached his contract by seeking employment . . . while negotiations for a settlement were going on'.

Wallis's departure was greeted with sadness by most of the people who had always taken for granted his presence at Burbank. As Julius Epstein put it to me, 'He was a wonderful executive in running the studio. When he was there, films always started on time and finished on time, and that was terribly important.'

As Hal now says, 'He was that kind of person. He held grudges. He tried to undo the things he had said good about me in print and in interviews. I just figured, "This is Jack Warner. It's the sort of man he is and he doesn't want to lose face".'

But he also adds, 'I owe him a great debt for what he did for me. He kept advancing me. He put me in charge of First National. He bought me three Cadillacs, and all in all I would say he treated me very well.'

When Jack wrote *My First Hundred Years In Hollywood* he didn't even mention Wallis's name once.

Hal's resignation was followed almost immediately by that of Joseph H. Hazen, a vice-president of the company who Hal in his own book *Starmaker* says had a similar relationship with Harry to the one Wallis himself had with Jack. He was Harry's right-hand man in the New York home office.

He had been with the company since 1927, when he joined as a lawyer, and was so respected by the other studios that when it came to the recent Federal suit aimed at divorcing the film companies from their theatres he was the man who was chosen to represent them.

Now he too was resigning because of 'personal differences with', as *The New York Times* put it, 'an executive whom he declined to name'. The executive was Harry, who saw Hazen as a threat to his own position. Harry believed he had two main faults—he was very clever, and he was not a member of the family.

Before long both Wallis and Hazen had set up an independent film company working closely with Paramount.

Jack, of course, needed a man on whom he could depend for fierce, undivided loyalty. He chose Steve Trilling, a tiny man with the hide of a mammoth. Trilling, who had been a Warner casting director, was now Jack's number two. He didn't have the power or the authority of Hal Wallis, but he did have the respect of the studio's employees from the top stars to the lowest office boy—'a darling man', as Bill Schaefer puts it.

Jack, who had previously seen only a selected few of the 'dailies', now made sure he saw everything—mostly in the house on Angelo Drive, although sometimes at Burbank, too.

Steve Trilling made the decisions that Jack wasn't concerned with. Frequently he was simply seen to make the ones that Jack didn't want to be seen making. These were principally decisions that involved firing people. Jack was every bit as accomplished a coward as he was a showman. When there was a senior man at the studio to sack he took off for the weekend and left the farewell message to be passed on by Trilling. It was a situation that lasted for the best part of twenty years. 'It got so', one former Warner executive, Hoyt Bowers, told me, 'that every time Jack left, we'd find ourselves asking, "Who's got the push now?"'

Other less touchy matters Jack would take on for himself. Like offering advice and handing down decisions on how the films bearing his name were to be made.

In 1945 Bette Davis starred in *Mr Skeffington,* a fairly lightweight story of a broke but once wealthy young woman consumed by her beauty and her thirst for wealth. In order to quench that thirst she marries a millionaire stockbroker called Job Skeffington, played beautifully by Claude Rains.

The picture was directed by Vincent Sherman—but Julius Epstein, who wrote it with his brother Philip, chuckled, 'No, actually, it was Bette Davis who directed it. She took control of everything.'

Half-way through production, Jack sent a memo to the Epsteins—it never worried him to go over the head of his director—and asked, 'Why is this picture so behind schedule?' The Epsteins replied as though writing a line of dialogue for the movie itself, 'Because Bette Davis is a slow director.'

The Epsteins, like a number of Warner writers, liked to think they had a say in the way their pictures were made. They thought that retakes were necessary, and Vincent Sherman agreed.

The only one who didn't agree was Bette Davis. She categorically refused.

Julius relayed her refusal direct to the top. 'She won't do a retake?' Jack bellowed, so that at least half the entire working population of Warner Bros could hear. 'Who the f... does she think she is?'

He stormed out of the office with the Epsteins in tow. 'She won't make a retake, eh?' he repeated, his face now appearing in glorious Technicolor.

Together they marched to the sound-stage where *Mr Skeffington* was being shot. 'You see all those sound-stages?' Jack roared. 'Who built those sound-stages?' For once, he didn't simply point to the name on the water-tower or the script above the front door. He finished his sentence with short, sharp, clearly delineated words, like rounds fired from a sub-machine-gun in *Little Caesar*.

'She won't do the retake! We'll see. She's going to do the retake!'

As he said it Miss Davis walked straight towards him, a confrontation he had neither expected in that form nor prepared himself for. 'Bette, darling!' he said—and put his arms around her. Nothing more was said about retakes.

When the film was completed Jack saw it in the Burbank projection room with as always his secretary, the director and the writers in attendance, sitting at the back of the small, comfortable room in leather chairs that made it all too easy to fall asleep if the action slowed.

At one point when Bette Davis was on screen he asked for it to come to a halt. The projector was stopped. The lights were switched on. Jack looked around him. 'People,' he said, 'are saying "Fanny" too much.'

Julius Epstein looked at him increduously. 'But it's her name, you know.' However, the number of Fannys in the script was reduced—not easy, since Bette's daughter was named Fanny too. In a number of scenes, therefore, deaf lip-readers could see 'Fannies' coming out of mouths that for that instant remained silent.

It wasn't the only thing to which Jack took exception. He was particularly concerned about the final segment of the picture in which Mr Skeffington goes to Europe and ends up in a Nazi concentration camp.

Jack didn't like that at all. He called Vincent Sherman into his office, and the writers went along too. 'Boys,' he said. 'Does this guy Skeffington have to be Jewish?'

'Of course,' said Sherman. 'Without his being Jewish we have no story.'

'Oh,' said Jack, who was once again frightened of encouraging more people to follow the Errol Flynn line and call him a 'Jew bastard'.

Flynn was particularly adept at the phrase when he went to New York for a publicity binge on behalf of *Objective Burma,* the film which almost led to a serious diplomatic incident between the United States and Great Britain.

Audiences in Britain had been used to seeing shots of emaciated, half-naked soldiers of their own Fourteenth Army up to their chests in the jungle swamps of Burma. They were plainly heroic, and their commander-in-chief, Lord Mountbatten, had dubbed them 'The Forgotten Army'.

The title seemed peculiarly apt when *Objective Burma* was released, showing to all intents and purposes the War being won single-handed by Flynn, aided and abetted by a squad of brave, all-American boys. The British were livid. Questions were asked in Parliament. Philip Zec, one of Britain's greatest cartoonists, filled his space in the *Daily Mirror* with the ghost of a Tommy asking Errol to move aside. 'Excuse me,' he says, 'you're sitting on my grave.'

Jack personally ordered a special prologue to be supplied for British audiences, explaining that the film merely told of a single specific incident in the campaign which in no way was intended to underplay the heroic actions of the British in the Burma conflict. But in truth he was more worried about Errol Flynn the man than the character he played in the movie.

It was essential to send him to New York to publicize the film. However, he made sure that his friend the Baron was carefully watched. Raoul Walsh, who had directed the movie, was appointed as chaperone.

'Remember,' Walsh told Errol, 'please—no trouble.'

'I promise, Uncle,' said Errol, who wasn't totally convinced himself.

Naturally, the first thing he did when he booked into the Waldorf

Towers was to order a completely stocked cocktail cabinet. 'Charge it to Warner Bros,' he ordered.

The first evening in Manhattan, he predictably went in search of a woman. Not completely predictable, however, was the result of that search. He fell in love, as completely and as foolishly as a teenager.

Shortly before his death, Raoul Walsh recalled for me, roguishly, the events leading up to one of Errol Flynn's few failures in love. Back at the hotel, he ordered a dozen red roses—on Mr Warner's account—and sent them round to the exquisitely formed, so very feminine, girl he had met at a cocktail party the previous evening.

The next day he bought two poodle pups which he asked to be sent over to her apartment. 'Your name, sir?' asked the assistant, convinced that she knew her customer but not really sure who he was.

'Jack L. Warner,' he replied, 'Warner Bros Pictures Inc., 321 West 44th Street, New York City.'

'Oh, yes, Mr Warner,' said the assistant, now grateful that her memory had been helped along by the man whose face she knew so well—obviously from pictures in the paper.

The episode threatened to end with Jack looking for a new leading man. The girl jilted Flynn, leaving him planning to throw himself out of the hotel-room window, and only stopping when Walsh, after a moment's desperate thinking, said that his erstwhile lover had asked him to hold back until she could get there to watch.

Had Errol in fact killed himself at that moment, Jack wouldn't have been very pleased, although it would have provided another subject for discussion at the lunch table.

It would have made better hearing than the occasional long-winded stories that a few of his guests—who were never invited again—couldn't avoid retelling in all their monotonous length. When that happened Jack looked to the ceiling, and Bill Orr and a few of his other close companions knew it was the moment for a rescue operation in the form of a quickly improvised story.

The guest had the word 'dull' noted mentally alongside his name. But in spite of everything, that was one appellation that could never be applied to Errol Flynn.

Jack's relationship with Flynn was characterized by the same brand of devout cowardice that he showed to some of his top women stars. It was a situation that would never change, as events four years later would prove.

Errol probably never gave him more trouble than during the making of *The Adventures of Don Juan* in 1949.

It was the movie that seemed to sum up everyone's impression of Errol Flynn—except that at only thirty-nine he was already exhibiting signs of the dissipation that was to kill him within twelve years.

He was growing fat, and no matter how the make-up experts tried to camouflage the ravages of his debauchery, there was little that could hide it.

Even so, that was only a minor problem compared with some of the other difficulties in making the film. Once more Errol refused to go on with the work until he had a rise. Then when that little matter was sorted out there was the trouble finding a group of minor actors desperately needed for an action scene that didn't involve Errol himself. Finally the men were found—cleaning up the Flynn tennis-court.

However, when his director Vincent Sherman dared to protest the Flynn charm was on hand to soothe all his agonies. He was the only director to whom Flynn—renowned for his parsimony—was known to have given a present, a gold cigar-cutter.

It didn't serve to ease Jack Warner's anxieties.

When he realized just how far behind schedule *Don Juan* was he rang Sherman and demanded action. 'You tell that goddamned son of a bitch . . .' he began.

But Sherman knew how far he would get.

'Mr Warner', he recalled that he said to his chief, 'I have to work with him. You tell him.'

'Well, I'm not scared of that bastard,' Jack replied, entirely courageous in the face of his director who had the power only to observe. Yet scared was precisely what he was. He didn't even pick up the telephone. It was safer to let the matter drop.

Finally the film was ready. As usual, it was run first of all at the Angelo Drive house. Jack said very little. But two days later a full-page advertisement appeared in both *Daily Variety* and the *Hollywood Reporter*—'Dear Errol. Just saw your picture. It was great. Sensational. Thank you for a wonderful picture. Jack. L. Warner.'

Sherman was less than impressed. 'One of the grips showed it to me. I went mad.'

It didn't mean, however, that the rows with Errol were over. They continued, and got louder and tougher. And as they did, they involved more and more people.

For all his extreme care, Jack was occasionally at the centre of a situation that Flynn would have regarded as par for the course, such as the time he heard that a star was using his dressing-room for an affair with the current Warner girl-friend. She didn't work on the lot, but the Hollywood community was comparatively small, and the actor didn't have the sense to realize that it would have been wiser to leave her alone.

When Jack heard about it he was furious.

He burst into the room to find the couple in the process of

copulation. He screamed louder than an assistant director calling for order—and chased the naked man through the door of a sound-stage supposedly protected by a red light. The shrieks of continuity girls didn't help the temper of an exasperated director struggling through the twenty-first take of the day.

Afterwards Jack could laugh at the proceedings. It wasn't, after all, as serious as the antics of some of his other actors.

Olivia de Havilland, for instance, never ceased to give him moments of anxiety, although he knew that he was on shaky ground with her whenever they came into conflict.

She had been faced with so many suspensions that her contract had by 1945 been extended by twenty-five weeks, to make up for the time when she wasn't working. She decided to petition the Superior Court of California for what was officially an interpretation of the law. In a historic judgment, the court ruled that Warners had been at fault. It was totally illegal to add any time to a seven-year contract without the approval of both parties.

They were in fact ruling not merely against Warner Bros but against the entire contract system at work in Hollywood. What Bette Davis had failed to achieve in London Olivia had been able to gain on her own doorstep in California.

Jack saw the writing on the wall, but was determined to try to erase it. He immediately appealed. At the same time he sent a telegram to 150 studios and independent producers (his mailing list was curling at the edges; at least seventy-five of these had not been in business for thirty years), advising them not to employ Olivia. It was a valid threat. Any studio going against Jack would face immediate revenge for this breach of the Hollywood gentleman's agreement.

But the appeals court sided with the plaintiff. Jack appealed again, sending a further 150 telegrams and another 150 warnings.

Finally and irrevocably, on 3 February 1945 the Supreme Court handed down its judgment. Warners had been involved in a totally illegal action.

There was nothing to keep Olivia at Warners, and nothing to stop Paramount from employing her in *To Each His Own,* for which she won her first Oscar. (Three years later, she won her second, also for Paramount, with *The Heiress.)*

Years later, writing in his memoirs—and once more stressing his belief that a contract was still a 'two-way street'—Jack said he accepted that it was 'probably good for everyone concerned' that the whole system was changed.

As for Olivia, she said long afterwards, 'I was sad not to have won [the Academy Award] at Warner Bros, because I could have said to Jack, "You see what I meant all along".'

167

She was luckier than Joan Leslie, who on her twenty-first birthday in 1947 asked to be relieved of her contract—because she said that it had been negotiated when she was a minor, and she could not be held responsible for it.

So, on legal advice, she 'disaffected her contract'—which immediately gave Warners, or so they believed, the right to exercise their own official right to take up an option on her services. Once having done that, they suspended her.

Joan's principal complaint was that she had not been handled properly. She thought she was entitled to star billing in her last Warner film, *Two Guys From Milwaukee*. But she said, 'I was reduced to feature status by malice and ill will.'

She sued for 2,725,000 dollars. When that seemed an unattainable target she changed her demands to a cancellation of the contract on the grounds that she was too young to be signed up for seven years. She didn't know how lucky she had been.

Joan was earning 1,250 dollars a week when the break came and the studio announced—the terminology on these occasions was particularly and intentionally biting—that she was no longer a Warner 'property'.

One effect of the decision was that all Warner contracts—to say nothing of those of other studios—were shown to have little or no binding force when it came to employing people against their will.

By the time that Joan's film *Cinderella Jones,* which had been made two years earlier and then inexplicably shelved, was released in 1946, she was virtually an outcast. A message had gone out again to the other studios.

The word from Jack was that Joan Leslie was difficult.

'Don't give her work,' he said—and they didn't. The girl who had been groomed as the star of tomorrow was at twenty-one decreed to be an actress of yesterday. For two years she didn't work at all, and thereafter only in unimportant subsidiary roles. Yet officially she had been the victor—and her victory was another nail in the contracts coffin.

Occasionally stars didn't know enough about what those contracts contained, or just how easy it could sometimes be to get themselves out of just such a coffin. George Raft made one of the biggest mistakes of his career when he thought it would be as difficult to leave Warners as it was for a visitor to get out of Count Dracula's castle.

Jack's rows with Raft—whose temper Warner often thought made him a lot tougher on the set than he sometimes seemed on screen—reached a point where after making five pictures he had had enough and wanted out.

Jack himself was far from averse to such an arrangement. Raft was not only difficult, there was clear evidence that his public appeal was diminishing.

In such circumstances the Warner board were content enough to take the usual procedure—pay off the money still outstanding on his agreement and hope they would part, if not friends, then certainly with the knowledge that he wouldn't be bothering them any more.

Jack decided to find an easy way out of contractual obligations that could have involved the studio in quite a financial headache.

He made his first bid. 'What do you say that we settle for ten thousand dollars?' he asked Raft—who promptly got out his cheque-book and wrote a payment for 10,000 dollars.

'I was never very good with money,' Raft himself told me, somewhat wistfully recalling the moment when Warner was trying to save the company at least a hundred thousand dollars by offering the star a mere ten thousand, and instead of paying the money received it.

If only Warner Bros had realized what an innocent they had had under their wing! They would have tried to pay him minimum scale. As Jack, recalling the episode, wrote in his memoirs, 'I practically ran to the bank [with the cheque] before he changed his mind.'

CHAPTER 17

HOLLYWOOD CANTEEN

He had tremendous instinct and always liked people to
laugh at him.

Paul Kohner

Nobody who worked for the Warner brothers was ever totally
spared the wrath of one or other of them, although most had reason
to know that where Jack was concerned, it could be tempered as
often as not with a smile, corny joke and well-meant pat on the back.

As Julius Epstein told me, 'You could tell him if it was—and it
always was—a terrible joke. He didn't mind.'

'On the other hand, you had to know when to laugh. A senior
studio executive began his career at Warner Bros as an errand-boy.
On his first day at the studio Jack tapped him on the shoulder and
said, "Say, sonny. What do you know about property?"

' "Nothing," said the boy, convinced that his ignorance meant he
was about to be put out of work.

' "No, son," said Jack. "You should have said "lots".'

The one thing the Warner writers had was an ability to deal with
those jokes in kind—frequently so deftly that Jack could never be
sure that an insult wasn't really a compliment. The suspicion that
cleverness bred occasional treason, though, resulted in a state of
attritional war between the writers employed by the company and
the brothers themselves.

The Epsteins were the first to discover that hostilities had begun.
They had long before decided that since few writers ever spent more
than a couple of hours at their Warner Bros desks each day—for
what they all appreciated were ridiculously inflated salaries—there
was little reason why they should come in at nine o'clock every
morning, as all the other studio employees were expected to do.

'One day,' as Julius recalled for me, 'we overdid it.' By coming in
at two-thirty in the afternoon. Just as they were walking through the
studio doors they bumped into Jack, who had left what was quite
clearly not a terribly convivial lunch.

He asked no questions. Instead he told them, 'Read your contracts. Bank presidents come in at nine o'clock. Railroad presidents come in at nine o'clock. You are coming in at nine o'clock.'

After Jack had chewed them out with his comparisons with the captains of industry, Julius forwarded him a half-completed script. Pinned on it was the message: 'Let the bank president finish it.'

Punctuality became an obsession with both Harry and Jack, and the Epsteins were for a time their principal target. All the writers were sent a memo ordering them in at nine o'clock in future. Again the Epsteins replied with a script, which they knew was more dreadful than anything they had previously written.

'This is terrible,' said Jack, when the brothers answered the summons to his office and had proceeded the length of the carpet to his desk. 'How could you write it?'

'It's funny you should say that,' said Philip, 'because it was written at nine o'clock!'

Jack was so exasperated by the behaviour of the Epsteins that he once thundered at them, 'I want back the money I've been paying you.'

Philip looked at him with what appeared to be an expression of genuine regret. 'Colonel,' he said in his most deferential voice, 'I'd like to give you your money back, but I've built a pool with it. However, if you're ever in the neighbourhood, feel free to use it.'

None of the writers escaped. One of Jack's main targets was Wilson Mizner, a brilliant raconteur whom Warner was convinced was single-handedly robbing the studio tills of every penny taken at the box office. Mizner never seemed to produce anything, Jack announced one day—and it was partly true, except that he came out with the best gags at the story conferences.

'I don't pay anyone five hundred dollars a week for ad libbing,' he declared. 'Do some work.'

Mizner's office was directly opposite Jack's. The day after the summary chastisement he could be seen sitting in the bright sunlight outside the office sharpening at least a hundred pencils. That, after all, was work.

Jack was even less pleased with William Faulkner, whom he had brought in at great expense because he believed the famous novelist's name would add a great deal of prestige to the Warner Bros product.

Faulkner too wasn't keen on the clocking-in principle. But he had a way round that. In a weak moment, Jack had consented to allowing him to work at home. A couple of days after his contract came into force Jack asked for him to attend a story conference two hours later. A secretary was asked to arrange it. 'But . . .' she stammered. 'Mr Faulkner works at home.'

'I know,' said Jack. 'He's got two hours to get here.'

'Yes,' said the secretary. 'But he lives in South Carolina.' Jack was not pleased. Faulkner did manage to produce some notable work from that South Carolina base, however—including the Bogart-Bacall picture, *The Big Sleep.*

Norman Krasna was another who clashed with Jack; and quite early in his Warner Bros career. In 1943 he wrote and directed the Olivia de Havilland-Robert Cummings film *Princess O'Rourke.* The trouble was he couldn't find an ending for it—and nor could anyone else sitting in on the story conferences.

'Goddam it,' said Jack. 'We have to have an ending. We have Olivia on salary at fifteen thousand dollars a week.' And he went on to berate Krasna for being like all his colleagues and failing to put in a full day's work.

Krasna glanced at his watch. 'I have the problem solved,' he said. 'I have the perfect ending.' No one was more excited than Jack himself. Everyone at the conference could see just how pleased he was. 'Well,' he said expectantly, 'what is it?'

'I can't tell you,' said Krasna.

'Why on earth not?' asked Warner, sure he was about to be crucified.

'Because,' Krasna answered, looking at his watch again, 'I thought of the answer after five-thirty.'

Jack agreed to relax his rule after that. But it didn't stay relaxed. He posted guards on the studio gates to note precisely the times when writers entered and left the premises, and to inform Colonel Warner personally of their findings.

Melville Shavelson told me about the ingenuity he and his colleagues had to use to avoid the Warner wrath. They decided to take advantage of the fact that one Warner writer had a ground-floor office, from which, by the simple tactic of climbing over a desk, they could get to the parking lot and escape without the guards noticing. If by chance they were spotted there was always a blanket under which they could hide on the car-floor. Since the driver couldn't hide quite so easily, they would take it in turns to do the driving.

'Our days lasted from nine to nine-thirty after that.' Except, of course, when there was a deadline to meet. Then they worked around the clock to get their work completed.

They worked when other people relaxed. Ideas for scripts were pitched around at the writers' table in the commissary during lunch breaks, with everyone providing thoughts for each other's projects. Sometimes they were more earnestly engaged in word games to decide who would pay the lunch bill.

That, of course, was another cause of distress for Jack. It was even more distressful to Harry, who took the view that all his employees were passengers riding on his back. When he saw the money that the commissary was losing he decided he had to take immediate remedial action. It was not difficult to see why the restaurant was a financial disaster area. It existed to keep people together, serving the best food at rock-bottom prices. And what was more economically unsettling, it only served one meal a day.

Harry decided that the only thing to do was to double all the prices. When Shavelson saw what had happened he suggested to his colleagues, 'Let's get out of here.'

They went to a near-by restaurant. When they got back to their desks there was a note from Jack: 'Dear writer. You are allowed an hour for lunch. You took an hour and a half.'

Shavelson planned the next step in the campaign very carefully. Since he was the only one of the writers who owned a stop-watch, he took charge. They went back to the restaurant the next day, but only stayed a clocked twenty minutes. The following forty minutes were spent standing in front of the front-gate guard, staring at him.

As Shavelson knew it would, the information found its way back to Jack. He himself responded with another note affixed to their typewriters: 'Dear writer. All's forgiven. Come back.'

The old prices were restored. Posters were put up all around the commissary declaring: 'Welcome back, writers.'

They had won. Or had they?

As Shavelson put it, 'We had underestimated Harry.'

A week later all the prices were up again—but only by a nickel. And they kept going up at the same rate. Within a few weeks they were back to what they had been before the writers' strike—double. 'He knew no one was going to leave for a nickel.'

As Bette Davis once said, 'The Warner brothers were penny wise and pound foolish. They would sack five waitresses to keep twelve producers on the pay-roll playing the horses.'

But Jack wanted to keep his writers happy if he could. He also made little secret of the fact that he admired them. A man who was unable to put two articulate sentences together in a public speech had a great deal of respect for those who could do with words what he himself was able to do with his business.

What was more, the writers were needed for more than just producing scripts. Melville Shavelson had as his specific task to write Jack's after-dinner jokes.

'He would usually ring me up,' he told me, 'and say, "That one played but the other didn't".' From a man of whom Jack Benny said, 'He would rather tell a bad joke than make a good picture,' the way a joke was received was a matter of vital importance.

So his writers knew their value, and took advantage of the fact.

They were not the only practical jokesmiths on the Warner lot.

The lugubrious Peter Lorre, who didn't instantly strike one as the biggest laugh in Hollywood, was as good at pulling the legs of the brothers Warner as anyone else. And better than most.

Once Harry was showing a high-powered delegation of bemedal-led Iranian Army officers around the studios. They were wearing the smartest uniforms seen in America for half a century.

'Good morning,' said the small, ingratiating Lorre as he passed them. 'Good morning,' replied Harry, not sure whether he had just greeted an actor or a garbage-collector. As the party moved away Lorre called after them, 'And as for you guys in the Chocolate Soldier outfits, get them back to wardrobe in ten minutes or there will be trouble.' If Harry wasn't amused—and he wasn't—Jack thought it was the funniest thing he had heard in years.

Harry found very little to smile about. His obsession was the company, and with feeling reasonably assured there would be someone in the family to follow him in running it.

With his own son long dead, and the plainly widening divide between Jack and Jack Junior, he started to pin his hopes on a third generation. But at first he had only granddaughters. A grandson would be a way of continuing the Warner line.

When his daughter Betty gave birth to a third daughter her husband Milton Sperling rang Harry and his wife with the news.

'Well,' he said, 'it's a little girl.'

There was a pause. Sperling thought the line had gone dead. At length Harry stammered, 'You know what the trouble with you is . . .?'

His wife tried to take the phone away from him. 'Wait a minute, Harry,' she said.

But now Sperling—who says of him, 'I loved him as a father'—wouldn't let the matter drop even if Harry was about to take his wife's advice.

'No,' he said to his father-in-law, 'what is the trouble?'

'Damn it,' Harry sobbed, 'can't you make a boy?'

He never got over the fact that he appeared to be living in a feminine world—and yet he was the Jewish father personified, caring, loving, wanting and providing everything that great wealth could offer his daughters.

He gave to Sam's daughter Leta the same love he showered on Betty and Doris. She was family, and that was all that mattered.

He was later rewarded. Doris (married to Mervyn LeRoy) gave birth to a son. The child became a Warner—Warner LeRoy—but he didn't take over the film business. He is now a New York restaurateur. (Doris later divorced LeRoy and married in turn director Charles Vidor and composer-conductor David Rose.)

Milton Sperling was injected with Harry's family commitment.

He was formerly a Twentieth Century-Fox producer, but Harry thought it was wrong for him to work for a rival organization.

Darryl Zanuck tried to persuade him to stay. 'Don't work for the Warners,' he said, with his own experience at the studio behind him. 'They're a lousy bunch of fellows.' But Harry won. Sperling joined Warner Bros.

Being a producer carried fewer constraints than those applied to writers and actors. Producers were expected to know everything about every film on the lot. Actors weren't even encouraged to know much about the pictures they were making themselves. They were, for instance, barred from seeing the rushes of their movies. Jack banned them because he thought that seeing the 'dailies' would give them too much of an opportunity to interfere.

Bette Davis for one was happy with that situation. She refused to see even her finished pictures. Loretta Young, on the other hand, told me that she often begged to be allowed to see them—and was always turned down.

Eventually subterfuge had to be used. She knew one of the studio projectionists. When everyone else had gone home she would sneak into a projection booth and watch the rushes then.

To the general public, seeing a sneak preview of a picture was one of the excitements of living within a convenient car-ride of Hollywood.

As far as the studios were concerned, it was a very good way of finding out what the public wanted. Jack would go to them all—and then study the cards that the audiences filled in afterwards.

There were numerous attempts to influence what they wrote, which tended to defeat the whole purpose of the exercise. Jack would stand at the door, and as people came out he would buttonhole them. 'Gee.' he could be heard to say, 'what did you think of that movie? Wasn't that a great picture?'

He later abandoned the practice. He suspected that too many smart-alecs used the opportunity to play film critic unfairly. He also believed he had a much more reliable guide to the public's interest in his products. He watched them in their seats. If they were still, all was well. If they shuffled around, it was not so good. Worst of all was when they went en masse to the toilets—and if they went more than once, the film was a turkey.

'No good,' he told Bill Orr after one such occasion. 'It was a two-piss picture.'

CHAPTER 18

MANPOWER

I may complain, but that's bullshit. They took an
unknown kid from Brooklyn and made him into an
internationally-known person. I bow to that.

Dane Clark

Dane Clark was not the easiest of people to have around a studio. A conscientious, deep-thinking actor who had made a handful of light films and thought he was worthy of something more demanding rarely was—especially when it came to crossing swords with Jack.

Dane, born Bernard Zanville in Brooklyn, a young Jewish kid who had been brought up to believe that if you needed something badly you would have to fight to get it, had come to Hollywood determined to build a career in films on to a couple of tiny roles he had had in New York.

Like most of the thousands of people who every year think the same, the hardest thing of all appeared simply to be getting through a Hollywood studio's gates.

He had been told that Phil Friedman, who was the Warner casting director, was the man to see. With the kind of *chutzpah* that children of his background were fed as part of their breakfast cereal, he managed to persuade one of the gate guards that he had an appointment. He also thought he knew how to do it. He carried a hat, an item of clothing he had never worn in his life.

Predictably, Mr Friedman was not in. But the hat would be the way to get to him. It was carefully left on a seat in Friedman's outer office, a good enough reason to go back the next day. Particularly since he had engaged the guard in conversation long enough to be recognized on a second visit.

When he did come back to reclaim his hat Friedman was in, and having a violent row with Jerry Wald, the ageing *enfant terrible* of Warner Bros, a writer and producer who was said to have been the model for the ruthless central character in *What Makes Sammy Run?*

Elia Kazan, then a young actor, had walked out just as he was about to play an important part in *Action In The North Atlantic.* Wald had tested forty-five people to replace him, and none was any good.

Zanville broke into their conversation. 'Why don't you test me?' he asked, as if he had been sitting in on their meeting all the time.

'Who are you?' asked Wald.

'What the hell difference does it make to you?' he replied. 'You wouldn't know if I told you. But if you've tested forty-five people, why not make it forty-six?'

You couldn't argue with that sort of logic. Clark got the part, and made his debut playing alongside Humphrey Bogart and Raymond Massey.

He was billed in the credits as Bernard Zanville, but Bogart took a fancy to him and suggested the change of name. Jack liked him, although he knew Clark had a reputation for being prickly, to say the least. He had a spirit that Jack appreciated, and, more important, the customers liked him too. The cinema exhibitors were before long voting him the most promising star of tomorrow.

He not only was the featured player in *Hollywood Canteen,* but starred opposite Bette Davis in *A Stolen Life* and did very well for himself and the studio in *The Very Thought of You* and *God Is My Co-Pilot.* He was being groomed as the new John Garfield, and indeed there were a number of similarities between them.

Winston Churchill, a film buff of no mean proportions, liked him and invited him for dinner. In New York he was pursued by a group of what today would be called groupies who followed him to his hotel—one newspaper reporter suggested he was having sex with them all night, which led to personal protests and a suggestion from him to the studio that they ought to hold courses for young stars in dealing with success.

He was overwhelmed with his own importance, a fact he now readily admits. After serving four years of his contract, he decided he wanted something better. Jack asked him to sign a new agreement to replace the one he had already, but the terms were not what he wanted.

It all happened at the worst possible time. Jack had had a huge row with his agents, MCA, and barred not only members of the firm from going through the studio gates but also any other agency that was willing to deputize for them.

It was part of a continuing war with the agents. Warners complained that the agency had done a deal over a star with an independent producer, rather than with the studio itself. Consequently the agents were not even allowed to pick up their stars' salary cheques.

The matter was settled only when the agency said that if the stars didn't get their money they wouldn't perform. It was the kind of language Jack understood.

It was not a completely unique situation at Warners, but it demonstrated the degree of pique that Jack could feel against a breed of men he always regarded as the parasites of the business. More than that, it showed the powerlessness of a young actor suddenly dealing with his own business affairs. If he had had no training in life, he had considerably less experience of the world of business. His relationship with his bosses had to be sweet—the agents were employed as much as anything to bear the brunt of Jack's swearing, and, if the occasion called for it, to swear back.

'Everywhere I went, I'd be pressed to re-sign,' he recalled for me. Finally the studio got the message and decided to act accordingly. From hounding him incessantly, the orders were to ignore him. For days Jack wouldn't see Dane, and for days the actor parked himself outside the art-deco office, waiting for the big confrontation.

It came when Jack decided he could take no more of what he saw as the ingratitude of a young kid whom he had brought from nowhere and made internationally known. He called him a 'ham' and worse.

To Dane that was a declaration of war that required immediate retaliation. And retaliate he did, in the way that came natural to him.

As he explained, 'In Brooklyn, when someone called you a name you belted him one. So I belted him.'

That was the end of his career at Warner Bros. 'I'll cut you up like a side of beef,' said Jack (seemingly no idle threat from an ex-butcher). 'Nobody goes for me like that. I'll see that you never work in the industry again.'

Jack had to be restrained from replying in kind by a coterie of executives standing by his desk. Clark was pushed along the length of the carpet and out of the door. Then he was told in no uncertain terms that his hopes of stardom were over.

A few days before the row began Jack had announced that he was going to remake *The Jazz Singer* with Dane playing the original Jolson lead. Now he let Clark know that the deal was off. The blow was softened very soon afterwards by Jack's decision—although it was never publicly announced; these things rarely are—to abandon the picture altogether.

The reason was that he knew that Columbia Pictures were going to make *The Jolson Story,* a fact that he resented and regarded as crass disloyalty from his friend Al.

Now, Jolson was never known as the nicest man in Hollywood. One of the world's great showmen, there was no doubt. A spell-binder on the stage, and to listen to on records, certainly, but the kind of man you would like for a father-in-law, absolutely no. Still, it was not his fault that the picture was to be made by a rival studio. Jack had been offered it, and turned the idea down flat.

The notion was brought to him first by Sidney Skolsky, one of that band of influential Hollywood columnists who could make or break careers by a seemingly inoffensive piece of gossip. Like Warner, he idolized Jolson, whom he considered, he told me, the king of Hollywood.

Warner Bros was the obvious place to take the idea. Skolsky was friendly with the writer Mark Hellinger, who put the plan to Jack. For reasons that now seem difficult to understand, he was somewhat less than enthusiastic. *Rhapsody In Blue* had not been the success he expected it to be. More to the point, few people were talking about Al Jolson's contribution to the film. It was mentioned in passing by a couple of critics, but apart from those who had seen the sensational Jolson performances entertaining the troops, it was clear they regarded him as a forgotten man.

Records had been made of Jolson's singing of *Swanee*—coupled with a dull, inept version of his *April Showers*—and they were gathering dust on the shelves. To add insult to what might have been considered a rather large injury, a number of newspaper advertisements had spelt his name 'Al Johnson'. Jolson, Jack decided, wouldn't make a nickel at the box office.

In fact, Al JOHNson would lose them a packet of dollars.

He said no and Skolsky had to peddle his idea all over town. Most producers agreed with Jack. Except Harry Cohn of Columbia, who always relished the idea of snatching success from Warner mistakes.

Cohn, who had also been smitten with the Jolson bug, was still infected. He said yes, and the idea was quickly buzzing through the clubs and bars of Hollywood, first as Cohn's folly and then as a brave, adventurous idea. When Jack heard about it he decided to change his mind.

He found out that Jolson was in New York to pick up an award for his services to the troops, and planned to waylay him. He did just that—first at his hotel, and then on the return train journey to the West Coast.

'What do you want to go to a crappy studio like Columbia for?' he asked Al. At the same time he promised him the world—in the shape of 200,000 dollars, the enthusiasm of a studio in which Al was a major shareholder, Mike Curtiz to direct and the Epstein brothers to write the story (Julius Epstein told me he refused to have anything to do with the idea: he hated Jolson), and the most tempting offer of all—he could play himself. This was an idea Jolson had had too, but which Columbia had rejected as totally unmanageable. Not only was Jolson not a very good actor, how could he play a twenty-year-old?

Al said he would think about it, but he was still so angry about once being rejected by Warners that he was prepared to hear all arguments against going back to Burbank.

They came from both Skolsky and Harry Cohn, who said that the as yet untitled *Jolson Story* would be treated as the major film of the year at Columbia, whereas it would be swamped by the massive output of Warners.

Columbia would make it in colour, while Warners always believed in using black and white for their biographies—as they had in both *Yankee Doodle Dandy* and *Rhapsody In Blue*—and would spend a great deal of money on it. Oh, yes, and Al could have half the profits. He signed there and then.

Once the idea was formally enshrined in a legal document the casting directors of Columbia got busy looking for their Jolson, a youngster who could act his way through the picture from early youth to late middle age.

At the same time he would also have to be able to do a little dancing—and, most important of all, mime to Jolson's own singing of songs like 'My Mammy', 'Rockabye Your Baby With A Dixie Melody' and 'California, Here I Come', to say nothing of 'Swanee' again.

And that is where Jack Warner came into the picture once more. Jolson asked for Dane Clark, whom he knew as a companion at Friday evening Hollywood boxing matches. Jack refused even to discuss terms. Hell hath few furies like those of a movie mogul scorned, and Jack made it very clear indeed that he considered he had been spurned more than a bride left waiting at the altar.

There was no way in which he would consider lending Dane Clark, even for a sum of money (which Warner Bros would pocket) far in excess of anything they would pay him themselves.

When Columbia finally contracted one of their own unknown 'B' picture actors, Larry Parks, for the role, Jack consolidated his determination to make things as difficult as possible for his competitors. He absolutely refused to allow them to see prints of any of the early Jolson pictures, so that Parks could more accurately perfect his imitation of the unique style. And in those days, when there were virtually no public film libraries, borrowing prints from the original companies was the only way of seeing those pictures.

Dane Clark himself was to have a similar experience. Once Warners had decided they were not going to turn him into a big, big star they used the old, tried Warner formula—and offered Clark parts that they knew any self-respecting actor would throw back in their faces.

180

When he did just that Jack put him on suspension.

Once more there were requests for him to be loaned out. Stanley Kramer wanted him as the boxer in *Champion*. Jack said, 'No. We'll make our own boxing picture' and, with the aggravation at losing what was plainly going to be an exciting part thumping through his body, Clark said yes to Jack's alternative. It was a dreadful piece of hokum called *Whiplash,* which was instantly and thankfully forgotten. Meanwhile Kirk Douglas became a superstar, largely through playing the lead in *Champion.*

In the course of the three years his contract still had to run after the big row with Jack, Dane Clark made just one movie that was acceptable, a 'B' picture called *Embraceable You.*

When his contract was over Warner Bros and Dane Clark saw each other no more. Now that he was free of his commitments, a Chicago businessman was prepared to star him in an independent film he was financing, but wanted to see footage which showed what he could do. Jack refused to allow any Dane Clark film to be shown outside a theatre.

He also made it very clear to the other studios that he didn't want Clark employed by them. The penalty for going against his wishes was the revenge each and every other studio knew he could exert, either immediately or at some time in the future. They all had their own Dane Clarks, whom they had treated in precisely the same way.

As a result, Clark had to go to England and France to work—and in the sort of pictures he would have turned down at Burbank. He was away so long that the rumour around Hollywood was that he had been blacklisted by Senator Joe McCarthy. It became so persistent that even the studio got worried, and paid for an announcement in the *Hollywood Reporter* that he had left by mutual agreement and for non-political reasons. But it had no effect. The heat had been on, and was now off. No one was interested in boiling it up again.

For fifteen years, Dane Clark says, he bore a tremendous grudge. It lasted until the day when in a Los Angeles street an elderly man called out, 'Dane! Dane Clark!' and put his arms around him. It was Jack Warner.

'That was when my view about him changed,' Clark told me. 'I had always thought of him as a wicked man who tried to ruin me. But then I realized it wasn't like that at all. He simply acted for business reasons in the way he thought most effective, but when it was long over I could see that if he bore no grudge, why should I? I don't think he even remembered what he had done, because it just didn't matter to him any more.'

And it was such a familiar story; so common, in fact, that Jack in all probability forgot who he did fire and who he did not—and why.

The rows with his actors went on and on and on. Always with Bette Davis, always with Flynn, and more and more with Bogart.

They would quarrel the moment they met, as though Bogie and Jack each had a dose of a certain chemical which exploded on impact. Once, Irving Rapper remembers, Bogart snarled so much when he refused to do a picture that Jack pressed a button under his desk top and, as if from nowhere, was surrounded by henchmen. It had been fitted as a result of the Dane Clark fracas.

'I thought he was going to kill me,' Jack told Rapper after the set-to with Bogart, whom he had wanted to star in a boxing picture.

Instead, Bogie pulled off his jacket and undid his shirt, revealing his somewhat puny chest. 'Look,' he said to Jack, 'make me a fighter and everyone will laugh.'

Sometimes they conducted their rows by correspondence, with the most biting of memos from Jack, who always ended them with the words 'Love to Mayo' (the Mrs Bogart of the time). The star would reply in kind, and sign his notes, 'Love to Ann'.

Love, of course, was the one emotion neither felt for the other. Joe Hyams in his biography *Bogie* recalls Jack's amazement when he discovered the actor wore a toupee. 'Good God,' he said. 'Some leading man I've signed up. He has hardly a hair on his head.'

Bogie, hardly surprisingly, knew how to annoy Jack. One of the most effective ways was to parade himself through the lot on a bicycle. Once when Jack complained Bogart called him a creep. That was when he knew he had gone too far.

He made an appointment to see Jack, whom he addressed as 'Colonel'. He then apologized. Jack never stopped admiring him for that.

'He's a big guy,' he said.

As for Bogart himself, he said of those times, 'I kind of miss the arguments I had with Warner. I used to love those feuds. It's like when you've fought with your wife and got a divorce. You kind of miss the fighting.'

Jack, however, was glad not to miss his acting. In 1945 came *To Have And Have Not,* the Ernest Hemingway story of gun-running in the Caribbean, which introduced both the world in general and Humphrey Bogart in particular to a sultry nineteen-year-old called Lauren Bacall. That really was chemistry!

But Betty (as everyone knew her at the studio) had enough memos from Jack to paper her dressing-room walls. In her biography *By Myself,* she recalls one from him that read 'Word has reached me that you are having fun on the set. This must stop.'

At one stage James Cagney told her, 'If you can survive even seven years at Warners, then you can conquer the world.' It was enough for her to conquer Bogart, who had now considered it worth while to sign a new contract with the studio; not for seven years, but for a record fifteen.

Bogart had little to lose by adding his signature to the document in December 1946. He would not only get 200,000 dollars a picture (also a record for the times) but the right to refuse stories and directors. Consequently, there was little chance of his being suspended for anything—unless, that is, he tried to interfere with any of Jack's personal obsessions.

Tennis remained the one that was closest to his heart. People who wanted to get on had to regard 'studio tennis' as important as showing up for work on time.

Jack was almost as proud of the studio tennis court as he was of the one at home.

In a generous mood—and, it has to be stressed, there were many—he said that anyone working at the studio could use it. It was an offer he began regretting almost as soon as he made it. That was when a group of mail-boys took him up on it. He was incensed, but there was clearly nothing he could do.

He worried over it for days. And then he found a solution. The question of a site for an aircraft-carrier scene in a new war film had constantly come up in studio conferences. The deck would have to be blown up by Japanese bombers, but that wasn't easy to do at the studio. The damage would be real.

That was when Jack's generosity took a new shape. 'I know,' he said. 'We'll use the tennis-court.'

Technical advisers rushed in to emphasize the gravity of the move. 'There'll be tracer bullets,' explained one. 'It'll all be broken up.'

'Do it,' said Jack. The court was destroyed, and he never had to see mail-boys playing there again.

CHAPTER 19

MISSION TO MOSCOW

He was captain of the ship—and tough with people.

Bill Orr

The status of Warner Bros in the nation was made very clear only three days before the end of the Second World War. The newly inaugurated President Harry S. Truman sent for Harry—a nice nose-thumbing operation to Jack, this, as far as the senior Warner brother was concerned—to seek advice on how the morale of the post-War public could be boosted.

Harry promised 'any help that the picture industry can give'. Note, he was patriotically speaking on behalf of the whole industry and not merely Warner Bros.

The President said that he believed 'motion pictures can assist in developing human beings out of barbarians', and desperately hoped that American films would be exported to enemy countries. They were sentiments totally geared to the way the film industry saw things themselves.

As far as Warners were concerned, they were going to put all their efforts into making entertaining and profitable films. In 1945, in a move they would take twenty years to regret, and as a first step towards that end, they divested themselves of their minority share interest in Decca Records, which amounted to about 1,800,000 dollars.

They were much more interested in showing that they were leading the way in the film business—even to the extent of giving away over a million dollars more to army charities, this time as a result of *Hollywood Canteen.*

In 1946 they celebrated the twentieth anniversary of the birth of the talkies with a giant birthday cake in the centre of New York's Columbus Circle.

Jack treated it all as a big party—and he loved parties, both when going to other people's and still more when holding his own, at which he could make all the jokes he liked, and at which no one would be discourteous enough not to laugh.

Occasionally, however, they would laugh at the wrong times, as when he and Ann held a party to unveil portraits of themselves painted by Salvador Dali.

The pictures were the talk of Hollywood, and hung in what had by now become the twin drawing-rooms, left and right of a huge hall. They were above the fireplaces at opposite ends of the two rooms.

Ann, who was exquisitely beautiful, was painted in an extremely low-cut gown showing a great deal both of her breasts and of her finest jewels. The only trouble was it was all in slightly sickly yellowy-green hues.

Paul Henreid insisted to me that he remembered that there was a desert scene as a background, and hidden in the corner of the picture was a birdcage, with Jack sitting in it. Loretta Young didn't remember the birdcage. What she did recall, however, was the way Jack looked in his portrait as a gift to any casting director. She told me, 'He looked like Douglas Fairbanks, with a gorgeous smile. But Ann's . . . I thought that if that were a picture of mine, I'd burn it. You could see who had paid for those pictures!'

But there was no getting away from the fact that, as the orchestra played and a hundred waiters passed glasses of champagne and plates of caviare from hand to hand, Jack was the perfect host.

Those parties really were quite remarkable. If David O. Selznick was renowned for having the most tasteful gatherings—and Ann could give him a run for his money as far as surroundings and the way the food was served—Jack's were the greatest fun.

He would order his studio wardrobe department to provide complete outfits in which his guests could dress up. On other occasions he would organize elaborate party games, like the time Rosalind Russell and director Edmund Goulding won a prize after swapping clothes with each other. Goulding totally destroyed the magnificent gown by Irene in which Rosalind had arrived at the party. It split in a different spot every time he moved, but everyone—including Miss Russell—enjoyed it immensely. And none more than Jack himself.

Despite what on the surface seemed a vast social circle, Jack was for a long time something of a loner. He was frightened of being betrayed by people he might befriend. So rather than be hurt, he would discourage close friendships.

Nevertheless, he went into the minutest detail to make his guests happy—even if he were trying to fire them.

For writer Mel Shavelson he provided a conducted tour of the magnificent house at Angelo Drive, explaining how the walls had come from the English stately home. 'And this parquet floor,' he said, 'if you look carefully you can see the old bloodstains. It came direct from Versailles, and the blood was from the French Revolution.'

'Gee, Jack!' said Shavelson. 'I could have sworn it came from your office.'

Jack laughed at that, although he appreciated that there was just a touch of sarcasm in Shavelson's riposte.

However, he wasn't so appreciative of jokes other people made at the expense of his guests. The eminent director Jean Negulesco said quite the wrong thing when Dali was a lunch guest at the studio just after the party.

Negulesco asked the chef to provide him with a half-cooked fried egg. When it was delivered, alone, on a wafer-thin china plate, the director looked at his dish, took off his wrist-watch and placed it square over the yolk. He then asked the waiter hovering behind his chair to place it in front of Mr Dali.

'Look,' he said. 'Still life.'

Jack could be seen to be involuntarily twitching his moustache in fury. 'You . . . you . . . you're fired,' he said. It was, of course, not a serious dismissal. Jack would have got someone else to do that for him. But he was very angry.

He was not, however, quite as upset as was Harry at some of the films the studio was turning out. Harry was constantly bombarding Jack with memos about the studio output. For the most part he didn't let any of the employees know: people remember him today as a gentleman. Jack knew him more as a prig who tried constantly to act the family patriarch.

It was largely through Harry's efforts that peace was finally made with the Hays Office, which by the end of the decade had become the Johnstone Office.

Jack Junior told me about that time, 'Uncle Harry was a puritan himself so he could usually agree with the Hays decisions, anyway. I don't think Uncle Harry would subscribe to *Playboy,* but I think he would have enjoyed it.'

Salaciousness wasn't really part of the Hollywood game at the time, although Howard Hughes was trumpeting his pictures of Jane Russell bursting the seams of her blouse in the advertisements for *The Outlaw.* They were much more concerned with the future of the industry after the massive changes brought on by the War. That was why Jack could proclaim, 'The future of the film industry has never lookd brighter—if we quit bickering, face the realities and really dig in to work for the peace we all realize we must have.'

Winning the other peace—the kind they fought the Germans and the Japanese for—was another matter entirely.

Early in 1947 Jack was awarded the Medal of Merit for the work the studio did in producing hundreds of training films, and for supplying prints of his other pictures to Service bases. That was a big plus for him later that year, when the Un-American Activities Committee started looking into Hollywood, and Jack and Warner Bros had to wriggle out of some very compromising situations.

Jack was the first witness called by the committee headed by Representative J. Parnell Thomas of New Jersey—in effect, Senator Joe McCarthy's predecessor. Before long Adolph Menjou told Thomas, 'Hollywood is one of the main centres of communism in America, but it is our greatest medium for propaganda.'

The suave actor, known as the best-dressed man in Hollywood, provided a list of names of communists and fellow travellers active in Hollywood.

He was merely following the example set by Jack Warner, who believed almost as a matter of religion that anyone disagreeing with him had to be a communist. In Jack's case it was partly no more than another row with his writers, only a much more serious one than that over timings and lunch tables.

He also said that he had failed to renew the contracts of 'at least a dozen writers because they held Un-American views'. It was music to the ears of the tribunal, but he had a series of ulterior motives. From his studio's point of view, it was a very good way of ending the contracts of people he wanted to get rid of.

He also foresaw trouble on the horizon over *Mission To Moscow*. It came more quickly than he would have imagined. The question came up very early in the hearings.

He acted, he said, out of pure patriotism. He was asked by the President to do it, and that was why he had done so. It was a sound move, that. To a lot of people Roosevelt had to be a communist, too.

Once he had asserted his unquestioned loyalty to his country Jack began to enjoy the hearings almost as much as he enjoyed his sessions in court. When he wasn't on the stand himself, noted *The New York Times*, he sat comfortably and played with his spectacles. They probably provided him with the same sort of comfort that in other places he got from his cigar.

Before long it dawned on him that he needed that comfort.

In fact, he was scared stiff by what had happened in 1943, and was using every weapon he believed to be at his command to pre-empt the trouble in which he thought he might find himself. Supplying the list wa a sure way, he believed, of getting the Committee on his side.

However, making his peace omelette with the Committee meant he had to break a great number of eggs, the careers of hitherto respected writers. The Epstein brothers, for instance, were at the top of his list. He had just had a big row with them, and wanted a convenient way of getting out of it.

He was before long forced to go into print, apologizing to a number of writers whom he had named. Julius Epstein told me, 'Because Jack was the first witness, his list with our names on it appeared on the front page. Looking down the list, we found that they were all people he either wanted to get rid of or who wanted to get out of their contracts. If you didn't want to work any more for Warner Bros, you had to be Un-American.'

(A little later on, when Martin Dies was running the Committee, it decided to get even tougher. The Epsteins, together with a lot of other people on the 'lists', were asked to complete a questionnaire. This read i) Have you ever been a member of a subversive organisation? ii) Name that organisation.

They wrote down 'i) Yes; ii) Warner Bros' and then never heard any more about it.)

Another who fenced with him about having his name included in the list was Irwin Shaw, later to be best known for his book *The Young Lions.* In a letter to *The New York Times,* he wrote:

> It is an example of the sick temper of our times that I feel forced to announce that I have never for a moment entertained the notion of overthrowing the Government of the United States, that I am not 'UnAmerican', which apparently is Mr Warner's way of saying 'Communist'.
>
> 'I am not and have never been a Communist and have fought the Communists in the American Veterans Committee.

He complained that as 'a citizen unjustly denounced in the nation's capital', he was not allowed a right of reply.

But he had advice to other writers:

> I say, "Come back children. Come back to Broadway. Leave the real movie making to the French, the Italians and the British who have demonstrated they have the courage to present life as it is and not as a political committee think it ought to be. . . .
>
> "Leave Hollywood now because the masters of Hollywood have defended you poorly and too late."

And he went on to list his other reasons for complaint:

> 1) I wrote a script for Warner Bros in 1941, which Mr Warner approved so highly he offered me a contract. I rejected this offer to go into the Army.
>
> 2) In the intervening years, Warner Bros tried to hire me again—again at constantly increasing prices—as recently as last Friday.
>
> 3) Among offers from Warner Bros was one last April to write a pro-democratic, anti-fascist, anti-Communist picture they were making.

Ambassador Davies, meanwhile, was fighting a lone battle over his *Mission to Moscow.* He denied that Warner Bros did not wish to produce the film, but did so only after being coerced into making it by Washington.

(A committee report published soon after the hearings declared that 'some of the most blatant propaganda films were produced as a result of White House pressure'.)

He denied, he said, 'categorically and unequivocally' that Roosevelt had had anything to do with it.

'It's a charge that defames the dead.'

On the contrary, said Davies, Hollywood 'to their credit were seeking material of the character of this book to aid the war effort'. He wrote it to help establish confidence in the Allies' cause.

Warner Bros came into the picture because I happened to know Harry Warner very well.

I had been impressed by his wisdom, his extraordinary public spirit, his intense devotion to our country, to our way of life and to our economic system of regulated competition and free economy.

Neither he nor I were Communists but we both felt intensely the necessity to beat Hitler and to protect the peaceful order in the world after the war, if that were possible.

He had told Harry about various offers made for the book's film rights, but he said 'he preferred his company to do it'.

The most damning part of Davies's denial of Roosevelt's alleged activity—Jack was squirming when he heard his evidence, to say nothing of his praise and admiration for Harry—was when he paid the organization a back-handed compliment. The Warners, he said, were 'three as fine and patriotic Americans as can be found in any industry.

'They are not the kind of people who can be coerced into doing anything that would be inimical to their beliefs, their convictions or the interests of their country.'

There was a great deal of truth in that last statement. The Warners, who, like Irving Berlin and other prominent ex-immigrants had for years been blowing the trumpet of their Americanism so loudly, now felt threatened. Would the country to whom they owed so much turn against them?

They knew too that there was more than a grain of antisemitism in the membership of the Committee. It was important to forestall any doubts of their loyalty.

Jack himself went overboard throughout the sorry period of the Committee investigations to show that his own sheet was as white as that of any rampaging Klu Klux Klansman. When Vincent Sherman was found to be on what was known as the 'grey list'—no proof of being a communist, but definitely left of centre—he was out of work for three years. As he told me, 'Warner didn't do a damn thing to help me.' And he added, in a telling phrase, 'If Jack had not been Jewish, he would have fought against McCarthy a lot harder.' In fact, he didn't fight him at all.

The brothers' fear of communism was much more a fear of what the Un-American Activities Committee could do to the studio. As was everything else, it became a topic of conversation at the writers' table—which was duly reported to Harry.

He called the Epstein brothers into his office.

'Boys,' said the President of the company, 'I understand you've been talking communistic.'

The eavesdropper was smiling to himself smugly in one corner.

Philip got up and punched the offending spy, who was fortunately both small and light.

'Shush,' said Warner. 'I have the same thing in my own family,' The word around the studios was that he had been complaining for some time about the liberal tendencies of Milton Sperling.

Jack meanwhile tried to explain that his antipathy to everything Russian was based on the folk memory of pogroms and Cossack assaults on the Warner ancestors.

The Committee inflicted a wound that would fester for years. In 1954 a judge dismissed a 51 million-dollar damages suit by twenty-three actors and writers who had been thrown out of work as a result of McCarthyism. Judge Elsworthy Meyer declared, 'The motion picture industry has a right to blacklist from employment workers who have refused to testify before the Committee.'

The Screen Actors Guild took a similar line. They even called on their eight thousand members to swear an oath of loyalty to the United States. 'No person who is a member of the Communist Party or any other organization seeking to overthrow the Government of the United States by force or violence can be eligible for membership,' it declared.

Edward G. Robinson's name came up before the Committee, not because he was proved to be a communist but because he had supported organizations which were considered left-wing. As far as Jack was concerned, it was enough to decide that Robinson's days as a big star were over.

After his stunning performance in *Key Largo* in 1948, Robinson was out of Warner Bros films until *The Mouthpiece* in 1955. He was no longer considered big box-office, or the sort that Jack Warner wanted to talk about.

And Jack thought he knew what big box-office would be. He cut his films minutely. 'Point to point' was his favourite expression, meaning that he didn't want to waste time seeing a door close or a car drive up if it didn't contribute something to the story. It was a philosophy he carried outside the studio too. In late 1947 he also thought he knew how the political box-office was working out. He became a member of the Board of Directors of the Draft Eisenhower For President League—five years before Ike himself was to make up his mind that *a*) he was a Republican and not a Democrat and *b*) that he was ready to run for the White House.

If only Jack had always been so right politically, and in his own business. Had he been, Warner Bros might have saved themselves a considerable amount of heartache in years to come when reflecting on Some More Who Got Away.

It was during the last year of the War that a maid employed by the Warners at their Angelo Drive home begged Ann to play a record to her husband. It wasn't an easy task, because Jack suspected everyone with whom he came into contact to be trying to get a contract of some kind or other.

When a girl called Maria had applied for a job Jack gave Ann his usual instruction: 'Make sure she hasn't got a script. She's coming to work here. Not in pictures.

'They are not going to sell me anything. I don't want to hear about the greatest story ever written.'

Ann would usually be more sympathetic, and when Maria came to her with a disc by a certain Alfredo Cocozza she promised to play it for Jack.

She did, and he was overwhelmed by the voice. 'He sounds like Caruso,' said Jack, who was not foolish. It *was* Caruso, with a hastily typed label pasted over the original.

However, Jack agreed to see the singer, who came along to the house and made the rafters ring. He was superb—the only reason he sent Jack a phoney recording was because he was in the Army and didn't have time to make one himself—but Jack didn't like his appearance.

The singer appeared to love spaghetti too much for Jack's enthusiasm to be whetted, and he thought he wasn't even worth offering a screen test. 'Sorry, young man,' said Jack, in one of the few instances of his announcing his own unpleasant decisions. 'I don't think the movies are for you.'

It was therefore up to MGM to offer a contract to Mario Lanza.

Something similar happened to a child who used to cycle past the Burbank lot to school every morning. By the age of sixteen she was brave enough to ask for a job at the studio. A casting director offered her a contract, at the lowest going rate of 65 dollars a week.

It was already too late to do anything about it when Jack spotted her on the lot. 'Who's that skinny, ugly girl?' he asked. He was told her name was Mary Frances Reynolds.

'That's a terrible name,' he told her when she was brought, somewhat trembling, into his office.

'No, from now on, you're Debbie Morgan.' He liked the name Debbie. But why Morgan? Because the biggest actor on the lot at that moment was Dennis Morgan—who was also giving a few problems at the time, hanging out at the neighbouring country club.

Years later she said of that time, 'I told him "Your ass it is!" [The memory of that moment is entirely hers.] I said, "I don't mind being called Debbie, but my name isn't Morgan. So if you like, I'll be called Debbie Reynolds".'

But Jack didn't think she was worth holding on to. He summarily fired Miss Mary Frances Reynolds as soon as he legally could do so. Conveniently for him—but totally in breach of her contract—she had another job behind a counter at the J. C. Penny department store. Her mother had advised her that that sort of job offered rather more security. But she eventually went back to the business, and was taken on by MGM. The rest—including *Singin' In The Rain*—is, as they say, history.

CHAPTER 20

THE BIG SLEEP

All the people who didn't like Warner, were the ones
who never worked for him. Those who worked for him
liked him very much.

Rudi Fehr

In July 1947 an announcement was made jointly by Warner Bros
and the RCA Victor company. They were together to initiate an
intensive programme of research into large-screen television.

It was not only a very prescient thing to do, it was also contrary to
everything in which the film industry in general and Warner Bros in
particular believed.

For while the research was initiated the studios were waging an
all-out war against the small screen, which was only threatening at
that stage to enter every home.

Much as they had with talking pictures, the studios first laughed at
the idea of TV catching on, and then became paranoiac about it.
Jack Warner himself was so terrified of the effect that television
could have on the motion-picture business that he personally issued
an edict banning the use of television to help in dressing the set for
any Warner Bros picture. Songwriters Paul Francis Webster and
Sammy Fain were ordered to rewrite the lyrics of a song because it
began, much to Jack's distaste, *I'm In Love With The Girl On
Channel Nine.*

It was the fear of radio all over again.

No one had thought that a tiny screen fitted into a wooden cabinet
would represent any threat at all. Until, that is, the film-makers
suddenly realized that there was a veritable stampede in the shops
to buy them.

By the end of 1947 the first signs of panic were apparent, and Jack
was leading the fear-mongers in no uncertain way.

Things were plainly beginning to affect the filmgoing habits of
people, and as their habits changed so did the takings at the box-
office.

Jack was issuing statements to the Press, making sure that people knew things weren't so good any more. And you didn't need a Warner glossary to understand what he meant.

'The spree is over,' he declared in one of them. 'We need more than mere showmanship to sell our movies.'

There was no clearer way of seeing how things were going than by studying the number of people who were slowly being laid off the Warner payroll. A few carpenters, electricians, scenery-painters. For the first time in modern history, the film industry looked as if it were contracting.

Significantly, when Irving Rapper had his last row with Jack he wasn't merely suspended. He was 'released' from his contract. The reason, said the studio, was an 'economy measure'.

Jack himself was reverting to the easy-going funsmith he always had been during (his phrase) turbulent times. With a clear conscience he could tell the truth and deny people rises—and say that everybody would just have to work harder. What was more, as one former Warner man told me, 'you'd end up feeling sorry for him'.

Jack knew that perfectly well. A week or so later he would call those same employees (a word he would use, much to their annoyance, when referring to the biggest stars on the Warner payroll) into his office and offer them half the increase in salary they had requested. They were so glad to have the cash offered without a second request that they accepted gladly.

He was always happier to give of his own volition than be pressed for money by other people. Vincent Sherman told me about him, 'He would take one step towards you and two steps back—in case you'd get too friendly and you'd ask for something.'

His fellow studio bosses felt much the same thing about him. They were intensely jealous of each other, which was one reason why the prices they charged to loan out a player—and sometimes a director—to another studio were always so inflated.

The business over *The Jolson Story* had soured completely what had been a fairly happy relationship between Jack and Harry Cohn, the boss of Columbia.

When Vincent Sherman was loaned to Columbia Jack told him, 'You'll be working for a no-good sonofabitch.' Which was precisely the terminology Cohn used to describe Jack.

Their row had been over money. Cohn had bought shares in Warner Bros, which might be regarded as hedging quite a few bets on his own outfit's success. Then he heard that Jack himself was selling some of his own shares. He rang the man he considered a friend to ask if it were true.

'Absolutely not,' Jack told him.

There the matter might have rested had it not been around the time of the Jewish High Holydays and he had occasion to go to a synagogue. He was sitting in front of one of the women of the Warner family, and happened to hear her saying to a friend, 'It might be a good idea to sell some of your Warner stock.'

Cohn was livid. He rushed out of the synagogue and immediately instructed his brokers—who had to be dragged out of a temple themselves—to sell. The brothers' plan was again to sell dear and then when the market was depressed buy back again cheap. It wasn't ethical, but it certainly seemed a good way of making some easy money.

As far as Cohn was concerned, it was the end of a friendship. It was also an indication of the way the economic situation was hitting the company.

Warners were continuing to divest themselves of subsidiary interests, although they kept their music-publishing division going and it made money, a state of affairs which led to yet another row between Jack and his brother Harry.

A meeting had been called by the three brothers—some idea of the importance of the situation was the fact that Abe had made the journey to the Coast to be there—to get home to employees that things were getting tough.

All the principal producers, directors and other executives were present, most of them men who had been told only days before that there was no chance of an increase in salary.

On occasions like that Harry liked to pose as the benevolent brother with the interests of the 'artistic' community he employed very much at heart.

At this meeting he allowed himself to be somewhat carried away. 'It is not only the money that counts in making a good studio,' he told them. 'With us it is the example we have always set for good citizenship.' It was like Jack claiming credit for making *Pasteur* and *Zola* and walking off with the Légion d'Honneur.

'Now,' said Harry, 'we have a music company. I don't know anything about the organization or what it does or how it does it. But I do know that it made four million dollars for us last year.'

Jack got up at that point and pulled Harry down into his chair. 'That's enough,' he said. 'You're talking too much.'

Harry had by then wondered whether it wasn't a good moment to retire, but he wouldn't do it unless Jack bowed out at the same time, and there was as much a chance of his doing that as of Senator McCarthy flying to Moscow.

To Jack being head of Warner Bros wasn't just having 50 million dollars in the bank—or more, if he were to realize all his assets. It was also having Cary Grant and Bette Davis calling him on the phone. It was having parties with Rosalind Russell as a guest. It was the odd invitation to dine at the White House. He knew he wouldn't

195

get them if he merely had the money. Discussions about the possibility of selling out only made his hold on power that much stronger, his resolve to keep it that way much more determined.

Abe, on the other hand, was all for not worrying at all about the future and getting out while they were still ahead. He had made a fortune on the stock exchange, and didn't need either the money or the headaches suffered by his two brothers.

'The movies were to him always an illegal business,' says Milton Sperling today. Jack saw it totally differently.

Now there wasn't a piece of film produced by his studio that he didn't see personally. He even saw the trailers before they were released, and there wasn't a director in the company who didn't get a message about them—usually saying, 'You're telling too much.' And he was most of the time absolutely right.

People—particularly Harry—would say that Jack was too much in control; a situation far removed from that of today, when the main complaint in Hollywood seems to be that there is no one to make decisions, no one to whom one can talk over problems.

That was always easy to do with Jack. When a star or a director could convince him that he wasn't after more money the pussy-cat in Jack Warner would start purring.

It was a marvellous opportunity, in the vaudeville parlance he loved so much, to be 'on'—which he nearly always was. When Red Skelton or another top comedian came to lunch it was like watching Errol Flynn and Basil Rathbone fencing with each other in *Robin Hood*. Except that the weapons were jokes, with Jack trying desperately to be as funny as the professional.

He was a delight to have as a party guest himself. Next morning he would report to his aides on the success or otherwise of the function. If he had thoroughly enjoyed himself he would discuss the guest list. 'Who's who and who's through was there,' was a favourite description of a party.

Julius Epstein sums up his character as being one of 'affable arrogance'. He was easy to talk to, even if he wasn't always so easy to listen to, although that was harder to stomach in public than it was at a private gathering.

As he got older, and as his surroundings in the house at Angelo Drive—by the end of the 1940s, there was a new house at Cap d'Antibes, the Villa Aujourd'hui, as well as two homes in Palm Springs, another house at La Jolla and a whole floor at the Sheri Netherlands Hotel in New York reserved only for his use—got even more luxurious and tasteful, Jack himself grew even more self-assured and more vulgar.

Surrounded as he was by pictures by Old Masters, furniture of the great craftsmen of Europe and—as a testimony to much of what was his own artistic sense—leather-bound scripts of every film Warner Bros ever made, the sight of Jack rising at his own dinner table was the signal for an exercise in masochism. Everyone knew there would be an entertainment—of a sort—but there was behind it always the not too hidden fear that someone was going to suffer. And it wouldn't just be Jack himself.

With Humphrey Bogart as guest of honour, he would raise his glass to 'the biggest ham in Hollywood', without apologies but also with the sure knowledge that he meant it.

At public functions he was just as predictably unpredictable.

Jack's speeches usually consisted of a dozen or more entirely unconnected thoughts linked together by his jokes. The language in which he expressed those thoughts was frequently suitable only for the lower decks of a warship. Whether he was addressing a group of Daughters of the American Revolution or of the Teamsters Union, he would attack people who didn't fulfil his own criteria of decency as a 'bunch of fuckers'.

When he got carried away by his enthusiasm he lost his line of thought completely. 'Wait a minute,' he'd tell them, sounding like Al Jolson warning that they ain't heard nothin' yet, but rustling through his notes, 'I have it . . . No . . . I've already told you that. . . . What the hell does it matter, anyway?' It was funnier watching him mangle his notes than listening to what he was trying to say. Although considering the trouble he went to in getting it all right in the first place, the exercise was quite remarkable.

Melville Shavelson wasn't the only one to write speeches for him. A team of Warner writers—and not just the funny ones—would be employed to do that. When he had their scripts in his hand he would go through each line as though an Academy Award depended on it. Every time he made a correction a page would have to be retyped. It was a task that was repeated perhaps a dozen or more times. But when he got up at the podium to make his speech the notes would come out, his glasses would be fixed to the bridge of his nose—and then he would say, 'I can't read this fucking nonsense, but I heard a great gag yesterday. . . .'

Harry's big mistake was to take Jack far too seriously and, while resenting him, to try to copy him. He decided it was time to move to the West Coast too. The stars liked him, he told his family, and he liked being with them. In truth he was flattered by their attentions, and they for their part thought it good policy to be nice to him.

He held his own lunches in the private dining-room. He wanted to know exactly what was happening in areas that had always been Jack's and not his. Consequently Jack resented Harry as much as Harry resented him.

As the rows between the brothers got more heated they also grew louder. Lowly employees could hear Harry berating his brother for wasting money, and Jack telling Harry that if he did more work he would be in a better position to complain.

'You should retire,' said Jack. 'We'll make you Life Chairman of the Board and you'll have a nice easy life.'

Harry's problem was that that 'nice easy life' was precisely what he wanted, but he was afraid to lose any of his responsibilities.

He sincerely thought that the life in California would make it easier for him to exercise his role as head of the family. When he bought a ranch in the San Fernando Valley as a suitable centre for his horse-breeding activities he had three homes built alongside it, for each of his daughters. He found it impossible to understand why none of the girls wanted to live there. The houses were never occupied in his lifetime.

That was never the sort of consideration that bothered Jack. Even now that he was getting older, the studio was the only thing that interested him. He wanted his life to be as tidy as the way he kept his desk, his family problems shelved the way he would put notes in the drawers behind him.

When things weren't going right the phrase that Bill Orr and the other studio executives coined for the temporary state of affairs was that he was 'scratchy'.

He didn't allow his relationship with Jack Junior to make him that way. He never saw his grand-daughters—Jack's children—because they might compromise his relationship with his son, who as far as the head of the studio was concerned was an employee but little else. His concession to family ties was to sign his memos to the younger man, 'Dad'.

It wasn't all roses for the girls in his family, either, although he was a lot warmer in his relationship with Barbara and Joy. It wasn't unusual, however, for him to send either of them rushing away from the dinner table crying after Jack had, to use his own expression, 'told them how things were'.

Joy experienced his wrath rather more than did Barbara, who was educated in Switzerland and was only home occasionally. But, as Bill Orr says, 'he came over rather strong'. Which was precisely how he came over at Burbank.

Abe managed to stay above it all, and because he did, the Warner employees loved him. He was, as he entered old age, still a huge bear of a man, but he was a teddy bear. Max Burcutt, who went to work in the Warner publicity department, had been there only a day when Abe told him, 'Hey, kid, you look as though you need a vacation.'

But there was more to him than that. Bill Orr recalls today, 'I used to think that he was the brother who knew most what was going on.'

Of course, he knew more than anyone else about the antipathy between Jack and Harry, which was now reaching crisis proportions. Although their fights could sometimes be heard in outer offices, employees were remarkably discreet in talking about them.

One fight, however, was more public—although, strangely, it has never been written about until now. It became so heated that Harry picked up a crowbar and chased Jack out of the office with it, shouting at the top of his voice as they ran through the open lot, 'I'll get you for this, you sonofabitch.'

As Milton Sperling, one of the spectators of the incident, told me, 'That was an expression of pure hate.' To say the least.

Afterwards Jack joked, 'The only reason he didn't hit me with that crowbar was because I could run faster than he could.'

Some of the stars wished they could run faster than Jack, too.

Too many bad films were being made. One of the worst, in fact, turned out to be one of the most momentous—because *Beyond the Forest* was the last film Bette Davis made for Warner Bros under her contract.

So bad was this story of small-town murder, adultery and wholesale misery that Bette had threatened to walk out before it was finished if she wasn't released. Jack could have held her to another ten years, but faced with that sort of threatening unhappiness, he decided that it was time to call the past eighteen years a day. She completed the film, with a symbolic last line that deserves one day in the far future to be inscribed on her tombstone. It said all that she had ever felt about Warner Bros, 'I can't stand it here any more.'

Writing in *Mother Goddam,* she says of this incident: 'I have always felt guilty for doing what I did to Warner Bros when I got my release. It was dirty pool on my part, but I was that desperate.'

And Jack wrote in his memoirs that she was in the hands of her agents—to him just about the lowest breed of humanity.

'Before long, the ten per-centers had Bette so confused that it affected her story vision and she was laying bigger eggs than an ostrich.'

CHAPTER 21

DEADLINE MIDNIGHT

These are turbulent times; turbulent times.

Jack L. Warner

Jack's principal recipe for success in running Warner Bros as well as he did was his penchant for detail.

Directors pulled out their hair at what they considered mere nit-picking, but it was the fact that he knew every face on the lot and what could be done with that face that raised him above his competitors in the film business. With no Hal Wallis to see things along, the title 'Jack L. Warner in charge of production' meant exactly what it said. He was the man in charge.

He wasn't always right. His insistence on banning TV sets was ridiculous, his concern over facial blemishes often stupid, because they could add character to otherwise benign expressions. His racial intolerance was downright unforgivable. At times his conversation on such subjects was nothing less than disgraceful.

Jack once ordered a scene showing two Blacks kissing to be not merely cut from a movie but the piece of film destroyed. 'It's like watching two animals,' he declared in one of his less charming asides to Steve Trilling. 'Terrible!'

But at other times, using the kind of instinct with which men can only be born, he could spot precisely what was wrong with a movie; identify the specific problem that had mystified other people working on the same project.

Back in his earliest days in the business, he had ruled that no one in a Warner Bros film should wear a particularly ornate tie. 'I don't want people looking so closely at a guy's tie that he ignores his face,' was an injunction that costume designers took to heart.

When George Raft made *Manpower* Jack sent a tetchy memo down to the set insisting that the actors' collars were too long and pointed.

Bill Orr's first mission on behalf of his future father-in-law was after Jack spotted something wrong with Ronald Reagan. It was long before anyone conceived of him being President of the Screen Actors Guild, let alone of the United States.

What Jack noticed was that Mr Reagan's shirt-collar looked loose.

It was up to Bill to find out why. 'We've been looking at the dailies,' said Orr, 'and your shirt seems to be very ill-fitting. Did it come that way from wardrobe?'

Reagan was very upset. 'I've lost a lot of weight,' he said. 'Don't you know what's happening? Jane [Wyman] and I are splitting up.'

Orr felt sufficiently chastened. The matter didn't end there. Not only did Jack insist on a whole new wardrobe being tailored for Ronald Reagan, but Harry regarded it as unnecessary interference which was going to cost a lot of money.

He also regarded it as an impertinence on the part of Bill Orr. 'Young man,' he called him next day. 'Come into my office and sit down.'

Orr went in, shaking slightly. But he was let down gently. 'I don't want you to get off on the wrong foot. And I think you're throwing your weight around and upsetting the actors.'

The truth of the matter was that David Butler, the director, had heard about it and reported what he considered to be Jack's interference to the one man whom he knew would share that resentment.

Reagan's big moment at Warner Bros came in 1950, when with Patricia Neal he was sent to London to make *The Hasty Heart,* about a group of patients in a military hospital in Burma. It was the film that made Richard Todd into a star as a kilt-wearing Scotsman. But Reagan—proving that he was much more than the 'B' picture actor recent folklore has made him—was quite outstanding.

The film was made in England because the post-War foreign exchange regulations meant that a great deal of Warner money was frozen in the country. Warners owned 40 per cent of Associated British Pathé and decided that a co-production with the firm would be a way of making the money work for them.

The picture, produced and directed by Vincent Sherman, was one of the big box-office successes of 1950.

It was lucky for Sherman that it was. His previous Warner film had been *Backfire*—'It contained so many flashbacks I didn't know where the hell I was'—which had been made on Jack's personal insistence.

'Look,' he said, persuading Sherman to do the job. 'Every film you make can't win an Academy Award. Besides, I've got eight actors sitting on their asses doing nothing, so I want to use them. For God's sake, put them to work.'

The Hasty Heart was a better idea from the first. But Reagan was beginning to upset Jack.

Two years later, in *She's Working Her Way Through College,* he declared that he didn't like his lines and inprovised his own dialogue.

Jack was furious. He called the director, Bruce Humberstone, into his office and demanded, 'What's this I hear about you letting a damned actor write his own lines?'

Reagan himself later allowed Jack to compare the two versions. 'You win,' said Warner.

By that time the studio had far more serious things to worry about. The whole industry was undoubtedly changing, and so quickly that not even Jack could be sure which way it was heading.

The past few years had seen their ration of successes, but it was a smaller bite into an already shrinking market.

Things had been slowing down for Warners since 1946, when *The Big Sleep* and *Humoresque* with John Garfield and Joan Crawford were the only really outstanding movies. The following year Irene Dunn had to put up with Jack's jokes for the compensation of co-starring with William Powell in *Life With Father.* Joan Crawford was in *Possessed,* and Bogart and Bacall teamed for the third time in *Dark Passage.*

It was a bit better in 1948—*Key Largo,* with Edward G. Robinson making his comeback but taking second place to Bogart; Jane Wyman getting her best-actress Oscar for *Johnny Belinda,* the story of a raped deaf-mute; and Bogart again in *The Treasure of the Sierra Madre.* The last was the film in which Jack sat exasperated watching Bogie gasping for sustenance while searching for gold in the Mexican desert. 'If this guy doesn't find water soon,' he said, 'I'll go broke.'

As it turned out, John Huston's direction of *The Treasure* cost 3 million dollars but made Warner Bros a fortune.

1949 was somewhat less vintage—Danny Kaye making *The Inspector-General* was the only title worth mentioning in a batch that was headed in every sense of the term by James Cagney's return to the studio in *White Heat.*

It was a tour-de-force performance in which Cagney brilliantly played a mother-fixated psychopath. The final line as he dies in a massive explosion—'Made it, Ma, top of the world!'—seems destined to be remembered for ever.

Warners heralded the picture as being a return to the gangster era. But it wasn't. Standing alone, it now looks all the better.

The year 1950 was, apart from *Hasty Heart,* best remembered for Warners' decision to return to the musical, aided principally by their biggest property of the decade, Doris Day.

She had made her debut for the studio two years earlier in *Romance On The High Seas* and was already sufficiently established for them to build stories around her.

Her second Warner film was *It's A Great Feeling*—which it was anything but for Jack Warner, who suddenly found himself without Dennis Morgan. Morgan was one of a group of actors for whom Jack used to send search-parties to the neighbouring Lakeside Country Club—in fact, he got so fed up with weeding him, Flynn and the others in their group from the Club that he decided to try to buy it; that way he could ban them from going there, but he found the price too high. Now Morgan was not available to make the film. He was quite suddenly no longer on the staff.

Jack's problem was that he had a *Two Guys* picture planned which was already booked into a couple of thousand cinemas all over America. With six weeks to completion date, there was not only no star but no sets either. And no story.

Morgan had been suspended for so long that no one at the studio noticed that his contract had expired. In short, Warners no longer had an option on his services at his former salary. For Jack that was terrible news. The *Two Guys* were by now an established part of the Warner output, and couldn't exist without Morgan's services. To inveigle him back to the lot with his sidekick Jack Carson, Warners had to quadruple his salary. The next problem was getting out a story.

That was sorted out by Melville Shavelson, who suggested using it as a vehicle for Doris Day, playing a waitress at the Warner Bros commissary.

The idea to adapt the story to Warners' own back yard was a good move, for not only could they use the actual Warner studios as a set, there would also be virtually free use of a whole host of players working for the company at the time.

Hence there were appearances by Gary Cooper, Joan Crawford, Danny Kaye and the apparently ubiquitous Ronald Reagan, to say nothing of Errol Flynn, who exacted suitable recompense from the studio for deigning to turn up.

Jack hadn't yet cured himself of the chronic indigestion from which he suffered at the hands of his writers, at the moments when he wasn't filled with admiration for them. His reactions took curious forms, such as blacking out what he considered unpleasant memories or disliked faces from his consciousness. When he met Jack Rose and Melville Shavelson, for instance, he would greet them with 'Hello, boys.' On one occasion he saw Rose alone. He still said, 'Hello, boys.'

Jack was calling them something else when they came to him with a story based on the Penrod and Sam stories, which in certain parts of the United States are as close to holy writ as *Huckleberry Finn* and *Tom Sawyer*.

Shavelson and Rose had been told to produce yet another tale for Doris Day, who would now be co-starring with the popular singing star Gordon MacRae. They came to the conclusion that a new tale set in a fairground and based on their own favourite childhood heroes Penrod, Sam and their dog Duke would fit the bill nicely. Jack didn't think so.

'We made one of those in 1937,' he said, 'and we're still trying to get the smell out of the theatres. Come up with something else.'

Shavelson did. He returned the same typescript only with the names changed—to Harry, Jack and Albert. 'I was fired not long after that,' he told me.

Before they went, however, Jack chose the film's final title for them.

Sitting behind his desk, with the ever-loyal Steve Trilling at his side, he ordered the Warner music catalogue to be brought into the office, together with a toothpick.

Without looking, he flipped the pages of the book and then stabbed one of them with his toothpick. 'Here's your title,' he said, and showed the writers where the instrument had landed. 'On Moonlight Bay'. As Shavelson says, 'That was the end of the story conference.'

Somehow they had to find room for a song that Warners already owned and build their story around it. And Jack's toothpick had already decided what song that should be.

Now, two very conscientious writers, determined that everything they wrote should be worth an Academy Award if not a Pulitzer Prize, would have come up with a brand-new script. Rose and Shavelson already had a script about a fairground, so henceforth the fairground would be known as Moonlight Bay. Jack was none the wiser, since he never read more than the first page of a script anyway.

It turned out to be one of the public's favourite Doris Day movies. Others came in remarkable profusion. *West Point Story,* co-starring James Cagney, was followed by the much better *Tea For Two,* supposedly a remake of *No, No, Nanette* but much more an excuse for Doris to show her teeth and sing the title song.

Within a matter of months of the other titles, came what was probably the best of the bunch, *Lullaby of Broadway*. This was another excuse to use more songs in the Warner catalogue, but since it gave a marvellous modernized airing to the Harry Warren-Al Dubin repertoire (as well as, among others, Gershwin—*Somebody Loves Me*—and Cole Porter—*Just One Of Those Things*) it was a delight.

Doris Day had now taken over from Bogart and Bette Davis as the studio's number one star and principal investment. Before long she was making *I'll See You In My Dreams* and *By The Light Of The Silvery Moon*.

Others were playing the musical game too. June Haver made *The Daughter Of Rosie O'Grady,* which gave a good idea of the paucity of ideas then current, and the nostalgia in which the new decade and half-century were encouraging people to wallow.

There was Ray Bolger in the filmed version of the famous *Charley's Aunt* story, *Where's Charley,* and Danny Thomas in a sorry remake of *The Jazz Singer.*

It was the golden age of what had become known as the musical biopic. *I'll See You In My Dreams* had been a joyous example of that. It told the story of Gus Kahn, one of the outstanding song-writers of the turn of the century. *The Story of Will Rogers* was moderately successful, and featured among others Eddie Cantor, who was himself portrayed in *The Eddie Cantor Story,* which was a disappointment to all.

Cantor himself had hoped it would do for him what *The Jolson Story* had done for his biggest rival in show-business, Al Jolson, who had now been dead for two years. To Jack it was an opportunity to revenge himself for what had happened six years earlier. He thought he had all the ingredients, a star who was so like Jolson in style and appeal, a story that seemed quite as warm, and the same director (Alfred E. Green) and producer (Sidney Skolsky). The result was a disaster.

For a brief time after that the studio reconsidered its musical policy and began to mark time on the genre.

There were Westerns, like Gregory Peck in *Only The Valiant* and Randolph Scott in *Fort Worth.* It was a time for spectacles like Burt Lancaster's *The Crimson Pirate* and Gregory Peck and Virginia Mayo in *Captain Horatio Hornblower.* Peck told me he wanted the English star Margaret Leighton in the Mayo role. She was more British than Mayo possibly could have been, he said. The director, Raoul Walsh, took Greg's request direct to the top.

A few days later Jack told him his decision.

'No dice with the Leighton dame,' he said.

'Why not?' asked Walsh.

The reply was succinct and unanswerable. 'No tits.'

Meanwhile there were also a few Warner dramas to concentrate on—a couple of terrible movies for Joan Crawford, *Goodbye My Fancy* and *This Woman Is Dangerous,* which signalled the end of her Warner Bros contract; James Cagney playing an alcoholic in *Come Fill The Cup*; Robert Walker and Farley Granger in *Strangers On A Train*; and a film that caused the biggest censorship rumpus

205

since Jane Russell's breasts, *A Streetcar Named Desire,* starring Vivien Leigh and a young unknown by the name of Marlon Brando.

That film not only had the Catholic Legion of Decency in uproar, it was the cause of a huge flare-up between Jack and his director Elia Kazan.

Jack personally ordered cuts in the picture after Kazan's work was finished. They weren't important, Kazan admitted, nor did they affect the kind of film it was, but the affair caused a flurry of discussion in newspapers throughout the world.

In a long article in *The New York Times,* Kazan said that the studio had been 'generous' to him, providing the best cast, cameramen and other artists and technicians. His work had been completed, he had gone to work on another movie, and *Streetcar* booked into the Radio City Music Hall. It was then cancelled, because the Legion of Decency had given it a 'C' rating, which meant that no Catholic would be allowed to see it.

Twenty years later a 'condemned' notice would guarantee a box-office sensation, but not then. Jack was afraid that a huge chunk of his paying audience would be lost. So with the help of a Catholic layman, he cut the film again to suit the Legion.

Kazan was furious. As he wrote,

> My picture had been cut to fit the specifications of a code which is not my code, is not the recognised code of the picture industry and is not the code of the great majority of the audience.

And he went on:

> As to the cuts themselves, I believe that if the audience—any audience—could see projected on the screen the footage which was cut out of *A Streetcar Named Desire* in order to protect the morals of that portion of them who are Roman Catholics, they would be overwhelmed by a bewilderment which would leave them, ever after, suspicious of censorship.

Among the cuts were the final three words of the sentence 'I would like to kiss you softly and sweetly on the mouth.' Which gives one some idea of how things have changed in a generation.

His final words summed up the total effect of the cuts. 'Meanwhile the box office is breaking records.'

It was a welcome fact, because not very much was doing anything of the kind in the early years of the 1950s. The trouble over *Streetcar* confirmed the fact that Warners, like other studios, were trying to play things safe and not take risks. Jack wasn't even going out of his way to find new talents or stories that would make the outstanding films. He wasn't making his pilgrimage tours to Broadway to see what the stage had to offer.

However, members of his staff were. Bill Orr saw Clifford Odets's play, *The Country Girl*, about an actor who hit the bottle and as a result was filled with self-pity. 'We have to buy it, Chief,' he said. But Jack's reaction was summed up by a staccato 'Oh, Jesus! Another story about a drunk! Who cares? No, thanks.'

Somehow or other Orr managed to get his father-in-law into the Broadway theatre. Throughout the first act he was shuffling around uncomfortably. When it came to the intermission Orr repeated, 'We must buy this, Chief.'

All the 'Chief' would say was 'No'.

Jack hated stories about alcoholics, and resisted them whenever he could. This time, it was difficult to turn down the arguments that Orr proffered. 'We've got Bogart for the lead. Jane Wyman could repeat what she has just done in *Johnny Belinda* and we could get Kirk Douglas to play the agent.'

Again the answer was no.

For once a Warner executive was not prepared to let the Colonel—a title that was infinitely more suitable than any other when a strategy had to be worked out—have the last word about a possible new film.

Steve Trilling and Henry Blanke backed him. But Jack still said no.

Finally he told his son-in-law, 'Just to get you off my back, I'm making an offer.' But he didn't tell Orr what that offer would be. He later found out—a mere 25,000 dollars. It wasn't accepted.

Paramount made a much more realistic offer, and the result was an Oscar for Grace Kelly and the warmest praise for Bing Crosby and William Holden.

'Jack never mentioned it again,' said Orr. 'Naturally, I'd give him a zing about it now and again.'

Had Warners done the deal that Bill Orr wanted, with Bogart in the Crosby role, things might have been very different for the studio. As it was, before long Bogart was off the list of Warner contract players, and even Errol Flynn was missing from the Warner roster.

Bogart had decided he had had enough after yet another row with Jack. The 'longest contract in Hollywood history' was cancelled. It cost Bogart 100,000 dollars.

After making two Warner pictures, Kirk Douglas too declared he didn't want to make any more. He paid a similar sum.

Soon afterwards Jack decided he had had enough of Flynn too. His generally bad behaviour had been in breach of their agreement. 'I think we should come to a similar arrangement,' said Jack. 'You pay us a hundred thousand dollars.'

Flynn's reply was predictable. He wasn't going to pay anything because it was Warner who wanted the deal ended. As far as he was concerned, he'd sweep up the men's room if that was what Jack wanted. He would turn up for work and do what was required. 'If you insist on ending the deal, why not turn things the other way? You pay me a hundred thousand.'

Jack said that he was willing to be charitable. He'd accept fifty thousand. Finally they did a deal. No one would pay anything, and Errol would be out as soon as he could get his things together.

It wasn't the end of his association with the studio, but at least Jack knew there would be no more rows like the one that followed the previous year's film *Starlift*, a kind of *Hollywood Canteen* for the Korean War. Almost everyone on contract agreed to take part in the film for a mere five thousand each.

All, that is, except Errol Flynn.

Bill Orr was asked by Jack to try to talk terms with him.

'What's in it for me, chum?' asked Errol. He was told about the 5,000 dollars.

'Well,' he replied. 'That doesn't seem to be a magnificent sum.'

'Do you want to come in?' asked Orr.

'Come in, chum? When not on salary?'

They agreed to meet after a tennis game. Errol arrived still wearing his tennis shirt—or at least one of the white ruffled shirts that had been made for *Don Juan,* one of the five of everything he somehow had managed to get the wardrobe department to supply.

He tried to persuade the company to furnish him with a car to cover the deal. In the end they decided it was safer to leave well alone.

Jack's trouble was that he liked Errol's company too much. When Errol met him soon afterwards in the South of France he suggested that the Warners might like to have use of his yacht, the *Zaca*—Jack's own vessel was, for some reason, out of commission.

Jack jumped at the opportunity. Errol shook his hand, bowed low to Ann and waved as the boat disappeared towards the horizon. What Flynn had failed to point out was that the fuel gauge was faulty, and that he knew there was only about half a gallon of petrol in its tank.

Within half an hour an angry Jack was jumping up and down on the deck, calling Flynn every vituperative word in his exceedingly wide vocabulary. He eventually got back to shore in a small motor-boat.

CHAPTER 22

I SELL ANYTHING

I always thought he was a clown.

Loretta Young

At the end of 1952 Jack Warner decided that it had been stupid to panic over the future of the industry. TV wasn't going to make it after all.

A film produced with the full intention of catching the great big television public called *Always Leave 'Em Laughing* left Jack first angry and then hilariously happy.

The picture, starring Milton Berle—'Uncle Miltie' to the hundreds of thousands of TV fans in the States—looked as if it were going to be the biggest Warner success story in the past ten years.

If reviews meant big box-office it was unbeatable. They were so good, in fact, that a few weeks later Jack called the producer Jerry Wald into his office and seriously accused him of buying up all the critics on the East Coast.

They weren't just good, they were sensational. The first week's business in New York confirmed the power of the Press, and then it took a nose-dive. No one came to see the film, and the reason, Jack decided, was because there weren't so many TV fans about after all. Either not nearly as many people had television as he feared, or if they did have it the small screen had stopped making any impact.

He came to London soon afterwards, declaring that it had all been an unnecessary fright.

'Even in America,' he said, 'it is finding its level; realizing its limitations.'

No, the film industry would not lose out to the newcomers. Not only was he not going to allow Warner films to be shown on television, but there would also be a ban on films made for TV being shown on the big screen.

Warner films were swinging to colour. Of the next thirty-three productions planned, twenty-seven would be in either Technicolor or his company's own rival system, Warnercolor.

But Jack nevertheless knew that a new dimension was needed to keep audiences going to the movies—and if it was not going to be forthcoming from the company who gave the world *The Jazz Singer* and everything that followed, then who else?

The result was that Jack decided to invest his all in 3-D—the 'deepies' as people began to dub them, following on the analogy of the 'talkies'.

He had been beaten to the post by United Artists with *Bwana Devil* in late 1952, but that was of no consequence. Warner's *House of Wax* in which fire and everything portable was thrust out into the audience would be better than anything else. Not only that, the company had developed stereophonic sound, a system first tried more than ten years earlier with Walt Disney's *Fantasia,* but with the twenty-eight speakers in use at Warner theatres it would be magnificent. Although, of course, it would be the pictures that would drag people through the turnstiles.

A certain millionaire optics-manufacturer by the name of Milton Gunsberg thought so too. When Jack Warner took out from his pocket an experimental pair of his 3-D spectacles and said, 'Soon everyone in the world will own a pair of these' it was Gunsberg who was won over more than anyone else.

He immediately committed his company to cash in on Jack L. Warner's philosophy. Could a man who knew so much about the cinema habits of the nation and who had heralded so much originality in the film business be wrong? He could—and the twenty million pairs of spectacles which Mr Gunsberg would still be happy to unload at a very reasonable price are a testimony to the fact.

Strangely, it was a studio of which no one had previously taken much serious notice that predicted it would all be a five-minute wonder.

Herbert J. Yates, head of Republic Pictures, had warned, 'I can't see how it can be expected to last. Now we are asking people to put on glasses to look at movies. It may be good for a while, but what do we do when the novelty wears off? Maybe some of us will expect audiences to stand on their heads, too.'

He was totally right. People didn't want to wear glasses when they didn't have to do so, and those who wore spectacles already didn't like the idea of putting on a second pair.

The real answer to the problem came from Twentieth Century-Fox, who in 1954 released *The Robe* in CinemaScope, a wide-screen system which had been known about for years but which seemed to be perfected. It came at much the same time as Cinerama —a far bigger and wider screen process, but with the distinct disadvantage that it required three cameras, three projectors and two lines down the middle which audiences were expected to try to ignore; considering the fact that the three images were unable to keep completely still, it wasn't easy.

Both systems were proudly advertised throughout the media as having a single special advantage: 'You see it without special glasses.'

The other companies didn't know quite what to do. Paramount developed their own system, which they called VistaVision. Warners announced that theirs would be WarnerScope. Before long CinemaScope was adopted by everyone, much to the relief of exhibitors who didn't know what kind of screen with which to equip their theatres. They needed something. Jack had been wrong again. Television was really sweeping the world now, and the habits of generations were being broken. People just didn't want to go to the movies any more.

That was what made Warner Bros decide to go into TV themselves. It was a reluctant move, one that Jack and everyone else hoped would have to be wound up—because people would want the excitement they could only get in a theatre.

It didn't work out that way. But he tried. In charge of the TV company was an executive who was chosen simply because he was the only one at Burbank who knew what a commercial or a time-slot was, but who knew next to nothing about production.

Before long Bill Orr was put in charge of the TV offshoot. One of the first things he commissioned was a series based on the greatest Warner success of all, *Casablanca.*

As usual, Jack was asked if he wanted to see the films before they left the lot. 'Yes, sure,' he said. But as if seeing something for television was a gesture of disloyalty to all that was good about Hollywood, he kept putting it off.

Finally, after a week he called his son-in-law. 'Let's see,' he said, 'what is it . . . *Casablanca?*'

'Sure,' said Orr. 'But it'll be just for your enjoyment. All the prints have been taken to the TV companies.'

'Nothing leaves these studios without my seeing it first,' he shouted. The thumps on the desk vibrated the ceiling of the room underneath.

'I insist on seeing it.'

'Well, you will, Chief,' said Orr. 'On Tuesday night with everyone else. That's when it's on the air.'

After that Jack and Bill were selective with each other. The Chief decided that TV was really too demeaning for him to bother in the way that he did with 'real' movies.

TV wasn't the only change that came about in 1952. It was also the year when the Government finally put its foot down and decided

211

it was illegal for studios to have their own theatres. Warners' practice—and that of the other film companies—was held to be in breach of every anti-trust law in the nation.

Nearly five hundred theatres had to be sold all over America.

If the present state of television wasn't the beginning of the end for the film industry, that piece of legislation certainly was.

But then, just as things looked their blackest, and as if once more deciding that today's newspapers were never more than tomorrow's toilet paper, Jack set about thinking of the big movies he was still going to make.

He could go on with his daily visit to the private barber shop, order a facial and then, as his fingers were manicured, ponder on the fact that life was still good and going to get better.

Once he himself had stopped worrying, he decided to start cheering up other people too. Early in 1953 he declared that Warners had 1,600 production workers employed full-time on a whole new batch of feature films.

'That is Warner Bros' answer to the state of the motion-picture business,' he declared.

But the box-office take kept dropping just the same.

He put part of the blame on his actors. 'Every sonofabitch is trying to win an Academy Award instead of making money,' he declared at one session around the lunch table.

A few days later he was taking an even more cynical approach. 'Gee,' he declared. 'Won't it be great when the actors are starving again!'

For a time the story was that Warner Bros would be up for sale before long. When a San Francisco syndicate seemed to be near finalizing a sale of the family's own shares in the firm the deal was suddenly called off. And without explanation.

The truth was that Harry told Abe he couldn't trust Jack's part in it all, and suspected he was trying to organize a coup behind their backs. Things therefore went on much as they had before, but with Jack himself more determined than ever to show that he was fully in control.

That still didn't go for firing people. Hoyt Bowers was pressed to sign a seven-year contract with the studio. 'I had been there for two years, but after the third year I figured I was high enough and didn't want to sign.

'The word came from the studio manager how Mr Warner felt. I still said no. So I was fired. I knew it would come at three o'clock because Jack left for Palm Springs at two-thirty.'

When the Warner Chief of Police retired Bowers returned to Burbank for the celebrations. Jack saw him and shook his hand warmly, as though nothing had happened.

Jack, uncharacteristically underdressed, receiving an award from General 'Hap' Arnold

Tennis made Jack feel young. His opponents knew it was better not to try to win – although on this occasion he and Solly Biano could only manage consolation prizes

Hal Wallis welcoming Harry at an Academy Awards evening

The happiest pose of all: Jack facing his own cameras

Jack and his empire

Marking the twenty-fifth anniversary of talking pictures in 1952, Jack with Abe and Harry cut a monster cake. Not forgotten in the background – a picture of Sam

Bill Orr with his father-in-law Jack Warner. In the centre, columnist Godfrey Wynn

Making his last big deal in the big office, with Rex Harrison and Audrey Hepburn after they had signed to make *My Fair Lady*

Audrey Hepburn and Rex Harrison in *My Fair Lady*

With Earl Mountbatten of Burma

But a great deal was happening now, and things would never be the same again.

Warner films had for the most part lost their old sparkle. Somehow symptomatic of the changes was the shape of the Warner shield. Throughout the 1930s and most of the '40s it had been an emblem that indicated something very exciting was on the way. Its silvery sheen represented both dignity and strength—and quite enough of each to assure the forces of good citizenship that Warners were still waging the fight against the onslaught of evil.

The shield was replaced by a wider, lack-lustre monogram inside a mere outline of its former glory. It was a true reflection on what was on offer.

The excitements were now very few. True, in 1954 Judy Garland shone from her updated version of *A Star Is Born* with James Mason acting magnificently opposite her. Nevertheless, anyone choosing to regard the downfall of a Hollywood star as a mere representation of what was happening in the film town itself wouldn't have been far off the mark.

There was absolutely nothing that year that came near it in prestige or good filmcraft. The year afterwards had the benefit of James Cagney teaming up with Henry Fonda in the middle of his career, William Powell at the end of his, and Jack Lemmon on the threshold of one of the great Hollywood success stories, in *Mister Roberts*.

There was also the promise of another brilliant career at its dawn in the shape of James Dean in both *East of Eden* and *Rebel Without A Cause*. Meanwhile Frank Sinatra tripped over to Burbank for *Young At Heart*—made at a time when he could do no wrong; it was just a couple of years after *From Here To Eternity* and he was at his peak. But these were mere isolated incidents.

If Warner Bros had had a magic touch, it seemed to have slipped. Even Edward G. Robinson's movie, *Illegal,* in which he played a slick lawyer, had none of his old fire.

In 1956 there was only the third James Dean picture, *Giant*—co-starring a magnificent Elizabeth Taylor borrowed from MGM —and *Baby Doll*, which involved even more censorship problems than *Streetcar*.

Even Gregory Peck was disappointed in his version of *Moby Dick,* directed by John Huston, which should have been a blockbuster. One of the most notable features of the picture was the rubber whale to which the star found himself clinging in the midst of a sudden pea-souper fog somewhere in the Irish Sea. The boat towing the whale broke its line and the two became separated, with Peck lost, it seemed, to all other human life. Eventually he was rescued—but the whale went on its way, and has not been seen

213

since. It could still be roaming the oceans of the world, like Captain Ahab, searching, searching. . . .

The Brothers Warner were similarly lost and searching for a formula at about the same time.

They talked about buying a record company—first suggested by film editor Rudi Fehr, a close friend of Jack's—an idea that would eventually bear fruit with the purchase of Frank Sinatra's label *Reprise*. However, it was the Warner film interests which, as ever, caused most concern. There were stories that Burbank was up for sale again.

The first indication came in March 1956, when the studio announced it was ready to sell its film library for television use—a surrender if ever there had been one. It ended up selling total rights to every film it made up to 1950—for 21 million dollars. They were bought by a corporation of investors (who later sold the films to United Artists) led by Elliot Hyman. Hyman is today head of Warner Bros.

The film city was by now certain that the studio itself would soon be sold. Errol Flynn sent Jack a telegram begging: CHIEF DON'T SELL WHO WILL I FIGHT WITH?

The rumours persisted. Jerry Wald was tipped to succeed as the new studio boss, but it didn't happen. What did come was news of an economy programme at the studio. Jack announced that eighty-five employees would have to lose their jobs.

It might have caused an even greater uproar in the industry than it did had not the brothers finally announced that they were after all selling out.

After all those years, could it mean that there would be no longer a Warner brother among the Warner Brothers?

The announcement was that the brothers were selling 800,000 shares for 22 million dollars to a group of investors led by Boston banker Serge Semenenko. As far as anyone could see, it was a united corporate decision. The brothers would remain on the board, but the authority would rest with strangers.

It didn't take long for the truth to be revealed. Jack had sold out with Harry and Abe—and then bought his shares back again for the price he had sold them for. Not only that, he wasn't going after all. He was to be President of the company, instead of merely Vice-President. His would now be the power—and the glory.

It was his big moment. He not only bought back his old shares, he bought more. He was now the undisputed mogul of Warner Bros.

You only had to see Jack in the private dining-room and walking to or from his office to realize how he was enjoying this situation. It wasn't so much that he was in charge that made him smile, it was the imagined look on Harry's face.

214

'I've got the old bastard by the balls at last,' he chuckled to one executive. 'He can't do a goddamned thing.' The laughter could be heard hooting through the lot.

Harry soon afterwards had a heart-attack. He never recovered from what he saw as his brother's duplicity. But he began planning for a very different and what he knew was a very difficult future.

His lawyers managed to draw up a scheme whereby he wouldn't have to pay capital-gains tax when he sold his race-horses. But there was nothing he could do about the studio. His younger brother was no longer simply in charge of production. He was the biggest single shareholder, and was very much in control.

It had been his scheme of things for a long time. He always said that Louis B. Mayer lost his hold on MGM because he didn't have enough shares in the company. 'He's stupid,' he told friends over and over again. 'They could get him out one day.' And they did.

Jack's name was always on the films. He wanted people to see who was boss in the way that proved it most effectively. Nevertheless, he didn't try to influence the Press. He wouldn't allow producers to talk to the newspapers either. It was for the films to speak for themselves.

When Jack did make statements they were geared towards making his investments more profitable. He looked optimistically to the future, he said. 'If all the man-hours spent in fear and trembling over the fate of the industry by too many motion-picture people were devoted to a strong and courageous effort in the cause of good picture-making, this industry would far exceed any feats it has ever achieved.'

When people were cynical about Jack's statements—and they were fully entitled to be—it wasn't easy to stop that cynicism reaching him. 'I hear they're still blaming me for letting Clark Gable go,' he said to Bill Orr on one occasion. 'Well, I let a lot of people go. I've made some big stars and some big mistakes. But what's the name outside this building?'

The name was still Warner Bros, and Jack Warner was undoubtedly still the boss. He still knew what the rest of the industry was doing; it was impossible to hoodwink him. Freelancing stars couldn't go to him and demand fees based on imaginary salaries offered by competing studios.

To prove him wrong, there was always a confidential guide, printed weekly and available only to top studio executives, which listed precisely the amount each actor was being paid anywhere in Hollywood. It was more accurate and more closely followed than any list of secondhand car prices circulating in the motor industry.

The moguls were in close touch on any matter deemed to be of mutual concern. They met together, they talked together, and sometimes they played together—at the races, on the golf-course at the sort of places where business was seen to be done as a casual incidental feature of a day's entertainment.

There were times when Jack even allowed that sort of business to encroach on his summers in the South of France. He was always in touch with what was going on at the studio. Packets would arrive daily. There would be a stream of telephone calls as he sat on the veranda of the house having breakfast or as he lounged on his private beach—Hollywood had to learn to keep European time when Jack was away. He still didn't want any decision to escape his attention—even when Ann was conveniently away and he was fondling the breasts of a starlet who just happened to be in the neighbourhood.

If it was a matter that affected Warner Brothers policy he was the one who had to say yes or no.

Some of his happiest moments were spent at the casinos of Cannes and Nice. He wasn't a Las Vegas gambler. The ambience of American gaming didn't entice him at all, but the elegance of the French casinos provided him with his idea of entertainment. In one night he could lose 100,000 dollars and think little of it. If he won 100,000 dollars, on the other hand, the people around him could be sure of a convivial night in which the champagne and Jack's ever-worsening jokes flowed until dawn.

In 1957 he achieved every gambler's ambition. In the company of Darryl Zanuck—as a demonstration of his attitude to fired former employees and fellow studio heads, they were close friends—and two businessmen, he broke the bank at the Palm Beach casino in Cannes.

His own winnings were said to be 114,200 dollars—40 million francs. Jack was so jubilant he had his French chauffeur drive over to Monte Carlo, where he lost every cent of his winnings. Zanuck was reported to have kept control of some 57,000 dollars.

In London he would stay at Crockfords until five-thirty in the morning, winning, losing.

It was a similar matter of gambling, running the studio. But Jack kept trying.

It was Jack's own idea to bring Errol Flynn back to the Warner lot—not under a new contract, which both of them would have found unpalatable, but to star in a picture which somewhat sadly would be perfect for him—the life of John Barrymore.

Not only was Barrymore the Flynn of his day, a hard-drinking roustabout with a contempt for authority, but the two had been close friends, and he often used to think of himself as Barrymore's adopted son—one of the sickest true stories to come out of the

Hollywood of the early 1940s was when Raoul Walsh and a band of buddies 'borrowed' the newly dead Barrymore body from the local funeral parlour. They brought the cadaver to Flynn's house and sat it in a chair awaiting Errol's arrival. When he finally saw it the actor had all but to be restrained in a straitjacket.

Now Jack had bought the rights to Diana Barrymore's reminiscences of life with her father, *Too Much Too Soon,* and he knew that Flynn was the only one for the lead role.

He was brilliant in it, which was not completely a tribute to his acting. He was simply playing himself, a bloated, drunken wreck of a man who had once been so handsome.

It took a kind of courage which may not have been attempted before. But then things really were changing. In 1958, a year in which Marlon Brando's *Sayonara* and Doris Day's *The Pajama Game* were the most exciting products on offer from the studio, the changing scene was more evident than ever.

The New York office was closed. A few months later the man who had occupied that office was gone too.

CHAPTER 23

THE MILLIONAIRE

They were the last of the robber barons.

Julius Epstein

Harry Warner died in July 1958 at the age of seventy-six, and a thousand people attended his funeral at a Los Angeles synagogue.

Edward G. Robinson, James Stewart, Michael Curtiz and the movie composer Dmitri Tiomkin were among the mourners at Wilshire Boulevard Temple to hear Rabbi Edgar Magnin kindly underestimate Harry's own opinion of himself: 'He was a plain, simple man who loved above all else being a farmer.' If it were true, it was a secret that he kept to himself.

He left 6 million dollars—half to his wife and the rest equally divided between his daughters. His legacy to Jack was greater—a sense of freedom. No longer would there be the spectre over his shoulder of a dictator who appeared to try to inhibit his every move, whom he was certain was consumed by a jealousy that began the day he was born.

A matter of days later, it seemed almost certain that Rabbi Magnin would be officiating at another Warner brother's funeral. Jack himself was seriously injured in a road accident on the main highway between Cannes and Nice. His sports car collided with a coal-lorry, and he was thrown clear. The result was severe head and chest injuries and what were described as other 'serious pulmonary complications'.

Ann and Barbara were by his bedside as the doctors shook their heads and warned them to prepare for the worst.

Jack Junior immediately flew to the South of France with his wife to be with him too. On arrival he made a statement which, through translation difficulties, indicated that his father was already dead.

Miraculously, Jack recovered. He said on his release from hospital that he had been gambling immediately before the accident and had won 50,000 dollars which the casino croupier had promised to keep for him. When the croupier heard the news it appeared that he was suffering from the amnesia Jack had surprisingly been spared himself. The money was permanently lost.

So was any hope of a reconciliation between himself and Jack Junior. He hated the story about the seriousness of his condition which Jack had given to the Press. He never liked talking about illness, let alone his own, and treated suggestions that he was dying as a sign of unforgivable weakness.

Early in 1959 the younger Jack Warner turned up at the studio as usual, to be met by a guard who refused to allow him to go any farther. The embarrassed man merely said, 'Mr Warner asked me to let you have this.' In a neat little bundle were the contents of his desk drawers.

The message was all too clear. He was no longer Vice-President of the company, in charge of television and industrial films. A statement issued to the Press at the time said that he had no idea why he had been sacked. He says today that he still doesn't know.

'Sure I felt resentment at the time,' he said. 'And I still do.'

Another victim of Jack's cruel streak was the ever-loyal Steve Trilling. Trilling had family problems, and had been very ill himself. But for thirty years he had been loyal to the company in general, and to Jack in particular. It was he who did most of Jack's firing for him.

One day Jack flew to the South of France. Trilling was there at the airport as usual to see him off. There was a mass of instructions that he had to digest about the way the studio had to be run in Warner's absence; which films to be given top priority and, as always, who was next in the firing-line. It wasn't pleasant, but it was part of the job.

When he returned to the office the studio comptroller was waiting for him.

The news he had was blunt and to the point. 'Jack wanted me to tell you,' he said. 'You have to clear out your things. You're fired.' A short time later Trilling committed suicide.

It was quite possible that Trilling had ceased to be the use to the studio he had once been, but there were kinder ways of getting the message home. Most senior executives had expected him to be kicked upstairs, with a sinecure vice-presidency that was no more than a tribute for past services. It was not to be.

Jack still considered himself irreplaceable and invincible. Other people seem to have thought so too. In 1960 he was made an honorary MBE for services to Anglo-American relations.

As far as he was concerned, he was by now on top of the world. He still enjoyed himself lavishly, entertaining the way he had always done, although Ann by now was very rarely seen. She decided that she no longer enjoyed the same functions that he did, so when Jack went out to dine he went alone.

When there were dinner parties at Angelo Drive she organized the shopping, chose the menus, looked after the table decorations—and then disappeared. 'Oh,' Jack would say, 'she's in Palm Springs.' In truth, she was upstairs. As the years went by she became more and more a recluse.

Jack's women friends, however, were still background figures too. He had his favourites, and stayed loyal to them—and they to him—for years. One had a teenage daughter to whom he was more generous than he was to most people. Ann had been known to phone the ladies to warn them off her 'property', but she was unable to influence the woman who was now comforting her husband in his seventies.

If he had been asked himself who his favourite companion was he would still say the studio. It still came first and last to him, seeing through Natalie Wood and Gene Kelly in *Marjorie Morningstar*—a 'Jewish' story, slightly watered-down Judaism, but remarkably a Jewish story nevertheless— Spencer Tracy in *The Old Man And The Sea,* Audrey Hepburn in *The Nun's Story* (which made the actress a million dollars), and the biggest gamble of his career, *My Fair Lady.*

Jack personally signed the cheque for the 5,500,000 dollars he paid CBS—who owned the musical—for the film rights. It was the most ever paid for a film story. Another 5 per cent of the gross, it was agreed, would go to Bernard Shaw's estate.

On Broadway and in London, the main sensation of the show had been Julie Andrews as Eliza Doolittle. It was Jack who surprised everybody, by deciding that he didn't want her for the film role.

'Who's heard of her, this English broad?' he asked the studio executives trying to make most people's forecasts into a *fait accompli.* Julie had become so well known in the role, her records were played on radios and record-players seemingly everywhere, that it had been taken for granted that the part would be hers.

Jack decided otherwise. Films were not sold just in New York or London. He needed a guaranteed success in the tiny towns where live shows never played. He got it, with Audrey Hepburn as Eliza. She wasn't as good as Julie Andrews had been, and the songs had to be dubbed by another artiste, but in Cecil Beaton's costumes she looked ravishing.

Julie Andrews, on the other hand, had the satisfaction of a much less expensive debut in *Mary Poppins* that not only made her a lot of money but launched her on an entire career as a saccharine-sweet heroine from which only now is she managing to escape.

Who knows whether *My Fair Lady* would have led automatically to *The Sound of Music?* What is certain is that the part of Henry Higgins could only have gone to the man who made the role his own on Broadway, Rex Harrison, although even in this case Jack was ambivalent. He at first wanted Cary Grant—a more marketable name, he believed—but even Grant said that if Harrison didn't get it he wouldn't go to see the film. And largely through him, it was worth seeing.

Needless to say, too, Wilfrid Hyde-White was a perfect Colonel Pickering and Stanley Holloway became an international name at the age of seventy plus, repeating his stage success as Eliza's dust-man father—although here too Jack had grandiose ideas. He wanted James Cagney for the part, but Cagney believed he was completely retired and turned it down.

Altogether the film cost 17 million dollars to make. It took 29 million. Jack Warner couldn't quarrel with that.

CHAPTER 24

ALWAYS KEEP 'EM LAUGHING

Oh, those terrible jokes!

Irene Dunne

Jack may have still been undisputed head of Warner Bros, but it was a world he no longer understood properly. The cinema had changed, and with it had altered the habits of millions.

It wasn't merely the advent of TV: to the man who had thrown bones to Rin Tin Tin, sat at the feet of Al Jolson in *The Jazz Singer,* wet-nursed Joan Crawford, tussled with Errol Flynn and Bette Davis and harangued Bogart, the small screen was a bastard industry. He was still great fun to be with, and a doughty opponent. Friends would still meet him at the Hillcrest Country Club or at other popular watering-places for the rich movie people and still become convulsed at his appalling sense of humour.

'What's new?' Mervyn LeRoy told me he asked him one day in the early '60s. Jack knew the answer—'New York, New Jersey, New Hampshire, pneumonia!' Quick as the screen credit for a technician he wanted fired.

But what was really new was that Warners were, like all their competitors, a studio without stars on contract, making films for whose success they no longer had a gut reaction. Without that, he could offer nothing more than a sense of continuity by his presence.

What seemed to continue unchanged was Jack's uncanny love of the law. He never despaired of achieving a calm, easy solution to a problem once he had exhausted all other possibilities.

When he brought out *My First Hundred Years in Hollywood* no one could accuse him of telling the truth, the whole truth and nothing but the truth. He not only ignored Irma, his first wife, his son Jack, and Hal Wallis, but just happened to say how much he missed Harry. He also said some unkind things about Judy Garland's husband Sid Luft, who had produced *A Star Is Born;* as a result of which Luft sued for a million dollars in libel damages.

It was finally settled out of court—as were most of Jack's legal tangles—although on one occasion in the midst of what he considered a highly enjoyable court experience he managed to ask the judge, 'Are you trying to make a Federal case out of this?'

The suits tumbled in and out of the Warner legal offices like fan mail.

In 1954 the studio's talented music department head Ray Heindorf sued for 20,000 dollars because Warners refused to describe him as 'Musical Director' in film credits. In one of those petty agreements so typical of the Hollywood community, the Directors Guild had decreed that only its own members could use the title 'Director'.

Jack Webb, star of the *Dragnet* TV series, was among those whose relationship with Warner Bros ended with a gaggle of lawyers around trying to sort out the details. He was dismissed as a TV executive producer while there were still three years of his contract outstanding. They finally settled the matter with Webb continuing to draw his 3,000-dollar-a-week salary for the remainder of his contract period.

Robert Preston sued, too—for 64,000 dollars which he said was owing to him in royalties for recording the soundtrack of *The Music Man*. Again it was settled out of court.

And yet Jack was not frightened of showing the human side of a legal situation.

One of the big early Warner TV successes was *The FBI Story* starring Efrem Zimbalist junior, who when he wasn't acting in the series was one of Jack's tennis partners.

Zimbalist was one of those who experienced the kinder side of the studio boss's nature. He hit a crisis in his life and told Bill Orr, 'I've got to get out for at least eight weeks. I must leave tonight.' And he left.

The studio's paymaster went to Jack and said, 'We've got to put him on suspension. Right?'

Jack replied, 'Wrong. We've got to show him who his friends are.'

Not many people would automatically have put Jack in that league. But some would.

One was a somewhat rotund producer who later became an international TV star, Bill (*Cannon*) Conrad.

Jack's introduction to Conrad was less than auspicious. He surveyed the young man's bulk and exclaimed, 'Good God! We're not paying you by the pound, are we?'

Conrad got into difficulties with Jack soon after arriving at Burbank. He didn't want to sign an exclusive contract—and, as in every other case, this rankled with Jack enormously.

He knew that Conrad had a lucrative sideline going—doing

voice-overs for radio commercials. The only solution, he worked out, was to offer to pay him, in addition to the money he earned on salary, the equivalent of his income from commercials. That was until he realized that the voice-overs were worth more than producing TV shows.

James Garner's brush with the studio was somewhat more complicated. The case was lost by Warners simply because Jack's showmanship was not appreciated by the judge hearing the petition in which Garner sued for wrongful suspension.

The studio in 1960 thought it had rightfully taken advantage of a *force majeure* clause in its contract with Garner, who was making the *Maverick* TV series for the company.

It was a time when Warners, like the other studios, was hit by strikes—by actors in feature films and by writers of TV shows. All studio contracts were formulated on the basis that employees worked for forty out of fifty-two weeks with the right of 'lay-off' periods after that. The usual practice was to pay them for three or four weeks after their working project was over and then lay them off if necessary. There was the same right to lay off in cases of *force majeure*—like the strike. There was the right, but it didn't make sense to exercise it.

The judge, who didn't think that Jack took the matter nearly seriously enough, agreed with Garner, and Warners lost the case.

When it was all over Jack merely shrugged his shoulders and said, 'It's water off the duck's ass. What the hell, maybe we shouldn't have laid him off.'

It was typical, in fact, of the way he ran his TV business. The more important this became for the company as a whole, the less Jack understood it. When the two worlds of television and feature films appeared to merge he understood it even less.

Bill Orr became head of Warners' production after being the top man in the TV division. In those days, they produced a TV series called *Days of Wine and Roses* about the hard reality of the life of an alcoholic. Orr liked it so much he wanted to turn it into a feature film. He knew too whom he wanted for the lead, Jack Lemmon.

His mistake was to send a kinescope recording of the series—a primitive film actually taken 'off the tube', long before the days of taped TV—direct to Jack. It was very dark—which to Jack just emphasized the wholly unsatisfactory nature of the whole deal. He wasn't interested. Worse than that, he was hostile.

'Bill,' he called to Orr on the intercom, 'come here.'

The tone indicated that there was trouble. 'If you're going to make another picture about a load of drunks,' he said, 'forget it. Anyway, what I saw was terrible. It was terribly gloomy.'

The series, starring Cliff Robertson, was not what he wanted to see made into a feature film. The answer was no—no matter how much arguing Orr or the people he tried to persuade to come on to his side did.

A weekend went by. On the Monday morning there was a more conciliatory tone in Jack's voice as he called Bill into his office.

'I've just read a wonderful script and we're going to do a deal with William Morris,' he declared in one breath, knowing there were going to be a few frowns.

'That's great, Chief,' said Orr. 'But don't you want to check with your head of production? That's me, Chief.'

'I know that,' said Jack. 'But this is great. It's called *Days of Wine and Roses*.'

The film was made and earned Jack Lemmon an Oscar nomination—he doubtless would have won the Award had he not faced competition from Gregory Peck in *To Kill A Mockingbird*. Somehow the old Warner instinct had resurfaced before it was too late.

He wasn't always so clever in his predictions. In 1967, during the Middle East Six-Day War, the Hollywood United Jewish Appeal campaign for Israel held a fund-raising dinner. Jack said he would personally double the biggest single contribution. It came from Herb Alpert of the Tijuana Brass—in the form of a cheque for 250,000 dollars. Jack blanched under his suntan. But he still made good his promise for 500,000 dollars—and without the usual expletives.

If that meant he was deserving of praise, people hearing him at a San Francisco dinner were not so fortunate. There had been a retrospective showing of Warner films. At the dinner Jack made a long, rambling speech which insulted almost everyone around and mingled the insults with his usual crop of obscenities. He thanked the people present for the trophy, which he had not yet received, and blamed all the world's problems on 'the Commies and the long-hairs'. It didn't go down at all well.

Next day he rang up the organizers and apologized. It was a similar story at a dinner given to him by a group of film editors.

At least once, he tried to avoid just that happening. He was at a film première with Rudi Fehr, one of his most trusted editors. The audience cheered loudly.

'What shall I do?' he asked Fehr.

'Stand up,' he was advised. Jack did—and took a bow. The audience kept cheering. 'Now you stand up,' he told his companion.

'Why me?' Fehr asked.

'Because it's an order,' said Jack.

And he still enjoyed giving those orders, although it was clear that he was no longer totally in touch. Little things revealed that the world was passing him by—and not just his attitude to television.

The man who once knew everything about his business wasn't really sure who the opposition now was, let alone who that opposition was putting up against his own output.

He still chose films on the basis of what he enjoyed, without realizing that his own tastes were those of his generation, and the survivors of that generation were mostly at home, falling asleep over those TV sets.

But he was content. He in his old age and Ann in her late middle age seemed to have an idyllic relationship, at least to those who didn't know that one or other of his current women friends usually accompanied him on his trips to New York. He still enjoyed studio tennis. Certainly there weren't many of his generation who even made the effort, let alone were capable of doing so. In short, he was a happy old man, and the organizations of the country were helping to make him so.

The awards came thick and fast. Mayor Lindsay of New York presented him with a medallion 'for his contribution to philanthropy and the arts'.

At another dinner Jack was given a special 'Humanitarian Award'. Among those who accepted invitations was Olivia de Havilland. She said, 'I'm all for encouraging humanitarianism—especially in Jack.'

As she moved away from the podium Jack went towards her to give her a kiss. 'He was embarrassed,' she recalled.

Anyone who was anyone in the film business—and outside it—had decided that this was the time to honour the man who, with the departure of Sam Goldwyn from the scene, was undoubtedly the Last Tycoon.

Very soon after being appointed 'Producer of the Year' by the Producers Guild he was given honary membership of the Directors Guild, which some of his old director employees might have thought took things a bit too far.

The supreme accolade had been the Oscar for *My Fair Lady,* which not only showed a sense of the theatrical but indicated he still knew when it was worth making an extra large bet. He had, nevertheless, made sure of the award—by giving himself the title of Producer on the opening credits.

The West Germans liked him too. They gave him their Cross of Merit—at about the same time that the American Hairdressers Union named him 'Glamour Champion of the Year'.

He could have enjoyed none of the tributes more than the one from his fellow-entertainers at the Friars Club—who provided a 'roast', an opportunity for the worst possible insults under the guise of ribald humour.

He was so overcome on this occasion that his rambles around the countryside of speechmaking were barely audible. *The New York Times* at the time quoted a friend who said, 'His very presence in front of the microphone can turn a hall into a disaster area.'

Jack Benny was more kind. 'He must ad-lib,' he said. 'No one could write that sort of stuff.'

'There are an awful lot of jealous guys on this dais,' Warner responded.

It was an occasion when the greats of American show business were out on licence. The stronger the diatribe, the more effective—and the more affectionate. Benny in particular had never been better. 'You're a very charitable man,' he told Warner. 'And I think charity is an excuse for a lot of lousy jokes.'

Dean Martin, who was to make a virtual profession of such evenings on TV, put it into song:

Jack L. Warner.
That Jack L. Warner.
He don't know nothin'. But he must say somethin'.
He just keeps yackin'
Keeps on yackin' a-long.

Jack was constantly appearing to make comments, but no one could be sure what he said. George Jessel, revelling in the opportunity to thank Jack publicly for giving the role in *The Jazz Singer* to Al Jolson, said, 'This is a lot better than some guy getting up with a lot of phoney tears. But what you said tonight, only God will know.'

Jack did, however, get the last word. 'The day you don't enjoy being roasted,' he said in all seriousness, 'you're cooked.'

Julius Epstein now says, 'The only people who really laughed at Jack's jokes were the ones who were insecure. I only remember one that was really funny. It was when Ronald Reagan first ran for Governor of California and Jack heard about it.

' "No," said Jack, "you've got it wrong. Dennis Morgan's running for Governor. Ronald Reagan for best friend".'

He would probably have enjoyed having one of his ex-employees as President. It would certainly have been another photograph to add to the collection of White House photographs he kept behind his desk.

In the early 1960s it was one of John F. Kennedy that had pride of place. That was because Warners had made a film of the President's wartime exploits called *PT 109*. JFK liked it more than did the ticket-buyers of America. The film was a turkey. But Kennedy wrote: 'Congratulations, Jack. It's a fine job.'

That note was compensation enough for the indifference at the box office which, one could fairly assume, he knew about to the finest detail. From the moment he and his brothers started the business he had carried in his pocket a typewritten memo which gave him the up-to-date situation on the company's progress.

The memo was changed every week, and told him in an age before computers precisely how much money every film under production was costing and how well or badly those already made were doing in the theatres of America and abroad.

Of course, that wouldn't have been made the subject of one of his speeches. There is no predicting how it would have come out.

As it always had been, his vulgarity was carried on into his private conversation. In the midst of an important discussion he could break off and say, 'I've got to go and take a piss.' Millions of dollars rested on the speed with which Jack could flush his toilet.

Ann may have been forgiven for thinking that above all Jack deserved an award for his prowess with other women; a matter that never ceased to cause her pain. He still refused to discuss his love-life, but those close to him knew that there was always some woman willing to share his bed.

Occasionally they were call girls whose services he bought for upward of 25 dollars. One was a retired prostitute whom he took to London in the belief he could palm her off as a lady of title. In the end an old friend had to pay the woman off.

Yet whenever Jack would try to ingratiate himself with stars, telling them how hard he himself worked, he would always add that he got into the studio late every morning—just so that he could start the day right by having breakfast with Ann. A great many people liked him for that.

If only they had felt the same way about his films. The golden age of Warner Bros had not just faded, it had, contrary to the rules of corrosion, gone rusty. There had been so little of note. *Look Back In Anger* and *Gypsy,* perhaps. And the occasional very bright spot.

Whatever Happened To Baby Jane? represented a macabre re-union on Burbank soil for two ex-Warner stars, Bette Davis and Joan Crawford, playing a couple of former show-business sisters who hate each other quite as much as Harry and Jack had done.

They were two *grandes dames* of the cinema returning in a magnum opus of bitchiness—Joan, the crippled sister constantly tormented by Bette, who dreams alternately of recapturing her short career as a child star and of driving Miss Crawford to her death.

Although Joan looked harrowing at times, it was Bette's picture from start to finish. She won an Oscar nomination and, as even Jack said, 'Bette came home to Burbank after fifteen years of self-imposed exile. As far as I am concerned, she can stay for ever.' Which was quite a compliment.

To emphasize just how happy Jack was to have both the 'old broads'—as they had been dubbed by the studio diehards—back at work again, he gave a lunch for them both in the private dining-room.

Joan called him her second father—Louis B. Mayer was the first. Bette stressed how glad she was they had kissed and made up.

She was to have another opportunity to go to work for Warners again. For the second time in her career she played twin sisters—the first had been in *A Stolen Life*—in *Dead Ringer* directed by Paul Henreid. In this she played both murderess and victim. It wasn't great. But *The New York Times* said it was 'great fun to watch'. The box office wasn't quite so enjoyable a view, but there continued to be other more pleasant spots.

Laurence Olivier made *Othello,* and then in 1966 came Elizabeth Taylor and Richard Burton in *Who's Afraid of Virginia Woolf?*

Things had changed so much now that Jack announced well in advance—not that here was a film that could be enjoyed by all the family, but that children would specifically be banned from seeing it. 'We do not think this is a film for children.'

The same might have been said for what was happening to the studio. Then in November 1966 it was finally all over for him.

The deal was that Jack—the only Hollywood studio head who had not been answerable to a huge conglomerate—would sell all his shares in the company to Seven Arts Productions, Ltd for 20 dollars a share. He held 1,600,000 of them, which meant that the deal which created Warner-Seven Arts was worth 32 million dollars to him. Since he was reputed to be worth a hundred million anyway, it wasn't done for the money alone. Nor did it seem he wanted to get out for his health's sake. At the age of seventy-five, he looked at least fifteen years younger.

Nevertheless, Burbank was a mere shadow of its former self, and so was Hollywood. It all seemed to have a ghost-like quality about it; a place where things used to happen and didn't any more. Joseph L. Mankiewicz has described it with a telling statement: 'I couldn't get rid of the feeling that any minute I'd look out and see tumble-weeds come rolling past.'

It certainly seemed strange for there to be a Warner Bros studio without a Warner brother around. Jack for one believed that was the case. Seven Arts were not above thinking it too, and encouraged him to stay in his office as an independent producer. Even Abe was officially still a member of the board, although he was more interested in lying in the sun in Florida and seeing his racehorses.

Then, a year after the sale, Abe was dead at the age of eighty-four, childless but well loved by those who knew him.

The new firm seemed genuinely glad that Jack was still there.

They encouraged him to make *The Frontiersman,* an old-fashioned Western in which the Indians were the bad guys. It was hopelessly out of touch with current thinking, and after Nunnally Johnson had delivered his script the idea was shelved without resurfacing.

There were times when Jack still played the big boss. When *Petulia* was being made at the studio he demanded to see the dailies.

Having seen them, he ordered cuts to be made. Walter McEwan, his right-hand man now, held him back. 'Colonel,' he said, 'I don't think we can do that.'

'So why did you make me see it?' Jack asked.

He still tried to see the rushes of other pictures, but before long the message got through that there was little point.

He remained a non-executive member of the board with the honorary title of Vice-Chairman, but it was very frustrating for him, and when the company decided to close his private dining-room he knew that the time had come to get out.

Several films were made by the new firm and never released. Their money was earned mainly from selling the rights of the existing Warner library to TV. Within two years they themselves had sold out, to Kiné Services, which now changed its name to Warner Communications. That was when he finally decided to leave Burbank after all those years.

'Hell,' he said to Bill Schaefer. 'These new people don't owe me a damned thing.' It was an admission of defeat.

In fact, there were a number of people who wondered why he had got out when he did. Had he waited another year he could have got at least twice as much for his investment. The studio was already in the process of making movies which were destined to become big money-spinners—like *Cool Hand Luke, Camelot* and the Audrey Hepburn thriller *Wait until Dark.*

But he wasn't finished yet. He was slower now, tired. But he still wouldn't admit it.

He bought a big suite of offices near his old rivals Twentieth Century-Fox in the burgeoning Century City, and announced that Jack L. Warner Productions was in business. As Schaefer told me, 'It didn't mean a thing to him if it cost him a thousand or two thousand dollars a week. It was somewhere for him to go.'

It was more than that. It was a palatial place, complete with paintings he had bought years ago, but which didn't go with the Renoirs and Monets he had had to keep him company at Burbank. He had ideas again to play it big.

He was again to play independent producer. There were two plans buzzing in his brain, a new version of the Billy the Kid story and a musical based on the signatories of the Declaration of Independence.

Having broken with Warner Bros officially, it seemed wise to make that break as physically as though it had been applied with a surgeon's scalpel. He went with his ideas to Harry Cohn's old realm of Columbia, where the lady was still standing proudly carrying her torch, although Cohn himself had long since departed the scene. (His was the funeral of which one wag had commented, 'Give the people what they want and they'll come along to see it.')

The only condition he had to meet in order to work for the old rival concern was that he really severed all his links with Burbank, including the owning of any Warner shares. That fulfilled he set about producing *Dirty Little Billy* and *1776*.

Neither was particularly successful, although the bigger disappointment was the musical, which Jack had fostered as much as a gesture of devotion to his country as a business venture.

It had been a moderately successful Broadway show, and even had a short, unsuccessful London run. Jack liked it, and if there was a subject with which he could demonstrate his business acumen this had to be it. The film opened for the Christmas 1972 season at Radio City Music Hall in New York, and was a tremendous success. Jack preened himself before a cluster of admirers who were convinced that the Colonel had masterminded a huge coup. The film then went on the road, and flopped wherever it landed like an oversized pancake.

But he didn't worry about it. Like an old man contentedly earning pocket-money sticking on stamps in the office where he had once been boss, nothing seemed to be worth bothering about.

His office surroundings gave him a great deal of pleasure, even though on most days there was little to do there. The torrents of mail had stopped virtually overnight the day he announced he was selling his Warner shares. Copies of the daily *Variety* and the *Hollywood Reporter* still came every day and were devoured—usually with a few disparaging comments over his desk to the ever loyal Bill Schaefer. Occasionally Schaefer would say to him, 'You know what they're doing up at the studio?'

But there wouldn't be a great deal of interest shown. It was too painful to him.

He was much more interested in the barber shop he had had installed next to his personal office. Serious film-production he could give up, his barber shop never. In a way, though, it was as much an example of Jack's ambivalent sense of loyalty as it was a pandering to his vanity. When he left Burbank he told his barber Don, 'If they ever close this shop, you can come back to me. We'll set you up. Just let me know.'

Don phoned three months later. A former lunch room at the luxury suite was converted. The barber brought a manicurist with him, and sinks and mirrors were installed. Jack was its only daily customer, although Schaefer used it too, and so did Jack's former Warner Bros accountant. Walter McEwan would come in from his home at Thousand Oaks forty miles away for a haircut or a shave.

Occasionally, like an old fire horse suddenly jumping to duty at the sound of a ringing bell, a newspaper or a TV story would spur Jack to new ideas. He had one when a dinner companion mentioned the name of James J. Walker, the colourful former Mayor of New York, whom Jack had known well. He thought it would make a great Broadway show. It was further proof that he was completely out of touch, but he refused to admit it, any more than he would abdicate his position, as he saw it, as the elder statesman of Hollywood; a pillar of an Establishment it broke his heart to realize was no longer there. However, he wouldn't let people think that was the case. He still nurtured the belief that whatever he did would be regarded as exactly right. The James Walker story would show them. Alas, what it showed was precisely the opposite of what he had hoped.

There had already been a film on Walker starring Bob Hope, and called *Beau James,* which hadn't done particularly well, but Jack wanted his old sparring partner Melville Shavelson (who had written the *Beau James* screenplay) to write the show for him. He was convinced he had a brainwave called *Jimmy,* but *Jimmy* was a disaster.

The show got as far as Philadelphia when Shavelson decided it wouldn't work. He phoned Jack. 'You've got to close this turkey,' he said. 'Nothing works. The sets are laughable, the costumes are terrible.'

To which Jack replied, 'What are you worried about? It's only a mill.' (Jack couldn't even bring himself to take a million dollars seriously when one of his own schemes was in question.)

When Shavelson pleaded with him to close it again he replied, 'If I close it now, who'll have dinner with me?'

The show reached New York and Jack checked into his Sherry Netherlands suite accompanied by his current girl-friend, a hairdresser. The reviews were terrible, but Jack kept it running for seventeen weeks. He had lost every cent of the million and a half he had invested in the show, but his pride had prevented his cutting his losses any earlier. The truth of the matter was that he had been out of active production for so long that he now had to admit he had lost his touch.

Those still close to Jack wondered whether he would now be happier with a family reconciliation. He hadn't seen his son for years. Apart from a brief meeting with one of Jack's daughters in a doctor's waiting-room, he had still never seen his grandchildren.

The opportunity seemed to come one day when Jack and Schaefer were having lunch at a restaurant near the Century City office.

Schaefer spotted Jack Junior there and told his boss.

'Ask him to come over and have lunch with us,' said the senior Warner. The lunch was eaten, but it was like a meeting between two acquaintances who hadn't met for thirty years, and were happy enough for that situation to remain.

There was nothing to talk about, and no emotion either from Jack senior. The two men never met again.

Jack continued to play, to enjoy life. When his birthday came around in 1972 he celebrated with a party. 'Don't tell anyone,' he whispered to Bill Orr, 'but I think this is the big 8-0.'

Two years later, playing tennis, he slipped and fell, hitting his head. He had had a stroke. He was never the same again.

His speech left him for a time and then returned. He was virtually blind, and his mental powers were mostly gone.

The man who had helped decide how millions spent their leisure hours, and who had in so doing been one of the governors of the state called Hollywood, was finished at the age of eighty-two. He lingered for four more years, with the Warner office fulfilling no more serious purpose than easing Bill Schaefer (who continued on the payroll) into retirement.

Then, on 9 September 1978, he died.

No final fanfares, no sunsets, no artistic fadeout. Just the death of a sick old man. Yet of all the stars of Warner Bros, he was probably its greatest.

CHAPTER 25

THE LAST TYCOON

There used to be giants in this town. Now all we have
are the Dodgers.

Melville Shavelson

Of course, Hollywood paid him the tributes everyone would have
expected. They turned out in their thousands to honour him at his
funeral. What was more, unlike the passing of so many of his
contemporaries, the mourning was real.

There have been a number of large-scale tributes to him and his
studio since then, including a US postage stamp marking fifty years
of talking pictures. The industry has laughed a great deal while
recalling his memory, and perhaps that is the nicest tribute of all.

When the University of Southern California—the repository of
the Warner Bros archives—held in 1979 an evening which they
called 'The Colonel', they most certainly laughed.

Julius Epstein, who had spoken of Jack's 'affable arrogance',
looked at the portrait hanging behind the podium and said, 'That is
just how he looked when he fired you.' Not true, because as
everyone there knew, he never personally fired anyone—although
the spirit of the words was understood.

After a similar tribute evening Loretta Young told me, 'It was
only then that I realized just what a terribly influential person he
had been. I always had thought of him as a clown. But he did so
much for our industry.

'Jack could have sabotaged the films we made at the studio. After
all, he had the power to do what he liked. But he knew how to make
them well. Zanuck didn't. He ruined more good films than anyone I
know. No one could say that about Jack. He did so much for us.'

Rather more, of course, than he did for his family.

In his will he left 200,000 dollars to Jack Junior, plus a 100,000
dollar insurance policy—enough to avoid an unseemly law-suit. A
trust fund was set up for his daughters and for his widow.

Sam's daughter Leta, however, decided to sue Jack's estate

—because, unlike Harry and Abe, Jack had left her nothing. She saw that as a breach of the brothers' promise on Sam's deathbed to look after her.

Bill Schaefer was left 15,000 dollars. 'I wasn't disappointed,' he told me. 'I didn't expect more than five thousand. Jack wasn't very generous.'

But then he did also leave behind him Warner Bros, and all those pictures made with the famous glinting shield at their head. And that in its way was generosity enough.

The Warner Bros were a giant chapter in the history of Hollywood.

The last of the brothers, the Last Tycoon of Hollywood, had survived his competitors, and outlived the people who had helped him along.

Al Jolson, Humphrey Bogart, Errol Flynn, Paul Muni, Edward G. Robinson had all gone before him.

In his way he had a bit of each of them inside him: showman, swashbuckler, actor—yes, artist.

You needed a special touch to make movies. But then a new generation is finding that out for itself. It too is discovering just how uneasy lies the head that wears the toilet seat.

INDEX